KEEPERS *of the* LIGHT

A History of British Columbia's Lighthouses and their Keepers

Donald Graham

HARBOUR PUBLISHING LTD.

This book is dedicated to the memory of Captain L.H. Cadieux. Whatever the future holds for lightkeepers, he certainly saved our past.

Copyright © 1985 by Donald Graham
Second printing January 1986
Third Printing May 1987

First paperback edition 1990 ISBN 1-55017-024-4
Second Printing, 1992

Harbour Publishing
P.O. Box 219
Madeira Park, BC V0N 2H0

Cover painting: Cape Beale by Buzz Walker (detail)
Cover design: Gaye Hammond and James Bradburne
Design & illustrations: Gaye Hammond
Maps: Daniel Cartography
Editorial assistance: Audrey McClellan
Printed and bound in Canada by Friesen Printers

This publication was assisted by the Canada Council and the BC Heritage Trust.

CANADIAN CATALOGUING IN PUBLICATION DATA

Graham, Donald, 1947–
    Keepers of the light

    Includes index.
    ISBN 1-55017-024-4 (paper)
    ISBN 0-920080-65-0 (cloth)

    1. Lighthouses—British Columbia—History.   2. Lighthouse keepers—British Columbia.   3. Pacific coast (B.C.)—History.   I. Title.
VK1027.B7G72 1985   623.89′42′09711   C85-091483-3

CONTENTS

FOREWORD

Ⅰt must be a great life!" gushes the clerk at the Prince Rupert grocery check-
out, waving away the proffered I.D. when she sees the unlikely address on the
cheque. "It must be fantastic to have all that time to yourself. Do you get T.V.?"

It is a moment a few lightkeepers, those who affect pea jackets and peaked caps
in town, might relish. Most come to loathe it. The only thing worse than explaining
the obvious is to be asked to again and again.

Some myths die hard. The childhood fantasies we all have about cowboys,
firemen, nurses or train engineers seldom survive kindergarten. But when it
comes to lightkeepers people never seem to grow up. Whether inspired by great
artists, pulp novels, or postage stamps, people persist in fancying lighthouses as
idyllic and romantic settings.

We all bring them with us, these notions, all the way from Regina, Montreal,
Los Angeles, wherever. I did, even though I honestly can't remember absorbing
them. My grandfather was a Prince Edward Island bluenose with a fair measure of
saltwater in his veins, so I may have learned of them on his lap. I can still recall
being mesmerized by the lighthouse stamped on the face E.B. Eddy's tissue
dispenser in Regina's Roxy Theatre in the early fifties.

Something seemed awesome and remote, and I may as well write it — *romantic*
— in the curl of that stainless steel wave against Eddystone's tower. Little did I
suspect that one wild, seasick night, thirty years and two thousand miles away I
would find myself and my family headed for a lighthouse in the middle of nowhere,
alone.

Even those who go on the lights cling to the illusion long after romance collides
with reality since they have little more insight into their past than do outsiders.
Out there on their stations they remain as cut off in time as in space. An
unmarked grave, an old dusty hand-horn, a few mildewed logs in an engine room
attic, rusting flywheels and boilers exposed at low tide, somebody's initials ornately
carved into a workbench — these are all that connect with people who have been
there — some of them a hundred years before. Between lies a void, though they
look out at the same panorama, perhaps even make out their weather logs at the
same desk.

The fact that the men and women who came before us to this life were among
the most ill-used in all of Canada's long and troubled labour history, who knew
real hunger, deprivation and despair as constant companions in the absence of any
others, who contemplated and sometimes carried out the ultimate escape from
their nightmarish existence subtracts nothing from their marvellous sacrifice.
The real story is stranger and so much finer than fiction.

They were a special breed and we shall not see their like again, even if the
federal government comes belatedly to its senses and abandons a flawed policy of

gradually automating their calling out of existence. Keepers of these lights willingly risked their lives time and again for people passing on ships in the night, knowing better than to expect any reward. For a hundred and twenty years on Canada's west coast, ever since the first light at Fisgard lanced through the night, no vessel went to wreck, not a single life was lost due to negligence on the part of a lightkeeper. We might all stand a little taller with a tradition like that behind us.

This the social history of a people who had no society and it is hard to make it believable to other lightkeepers, let alone readers in the real world. Sometimes as disaster and death piled so high, I pushed away from the table, angry and depressed, leaving as much venom on paper as ink. To overcome disbelief (Lord, it couldn't have been that bad!) I have drawn heavily on the rich reserves of the keepers' own experience. A man who writes, "Would you please send someone up here at once as my wife has gone crazy and I want to get her to town at once" means business. There is an essay in terror written between those lines, and we have no better way to feel the tightening coils of tension inside at his island outpost, as it reeled against wind and waves that ugly September in 1919.

Unfortunately there are many gaps. Whether by accident or design, many records have been destroyed, condemning whole generations of lightkeepers to obscurity. Many live on only in names or faces staring out from faded tintypes but surely their common experience allows some inference that their lives were much the same as others who emerge, large as life, from their log books, letters and diaries. In one sense these places have barely changed since life crawled out of the sea, up and over them. Isolation still exacts the same heavy taxes and pays the same handsome dividends to those souls who choose it.

Readers of this volume will also quickly realize that its scope is limited geographically to the lightstations of the colonial period, the harbour lights of the south British Columbia coast, and the lights of the west coast of Vancouver Island. Those of the inside passage and the north coast will be dealt with in a later volume.

This is intended as a popular history, and rather than lead readers through a tangled thicket of footnotes, I have chosen to cite only those references which might spark controversy or, more likely, seem beyond belief. As for the original sources, the entire collection I inherited from Captain L. H. Cadieux can be found at the Maritime Museum in Vancouver. The Canada Coast Guard has a fine collection of files dating back to the 1870's at their base in Victoria. The rest of the written record, which would have remained out of reach without timely Explorations grants from the Canada Council, can be found in the Public Archives in Ottawa.

Whatever remains is locked away in the memories of those who lived through it all, survivors stranded now back in civilization by the doldrums of age. Some are isolated for the first time, but a large part of them remains, as it always will, out there, under swarming stars above a heaving sea, with the lantern turning and horns blasting away in their dreams.

Section divider photos: Imperial Lights—Race Rocks, 1981. Jim Ryan photo. Safe Harbours—Point Atkinson. Pacific Graveyard— Bamfield Lifeboat.

1 *The Imperial Lights*

W e share a kinship of sorts, in our time and place, with the men who took the helm during the golden age of navigation two centuries ago. Cook, Vancouver, Quadra, and the nameless seamen who trimmed and set their sails, would have been as stirred anticipating daily ferry traffic from Tsawassen to Prince Rupert as we are by the prospect of transplanted towns on the plains of Mars.

Imagine, if you can, their task of charting a contorted coastline—hundreds of thousands of miles in overall length, scarred and convoluted by countless fjords, channels, and inlets, ringed by buffers of breakers and foul ground—with only a compass and sextant, and anxious eyes on the stars. Each time the cartographers unrolled their charts in their lurching cabins, they watched them grow in detail.

If we take the same voyage for granted today, with only an occasional glance up from cafeteria trays, video games, and newspapers, it is only because the treacherous has become so well-defined. The north-south sea lane today is a constellation of lighthouses, beacons, bell buoys, and assorted markers stretching from Race Rocks in the south to Green Island on Alaska's doorstep.

"It is in this very latitude where we now are," Captain Cook confided to his log while passing Cape Flattery in 1777, "that geographers have placed the pretended Straits of Juan de Fuca. But we saw nothing, nor is there the slightest probability that any such ever existed." With no light or sound on shore, nothing exists beyond the horizon when fog drags it within arm's reach.

The first light intended to assist commercial navigation on the west coast attracted Spanish galleons to the harbour at Salina Cruz, in California. Cortes, the self-styled conqueror of Mexico, established the beacon, which seems to have been a feeble improvement over open fires, fueled with faggots of wood or coal. Burning atop a square adobe base, it was often obscured in smoke.

Two hundred years later, and several thousand miles north, the Imperial Russian Government built Baranof Castle at New Archangel-Sitka. The castle supported a cupola one hundred feet above sea level. Attendants laboured up the stairs and poured seal oil into four square cups leading to a central wick displayed in front of a reflector. Legend has it that a Russian princess, forced to marry against her will, fled the ceremony and took refuge in the lantern room, where her body was found. Later residents swore that her ghost frequently stalked the chamber.

At a mere $4.7 million, Alaska was the greatest bargain Uncle Sam ever struck, though the press and public, still reeling under the exorbitant cost of the Civil War, ranted that "Seward's Folly," this "ice box," was an extravagance they could ill afford. Castle Baranof passed into Yankee hands, along with all the Czar's American possessions, in 1867. For ten years the castle served as headquarters and guiding light for U.S. Commanding Officers (doubtless an unenvied posting), and burned to the ground in 1894.

In 1852 Congress authorized construction of sixteen lighthouses along the Pacific Coast. Owing to the usual limitation of budgets only nine were completed. The first went up on Alcatraz Island in San Francisco Bay in 1854—later the

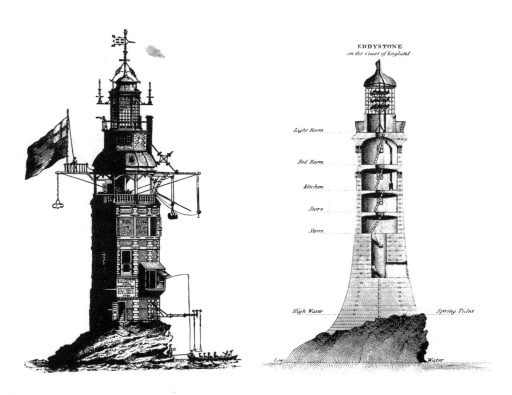

EDDYSTONE
on the Coast of England

Light Room

Bed Room

Kitchen

Store

Store

High Water

Spring Tides

Low Water

Water

The cause of much romantic lighthouse lore, Eddystone Rock near Plymouth, England, has had four lighthouses built on it since 1696.

domain of Alvin Karpis, Al Capone, the celebrated "Bird Man," and the American Indian Movement. When completed, the ninety thousand candlepower beacon drew shipping from a range of twenty-one miles. By 1857 the Tatoosh light at Cape Flattery, and the New Dungeness light, marked the entrance to Juan de Fuca Strait, perhaps the most crucial corner to be turned by shipping anywhere. For years to come, failure to see or hear Flattery cost hundreds their lives.

Sandwiched between Cape Flattery and Castle Baranof lay more than fifteen hundred miles of Canadian coastline, wrapped in abysmal darkness from dusk to dawn, pounded by monstrous swells gathering strength across the open Pacific, and shrouded in perpetual rain and fog. As early as 1786 the first British pelagic sealing venture lost two ships and a hundred men here. No one will ever know how many other vessels sailed to their doom. The first recorded wreck was the *William*, driven ashore four miles east of Pachena Point on the West Coast of Vancouver Island on New Year's Day 1854, with the loss of her cook and captain. Local Indians sheltered and fed the remainder of the sixteen-man crew and rowed them down the coast to Sooke.

This scenario would be repeated again and again. The finest sailing vessels afloat were salvaged and the best crews to be mustered were pulled from the shoals by "savages" in dugout canoes. Expecting no reward for their effort, the Pacheenas, Nitinats, Ohiets, and other tribes were the pioneer search-and-rescue teams, venturing with nonchalance born of a millenium's experience into waters which proved too much for the sophisticated technology of sail and steam.

Once the fixed American lights were burning over at Dungeness and Cape Flattery, the need for similar aids on the Canadian shore became obvious and urgent. By 1860 more than a thousand vessels had sailed into Victoria Harbour from ports as far flung as Melbourne, Shanghai, and Valparaíso. Local traffic, mail, freight, and passenger carriers sailed beside foreign ships that were seeking, in the words of one writer of the time, "The Various and the differing resources . . . which have so strangely been concealed for ages, which are now so suddenly brought to light." Captain George Richards, master of the *Plumper*, who was surveying the coast for safe harbours for the Admiralty in London, foresaw an unprecedented shipping boom, "a marked and permanent change in the commerce and navigation of the known world."[1]

With no navigational aids, however, the commercial boom was rife with dangers. If they could see Flattery, captains knew when to turn into the strait and steer for the Dungeness light. Once that beacon slipped over the horizon astern, all was echo and guesswork, dead reckoning in the dark.

The first Canadian light was a private venture. In late November 1859 Captain Nagle, Victoria's harbourmaster, paid one hundred dollars for a lantern and placed it on MacLaughlin Point at the entrance to Victoria's harbour. Three months before, the American steamer *Eliza Anderson* overshot the harbour entrance on a rainy night and ran before the wind well past Esquimalt.

By April the tubes in Nagle's lamp overheated and melted down. He had no funds to replace them. Within a month Victoria's merchants, knowing full well that a dangerous harbour ate into their livelihood, petitioned their Colonial Assembly to appropriate funds to replace Nagle's light. In late August a Victoria Lighthouse Bill was laid before the legislators, providing for a manned light on Work's Rock in the harbour. By September the bill called instead for the re-establishment of the MacLaughlin Point beacon. It never passed. By October 1860 Captain Richards had convinced Nagle that lighthouses he had already proposed for Fisgard Island and Race Rocks were far more crucial.

Richards stated the obvious. If a light were placed at Bonilla Point on the Vancouver Island shore across from Flattery, the entrance to the strait would be bracketed, almost impossible to overshoot. Once into the funnel of Juan de Fuca, all a mariner needed was a light on Race Rocks, eleven miles southwest of Victoria, to mark the limit and warn him off its tide-swept shoals. From there, another beacon on Fisgard Island at the entrance to Esquimalt Harbour would bring him to safe anchorage off the city that was "destined to become the emporium not only of Vancouver Island, but also in a great measure of the new Colony which has just been called into existence under the name of British Columbia."

Richards' report went to Governor Douglas on 23 October 1858. From there it travelled to the secretary of the Admiralty in London, along with a letter from Richards' superior, Rear-Admiral Robert Baynes, which directed their Lordships' attention to "the great want which is felt by all vessels coming to Vancouver's Island of a light on the North Shore of the Straits of Juan de Fuca." He advised that a light be placed on "the Race Islands or Rocks," with a harbour light at Esquimalt. It was "almost impossible after dusk" to make the harbour, he declared, "the entrance being so difficult to distinguish." Richards also recommended mounting a light on Bonilla Point opposite Cape Flattery, claiming it "would render the navigation of the Straits at all times easy."

Victoria in 1860 was far removed from the cloistered intrigues of the British Admiralty with its expanding empire, and all those waves to rule. Baynes' letter met with a cool response from James Booth, a Board of Trade official. He opined that the board, though charged with overall responsibility for navigation to and from the colonies, should not consider the proposal to "belong to the class of Imperial Lights."

This imperial designation was crucial since it meant that all material and construction costs would be assumed by Great Britain. For its part, the colony was in no better position than Captain Nagle to construct lighthouses. Unless Booth could be dissuaded or overruled, the project was likely to be stillborn.

Booth handed the package to Captain Sulivan, nautical advisor to the Marine and Harbour Departments. Sulivan, a career naval officer who had served aboard Darwin's *Beagle* and who had enough sea time to recognize the importance of the suggested lights, championed Richards' proposal, asserting that the establishment of the American lights argued for quick completion. He also recommended building an additional light midway between them. Presuming that the colony would need assistance, Sulivan proposed that lantern and

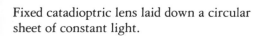

Fixed catadioptric lens laid down a circular sheet of constant light.

Below: Old gas vapour burner from a B.C. lighthouse converted into a table lamp. Right: Fifth order light used at Capilano Lighthouse. The crank handle wound a spring works which turned occulating (flashing) mechanism.

apparatus be sent out directly from England. Since the American lights were fixed beacons, he suggested installing revolving types: Race Rocks flashing at ten-second intervals, with a one-minute interval at Bonilla Point.

Sulivan calculated the cost of lanterns and apparatus at 2800 pounds sterling each, with additional freight charges. As for the harbour light, the Admiral foresaw a fixed beacon costing 600 pounds. Noting that the construction costs of a single iron lighthouse in the Bahamas, built "with Engineer and Workmen from England," were 20,000 pounds, he calculated that the same figure for the three lights in question ought to be the outside. Sulivan stressed that the wreck of a single British vessel might entail. . . a loss far exceeding the cost of these two lights."[2] He suggested that costs could be reduced by employing the assistance of idle seamen from British ships-of-war moored at Esquimalt.

J. Washington, an Admiralty hydrographer supervising surveys of the Pacific Northwest, laid down the cardinal principle of lighthouse construction: "They should not be placed at an Elevation exceeding 150 feet above the level of the sea on account of the prevalence of fog."[3] This maxim, born out of three-and-a-half centuries' experience at Trinity House—the Venerable General Authority for England, Wales, the Channel Islands, and Gibraltar, which had erected, staffed, and maintained lighthouses since 1514—along the British coast, would be disregarded fifty years later, with catastrophic results.

Fisgard

With Governor James Douglas' backing, construction began in 1860. H.O. Tiedeman, renowned architect of the day (who also built Victoria's first Legislative Building), engaged a local contractor, John Wright, to build Fisgard light first. The foundation was of solid granite, two feet thick, surmounted by four-foot-thick brick walls. The top was also granite, ten inches thick by four feet. Bricks for the "well plastered and finished" keepers' quarters were imported from England. The dwelling consisted of two rooms on each floor measuring eighteen by fourteen feet.

Fisgard light made a grand impression on Victorians of the day. The *Colonist* gloated over its distinctive iron spiral staircase, cast and shipped from San Francisco. "There is no stairs of a similar pattern on the continent, except at Toronto," the editor affirmed. "It certainly reflects a great credit on the designer and to see it will amply repay a visit to the Lighthouse." Standing atop the tower, he waxed eloquent upon the "admirable scene commanding a view of Esquimalt Harbour" from Beacon Hill to Dungeness light over on the American shore, and westward to a new light-tower reaching up at Race Rocks.

George Davies enjoyed the distinction of becoming the first full-time lightkeeper on Canada's West Coast. Recommended by a lighthouse engineer in England, he signed a contract on Christmas Eve 1859 which guaranteed a salary of "150 pounds per annum without rations," as well as a dwelling "exclusive of bedding and linen." In return, he agreed to serve one year after his arrival or to forfeit 50 pounds. "In case you are guilty of drunkenness or misconduct," he was warned, "you will be liable to be dismissed by the Governor without notice." The Colonial

Top: Fisgard, built in 1860, was first lighthouse in British Columbia, Bottom: The celebrated cast-iron staircase inside Fisgard tower. Jim Ryan photo.

Office agreed to advance the price of passage for Davies' wife and three children, to be repaid at the rate of five pounds deducted from his monthly salary.

He set sail on the *Grecian* with his wife Rosina on 19 January 1860. Davies' yellowing ticket lists their ages as twenty-eight; their children were six, four, and two. The youngest son was sick and made the journey later on another ship. The view from the *Grecian's* stern would be their last of England. Before them lay a grueling voyage of 196 days via Honolulu. Had they any inkling of the fate awaiting them in the New World, they would never have clambered up the gangplank.

Victorians have always nurtured an excessive pride in their colonial ties, but Davies' imminent arrival turned their pride to anger. The *Colonist* scarcely veiled its contempt. Noting that the colony "would have to find means for the ordinary support of the lights," the editor complained, "We ought to have had the right to select the keepers, as there are as many persons here just as well qualified as any that can be imported from England." Blissfully ignorant of the slight upon their arrival, the Davies family disembarked at Esquimalt in late August and took up residence by the new lighthouse built "to endure for a century," hauling their water from a nearby stream.

Davies superintended the fitting of the new light apparatus in Fisgard's tower, and then made ready to take charge of "either or any Lighthouse in the Colony, as the Governor may direct." Five months later, on 9 February 1861, Davies transferred to Race Rocks aboard the gunboat *Grappler*. At both stations Rosina

Left: Inside the Fisgard lantern room 1982. Jim Ryan photo. Below: Fisgard from shore.

alternated watches with her husband. The colonial secretary allowed her 40 pounds in recognition of her "services rendered at the Light House."

If the Davies family survived their voyage and icy reception unscathed, the apparatus down in the *Grecian*'s hold fared much worse. Of six ruby-tinted shades for the beacon, only one arrived intact. When half of a replacement shipment arrived, Davies hauled them up the celebrated staircase and discovered they had been cut to the wrong size. Six more arrived shattered in late August 1863, and yet another six were unloaded in pieces the next February. When all the tinted frames were finally fixed in place, Fisgard advertised the harbour's entrance with red, white, and green flashes.

The new beacons at Fisgard and Race Rocks were the culmination of four centuries of British lighthouse technology. Their mantles and reflectors floated upon a tub filled to the brim with mercury, and were driven by a clockwork mechanism, identical in design to the lead pinecones which power antique cuckoo-clocks. Four hundred pounds of cylindrical counterweights were cranked up from the floor. Once the dog was tripped, reduction gears spun the lens on top of its mercury bath for three hours before the weights settled on the floor again. Davies, like all B.C. keepers to follow in the next hundred years, catnapped through the night, rewinding the weights when necessary.

The primitive though highly effective use of mercury for bearings posed a sinister threat. Even today doctors can easily misdiagnose mercury poisoning as rheumatism, senile dementia, emotional instability, or psychosis. Whether it was absorbed through the skin or entered the lungs, metallic mercury wound its way through the central nervous system to the brain, short-circuiting the processes of

Fisgard was barely broken in when the warship *HMS Bacchante* ploughed into the rocks at its base in July, 1862.

emotional response and rational thought. Silent, insidious, incurable, its effects compare in their severity to long-term exposure to radioactivity. Lewis Carroll did not invent the "Mad Hatter"; there were lots of them around in his day, driven mad over time from rubbing mercury into pelts to stiffen them into top hats.

There were at least five hundred pounds of mercury in the tub under the light. Log books describe how a keeper would routinely lower the bath, wipe dust and debris off the gleaming surface with a rag, drain the deadly metal off, strain it through chamois leather, then top it up as required. At a temperature of twenty-five degrees celsius or more in summer, he was inhaling mercury vapour in the beacon room like steam in a sauna. Family members could be contaminated by residue on clothing, wives through sexual intercourse. No one will ever know to what extent lightkeepers fell victim to the ravages of contamination. There was insanity enough on the lights, but the tendency was always to dismiss madness as "cabin fever," contracted through prolonged isolation.

As for the lens, the "Rules and Instructions for the Guidance of Lighthouse-Keepers" devoted whole pages to "the great art of keeping the reflectors in order," calling for "daily, patient, and skillful application of manual labour in rubbing their surfaces." Any flaws or scratches in their surface "must be due to dust and careless work," and the lightkeeper was held responsible for them. Each reflector was to be cleaned every day, and twice a week they were to be dismantled and carried to a bench in the lightroom where they were rubbed and polished to a sheen. At least once a year the lantern "and all its appendages" were to be scraped and painted inside and out.[1]

An absorbent sock-like wick soaked up colza oil from a reservoir below the reflectors, at the base of the revolving mechanism. Colza, an imported vegetable derivative, later gave way to cheaper dogfish oil, freighted down from the Haidas in the Queen Charlottes. Both fuels were viscous and dirty, leaving the sort of thick sludge which accumulates over time in a deep fryer. They were replaced by cleaner-burning kerosene in the 1890s. Keepers pumped the new fuel under pressure in a cylinder, lit their wicks with a "spirit can" of methyl hydrate, and then opened a valve to direct a stream of "petroleum vapour" up into a gas mantle. If the mantle clogged, pressure built up until it blew out, engulfing the entire beacon room in a sheet of flame and coating its inner surface with oily soot. With a particularly "bad batch" of fuel, a keeper might have to clean up three or four times a night—and quickly too.

Catoptric reflectors were arranged on their turntables, like gleaming flower petals around the light source, with space between each to produce a narrow beam from the one opposite. By the 1880s dioptric lenses invented by Augustin Fresnel, which magnified and focused the flame, were imported from Chance Brothers "near Birmingham," the world's leading designers and exporters of lighthouse apparatus. They came in five sizes or "orders" ranging from three to nine feet in diameter. Tinted panes were often puttied into place around the beacon room to cast a slender cone of red or green light over dangerous shoals.

The lights may have been at the cutting edge of technology, but the lightkeeper's cramped quarters were anything but modern and comfortable. William and Amelia Bevis, who arrived at Fisgard in March 1861 with two assistants, reported, "Every room...is so Damp that when the Frost sets in, all the plastering and whitewash will come off." If the fire flickered out in the night, Bevis complained, the bedroom became "so Damp that myself and Mrs. Bevis are so much troubled with pains in the limbs such as we have never before experienced." When gales blew into the funnel of the harbour, driving rain had "a complete run through doors and windows," pooling inside as fast as the Bevises' encroaching rheumatism permitted them to mop up.

After a "protracted illness," during which his wife and niece performed his duties, Bevis died at Fisgard on 5 August 1879. Captain F. Revely, the marine agent, wrote Colonel Francois Gourdeau, deputy minister of Fisheries and Marine, recommending that Amelia Bevis and her niece, "a strong and active woman," be appointed in his place. They were "in very poor circumstances," he confided. Gourdeau replied it was "against the rules of the Department to place Lighthouses in charge of women." The two were allowed to stay only until Henry Logan replaced them on 6 January 1880.[2]

Logan asked to be relieved in late February 1884, and Joseph Dare took his place that April. Dare, like scores of lightkeepers and their families to follow, fell victim to tragedy. On 28 February 1890 he was walking along the shore, shooting mink for sport, when he slipped. The rifle fell, clattering down on the rocks and discharging a load of shot into his eye. Severely wounded, Dare languished in a Victoria hospital for four months. The department refused to pay him during that time, and Dare, half blind and bankrupt, took up his duties again in June. In July he drowned while attempting to row home to Fisgard.

Fisgard light went through a succession of keepers until 1928 when it succumbed to the same fate intended for all the lights: automation.

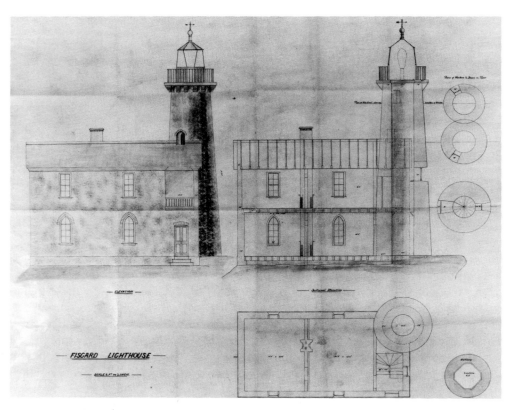

FISGARD LIGHTHOUSE

Above: Architect's plans for
Fisgard tower and residence.

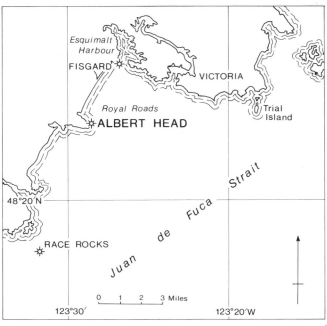

Race Rocks

No one ever questioned the need for a light on Race Rocks. Hudson's Bay Company officers bestowed that fitting title in 1842 as they watched the terrific eight to ten-knot rip tides sweep around them, surpassed in violence only by the tides at dreaded Ripple Rock up in Seymour Narrows. In the course of his 1846 survey Captain Henry Kellett retained the ominous name, noting, "This dangerous group is appropriately named for the tide makes a perfect race around it." Captains Richards of HMS *Plumper*, Fulford of HMS *Ganges*, and Nagle selected Race Rocks as the site for a light on 10 August 1859, the same day they decided upon Fisgard.

If Fisgard was an inspiration to Victorians, Race Rocks would be an enduring monument to lighthouse architecture. Scottish quarrymen cut and numbered each stone, stacked them in a ship's hold, and the tower made its way to Victoria as ballast. All through the hot spring and summer of 1860 the stones were wrestled up the ascending scaffolds and cemented into place.

Sixteen thousand sea miles away, while masons were piecing together the tower at Race Rocks, the *Nanette*, a three-year-old vessel of 385 tons loaded with $165,000 worth of cargo, cleared London bound for Victoria. Captain Main, her master, succumbed to dysentery soon out of port and entrusted the helm to his less experienced mate, William McCullogh.

On 23 December *Nanette* began her run into the harbour, under a lifting curtain of fog. McCullogh logged an account of how helpless a vessel could be once in the tide's grip off Race:

At 8 o'clock saw a light bearing N by W [Fisgard] could not find the light marked on the chart. At 8-½ o'clock it cleared somewhat, and then saw the point of Race Rocks for the first time, but no light. Called all hands on deck, as we found the ship was in a counter-current, and drifting at the rate of 7 knots toward the shore. We made all possible sail, but there was nearly a calm at the time and the sails were of no avail.[1]

All the crew's efforts only postponed the inevitable. *Nanette* careened into the rocks shortly after midnight. The construction gang was there to assist her crew, but they swamped the lighthouse boat. The remaining seamen, many wracked by spasms of dysentery, shivered through the night, crouching in the lee of her crippled hull. HMS *Grappler* took them off next day.

The impact of all that precious cargo up for grabs hit Victoria with a force not seen since the gold fever of 1858. Five days later the scene at the wreck "baffled description." The *Colonist* disdainfully reported, "Disputes as to the possession of packages fished up are constantly taking place, and not a few rough and tumble fights have taken place. Everyone seems to be working on his own hook, and in every case demands salvage for what he brings up." Faced with the prospect of losing everything should a new storm drag *Nanette*'s splintered remains into deeper water, her underwriters "dared not outlaw freelance salvage efforts." So the free-for-all went on day after day, fueled by gin from the cargo. The *Colonist*'s reporter cautioned that, owing to the hard drinking and "rowdyism" at Race Rocks, "black eyes and broken noses are quite fashionable there." The greedy comedy was finally marred when, loaded to its gunwales with plunder, a canoe carrying five men, an Indian woman, and her eighteen-month-old child capsized off Albert Head. Only one survivor made shore after three hours in the water.

On Boxing Day 1860 the beacon, which would surely have warned *Nanette* away from danger, had it been operational three days earlier, was lit atop the stone tower at Race Rocks. On New Year's Day 1861 the Colonial Secretary's Office issued a notice to shipping, warning mariners of the vicious tides. The rocks "should not be rounded nearer than from half a mile to a mile."

George Davies' first task as Race Rocks' keeper was to haul himself up in a bosun's chair and paint black and white stripes around the tower. Mariners had complained that its day shape blended into the landscape behind. To this day, the stripes set the tower apart from all others on the Pacific coast.

Receiving visitors on a lightstation, however short their stay, breaks months of monotony. As Christmas 1865 drew near the Davies family's excitement mounted in anticipation of a visit from Rosina's brother, his wife, and three friends. After weeks of baking, scrubbing, wrapping gifts, and planning a Yuletide feast, the Davies were up with the sun Christmas morning, watching the horizon.

As the boat drew near they ran down on the rocks and stood waving, waiting to help unload the guests and their gifts. Twenty feet from the landing the boat happened upon a whirlpool and capsized, hurling all its occupants and their cargo

Race Rocks Lightstation showing original residence attached to tower. Historic dwelling was recently demolished.

Right: Thomas and Ellen Argyle and with six of their children, 1880. Left: The Argyles in retirement after 21 years on Race Rocks.

into the frigid, swirling water. The surveyor-general had recently withdrawn the station boat, and no rope or life buoy lay at hand. William Saunders, one of the friends, clung to the overturned craft and drifted screaming within a few feet of the shore, but was snatched back and swept out into the strait. Within minutes all that remained of that black Christmas were a few floating parcels.

Broken in heart and spirit, the Davies family had less than a year before them at Race Rocks. In the winter of 1866 George was deathly sick. Rosina tried to attract the attention of passing ships by flying the Union Jack at half mast. No vessel took notice. Her husband's condition steadily worsened for nine days. He died shortly before Christmas. The *Colonist* expressed amazement that the family had no station boat "to send to the city for succor," a fact that called "aloud for the adoption of a system of signals whereby the wants of the lightkeeper may be made known in town."[2]

It is a chilling thought that George Davies' vocation could bring so much suffering and cost him his life. One can imagine Rosina's desperation as she stood at the rails watching every ship pass by, passengers and crew waving gaily back at her, waves slapping derisively into the rocks. George Davies was the first to pay the ultimate price of isolation on the lights. He would not be the last.

Davies' replacement, Thomas Argyle, had grown to manhood in Birmingham, England's dirty industrial hub. He joined the Royal Engineers and set out to serve in the fledgling colony of New Caledonia, western terminus of the Hudson's Bay fur empire. His ship, *Thames City*, slipped up Juan de Fuca Strait in April 1859 after a grueling six months' passage from Gravesend round Cape Horn, passing by the heap of quarry stone at Race Rocks.

The engineers' arrival was timely. Gold fever had struck with all its baffling symptoms. Some thirty thousand gold seekers poured into the colony. Many were Americans with little love for Great Britain; infused with the unsettling notion of Manifest Destiny, they were determined to "twist the lion's tail."

As they flocked up the Fraser to the gold fields they met the Royal Engineers, who were charged with maintaining a British presence. For the next five years the engineers toiled from a base near today's New Westminster, surveying and clearing wagon roads up the Fraser Canyon, through Yale and Clinton, and onward to the Cariboo. Once having tasted life on the frontier, most of the transplanted Englishmen elected to stay and claim a free land grant of 150 acres. Only fifteen engineers returned to England. Thomas Argyle picked out a prime piece of waterfront property at Rocky Point in Metchosin.

Ellen Tufts' roots ran deep into the Loyalist community of Tuft's Cove near Halifax, but she left them in 1862 and set sail alone for Esquimalt via Cape Horn, passing the new Race Rocks light as her ship entered the harbour. There she met and married the strapping, full-bearded engineer and settled on his parcel of land to raise three children and tend a flock of sheep. Little did she expect that, five years later, she would be living on Race Rocks, watching thousands of other passengers looking over at her.

Lighthouses were nothing new to her husband. As a youth Argyle had worked as a lighthouse mechanic for Chance Brothers of Birmingham. He was a natural candidate to fill the vacancy at Race Rocks in 1867. The colonial government engaged Argyle as chief keeper at an annual salary of $630, and Ellen as matron at $150. They also hired two assistants for a total of $780, and provided supplies, the same rations issued to ships' crews in the Royal Navy, amounting to $900 a year.

Supply always depended upon wind and weather. In 1869 Argyle complained, "the meat boat has not been regular." In April 1870 they had exhausted their "fresh" meat and he had to row out to the *James Douglas* and buy some from the steward. "I have rote to Mr. Fell & Co. and requested them send the boats regular. But they do not notice my request," he informed the agent, "& Sir I wish you would please send me a copy of the contract for this year so that I may know when the meat boat is dew at the Light House." Sometimes when the "meat boat" arrived, the hands were only too anxious to get their cargo ashore. One Friday Argyle's nose told him to send a shipment back as it was "not fresh after Laying in a Box. . . since last Tuesday." But even rotten meat may have looked good in January 1870 when Argyle advised, "We have been out of meat at the lighthouse for 3 days and Sir I hope you will supply sum without delay."[3]

The station was supplied at great risk and cost, whether Argyle rowed to town or friends brought the goods out. In January 1871 John Costello, better known as "Billy the Bug," left Victoria bound for Race Rocks with their supplies. A sudden gale swept him past the station to the American side, snatching away sail, oars, and rudder. Costello was buffeted about for two days and nights. On the third day, borne near the lighthouse on the notorious tide, he ripped a plank loose and thrashed his way ashore. The Argyles did their utmost to battle the effects of hypothermia on their ravaged friend, but it was all in vain. A passing boat took his corpse home the next day. Known for his selflessness, Costello was described as "his own worst enemy. . .ever foremost in relieving distress while he neglected his own wants." On the day of his funeral all flags in Victoria were lowered to half mast.

But Thomas Argyle was obviously a man who was at home on the water. On 17 September 1874 he spotted two men clinging to logs as the tide swept them past on their way into the Straits. He rowed out, pulled them aboard his skiff, and brought them back to the lighthouse. He might as well have let them drown. The two were "seamen deserters" from HMS *Shah*, so instead of receiving recognition for the double rescue, Argyle found himself sitting in the prisoners' dock at the courthouse in Victoria. The magistrate found him guilty of "aiding and abetting deserters" and fined him $100—more than two months' pay—or a penalty of six months' imprisonment.[4]

Under most circumstances, the arrangement between Argyle and the colony was a comfortable one indeed; in fact, it represented the highest pay and best conditions to prevail on the lights for more than a century to come.

When British Columbia joined the dominion in 1871, the lights came under the jurisdiction of the Department of Marine and Fisheries. Lightkeepers' working conditions deteriorated almost overnight. In 1880 the department sacked Ellen Argyle, cut Thomas's salary by eighty percent, to $125, and informed him that he

Automatic electric lamp, Race Rocks 1982. Jim Ryan photo.

would be expected to hire and pay his own assistants and purchase provisions as well. The Colonial Lighthouse Board's free medical care for keepers and their families was discontinued, as was the circulating library for Fisgard and Race Rocks that had been set up by the colony in 1865.

Argyle was incensed. The cut in pay and loss of benefits seemed a shoddy reward for thirteen years' service, especially when unskilled labourers were earning a minimum of $400 a year in Victoria. Accustomed to the prestige and pay accorded lightkeepers in Britain and her colonies, Argyle applied to be pensioned off but was refused.[5]

The hard-hearted policy prompts the question: why, if they were the very linchpin of waterborne commerce, were lightkeepers suddenly and deliberately reduced to paupers? Surely their services merited a living wage.

In 1872 a commitee of Elder Brethren of Trinity House arrived to inspect the fledgling lighthouse systems of Canada and the United States. They were appalled to discover that "both systems seem to be ruled by political considerations rather than fitness or previous knowledge on the part of the keeper appointed."

Accustomed, like Thomas Argyle, to a highly professional and prestigious role

for their keepers (many of whom had passed stations from father to son for generations), and to a dedication which caused watches in the lightroom to be relieved "with as much punctuality as on a man-of-war," they could scarcely mask their contempt for the new dominion's mistreatment of its keepers. "The office of lightkeeper is looked upon as an unskilled occupation requiring no special knowledge or training," they reported, "and the keeper has neither increase of pay, promotion, continuance of service, nor pension in the future to look forward to as an incentive to good behaviour. . . ."[6]

For forty years after British Columbia joined, Canada was virtually a one-party state. With a brief interregnum when MacKenzie's Liberals capitalized upon the overpowering stench of successive CPR scandals, Tories ruled as if by di-

Foghorn motor, Race Rocks. "You'd start it by climbing on the spokes." Note hand-painted ceiling border.

vine right. Patronage oiled the gears of government. Now a defeated cabinet minister can find as much power and more income in a law firm, bank boardroom, or as head of a Royal Commission; then, every single job went to those whose politics were "right," who had licked stamps, opened their wallets, and invested shoe leather at election time.

Each lighthouse was "the gift of the Member." Captain James Gaudin, marine agent at Victoria from 1892 to 1911, took great pains to explain his helplessness in appointing qualified men. Writing in 1907 to James Forsyth, an experienced and proven keeper who wanted a transfer, Gaudin reminded him, "These appointments are never left to me. Rather, they are the patronage of the Member of the constituency in which the lighthouse is situated." Allowing that he "would very much like to see" Forsyth in charge of one of the stations again, Gaudin could only recommend that he apply to his MP to have his name placed on the applicants' list.

Patronage, though no more brazen than today, was far more commonplace, a political convention. Though politics need not rule out performance and expertise, the bizarre situation of lightkeepers virtually guaranteed that the best qualified keepers—sons and daughters who had grown up trimming wicks, polishing lenses, overhauling engines, handling boats—were given short shrift. Isolation insured that they grew up with no access to the partisan political process.

For the Argyles, lightkeeping after Confederation was suddenly a tough life, with no prospect for improvement. The dwelling at Race Rocks was wholly at the mercy of the elements, with no barriers against moisture. "Violent Stormes which we have witnessed of Late as carried the ole of the shuttering away from the s.w. side of the House," Argyle wrote in March 1871. "I also Beg to inform you that all Hands at the Lighthouse are complaining of Paines and for my Part I have not Been fre from Paines for the last month . . . as Everything is in a Veary damp state at this time."

Ellen gave birth to six more children during the years at Race Rocks. Even taking contemporary prices into account, when meat and potatoes fetched twenty-five cents and one cent a pound respectively, the family of eleven found itself in desperate straits. Thomas Argyle, however, had a great skill and even greater luck which allowed him to scrape a living from the ocean floor.

Doris Gilbert, Argyle's granddaughter, recalled that the barrel-chested light-keeper was a powerful swimmer, "a bull seal in the water." With this talent and the incentive of his barely subsistence wage, Argyle became the first skin diver on the West Coast. In 1885 the *Colonist* printed a rumour that the keeper from Race Rocks was paying for his weekly supplies in Victoria with gold sovereigns. Much to the astonishment of local merchants and onlookers, he strode up to their tills with his list, dropped a single gold coin clanging on the counter, and pocketed the change. It happened month after month. His supply seemed unlimited. In fact, when he died thirty years later at the age of eighty, he still had some gold sovereigns left to bequeath to his descendants.[7]

His granddaughter also possessed a silver teaspoon with the name "Barnard Castle" engraved on the stem. "Legend has it that Grandfather Argyle found this spoon in the hull of a sunken ship off Race Rocks," she recalled. The *Barnard Castle* struck the rocks early in the morning of 21 November 1886 and flooded so fast that compressed air in the hold blew her hatches off, spewing a geyser of deck timbers and debris fifty feet into the air. She went down in six fathoms. The *Barnard Castle* was a lowly coal freighter and the spoon probably stirred coffee in the officers' quarters. Present day scuba divers think twice about diving into the swirling waters around Race Rocks. Only the reckless and foolhardy would attempt it alone without the warmth of a wet suit. Yet for Thomas Argyle, gliding naked through the kelp forest over the sea floor was all in a day's work.

Argyle's term at Race Rocks stretched into twenty-one years. Always disgusted by his treatment at the hands of the dominion government, he tried in vain each year to be pensioned off. Always the answer was the same as in 1884: "The Minister. . . decided that at present you have no claim to be placed on the retired list at your age and present condition of health." There was some consolation in a pay raise to $800 when a steam fog alarm was installed. He was instructed to claim $500 for himself and pay an assistant $300. Fortunately, he was allowed to retain his eldest son, Albert. In 1888, after a total of twenty-nine years' service to colony and Canada, he was retired and granted a paltry pension of $21 a month.

The family now pinned all its hopes upon Albert. The department had appointed him keeper during his father's illness. In April 1888 the marine agent visited the station. He assured Albert Argyle that his permanent appointment "would be out in a short time," and advised him to write the minister for the position. With his application, Albert forwarded a letter which Senator MacDonald had given his father years before, "which stated the Government intended appointing his son to the position."

Albert heard nothing for seven months and never even received his pay. He used all his savings to pay an assistant, and ran up a bill of $100 "in extra trouble and expense going to and from Victoria." Two months before he was dismissed he received a letter from the department advising that they desired to appoint a married man and "a practical engineer." It was, he fumed, "a mean and cowardly imputation" upon "the very things that I had given 9 years of my life to attain pro-efficiency in."

The deputy minister came to the station on the heels of the insulting letter. Though he knew that the appointment had already gone to W.P. Daykin, a "special friend" of the local MP, he intimated that he would "use his utmost endeavours" to have Argyle appointed. He advised Argyle to cut costs by hiring "Chinamen to assist" on the light, and suggested he "could live on fish the whole year."[8]

The fateful telegram arrived from Ottawa Christmas week, advising him he was through as of 1 January 1889. Argyle immediately wrote Senator MacDonald pointing out that he had been paid even less in the interim than his father had

Left: Mr. and Mrs. Frederick Eastwood, appointed keepers of Race Rocks in 1891. Right: Race undergoing refit in 1920.

paid him as an assistant. "I am not afraid to stand before the world," he declared, "and prove that if not the best and most able lightkeeper in B.C., at least I have no peers."

It was all fruitless. By this time politics rated much higher than ability and excellence in the lighthouse service. W.P. Daykin, who benefitted in the short run from his connection with Gordon, would have two decades to learn that political favour and influence were relative things on the lights: those who had most went where they wanted; those who had least were ignored. Albert Argyle, born and reared on Race Rocks, had none, and his twenty-one years' service counted for nothing.

By the time Thomas died in 1919, leaving Ellen with no income, Albert Argyle had become a lawyer. Once again he took up cudgels with Marine and Fisheries. Fighting fire with fire, he wrote Simon Tolmie, British Columbia MP and Borden's minister of Agriculture, reviewing the shabby treatment his parents had suffered at the hands of Tolmie's colleagues across the Cabinet table. Comparing wages and benefits once paid by the colony with those of Canada, he rightfully calculated that over twenty-one years "the Dominion had made a saving of $145 per month ($36,540 altogether). Most of it at the expense of [his] father and mother." Ellen had served thirteen years and worked without pay for eight more. Argyle pointed out that under the "terms of service. . . adequate pensions should be provided to persons employed by the Colony at the time of Confederation."[9]

Argyle's letter travelled from Tolmie to Ballantyne, minister of Fisheries and

Marine, and finally landed on the justice minister's desk. He determined that Argyle was right in law—"The Dominion had agreed to provide pensions for certain servants of the Crown colony"—but he gingerly sidestepped the issue. Ellen Argyle's claim should be refused, the minister recommended, because there were no specific references "to such positions as that of matron of the lighthouse."

Even if the position were not spelled out (hardly surprising since Ellen Argyle was one of a kind in 1871), it would have cost a pittance, at $21 a month for the few years she had left, to provide some semblance of gratitude and a measure of

Race Rocks Lightstation from the air. Jim Ryan photo.

dignity to one lonely widow who had lived, worked, and raised nine children on a barren rock hardly big enough to hold them all. Why, of all people, did lightkeepers deserve such shabby treatment? The answer, as the story unfolds, is puzzling only because it is so obvious. Out of sight, out of mind; they were the easiest victims of patronage, cost-cutting, and bureaucratic intrigue. After all, whom could they tell? Most of them did not even get to the polls come election day.

W.P. Daykin moved over to Race Rocks from Sand Heads light at the mouth of the Fraser River. The marine agent accompanied him, possibly anticipating some difficulties from an enraged Albert Argyle. Daykin stayed only three years before setting sail in 1891 for Carmanah light on Vancouver Island's West Coast.

The Conservative party appointed Frederick Eastwood to replace him in April 1891. Eastwood had three school-age children and found an ingenious way of seeing to their education. He learned from a farmer that three more children were needed to qualify for a teacher and provincial grant at nearby Rocky Point, so he built a house there, rented it to the teacher, and sent his children to school.

Race's keepers frequently left the station in care of their assistants during the day, in order to row over to Victoria for supplies and mail. Unfortunately, Eastwood had problems with assistants. His wife found one snoring under a boiler in the engine room one night. Eastwood cautioned him about sleeping on watch. "Three or four days afterward," Eastwood related, "I went there myself, at night. . . down into the engine room, but I couldn't find anybody; and finally I went into the boathouse in a loft, and found him fast asleep there." Eastwood then took the highly unorthodox step of hiring Japanese, who proved to be far more diligent than "white men."

But he was far out of step with the racial temper of the times and his deviation was quickly brought to the department's attention. Colonel Edward G. Prior, Victoria's MP, wrote the minister in the autumn of 1900, charging that Eastwood was negligent and was often absent without leave. Worse, Prior revealed, "For a long time past this lighthouse has been in charge of two Japanese instead of a whiteman." This was the first charge of negligence in the service, and Louis Davies, minister of Marine and Fisheries, reacted quickly, appointing James Gaudin to head an official enguiry. Davies emphasized, "The Department is not desirous to encourage in any way the employment of these men. . . white men should have the preference."

At the enquiry all Eastwood's neighbours testified to the rumour that he was often absent, but none could substantiate the slur. On the contrary, to a man they claimed he gave good service. Captain John Walbran of the *Quadra*, and his first and second mates attested they had always found him on the station. "He is a careful lightkeeper, and I never had any fault to find in any way," Walbran remarked.

Thomas Argyle gladly came out of retirement to take the stand and explain that it was hardly surprising that Eastwood was frequently seen off the station. Mail service, delivery of supplies, and paid assistants had once been provided by the colony, but "after Confederation," he pointed out with relish, "this was all knocked in the head."

By the time Eastwood took the stand, he knew that the charge of absenting himself had evaporated; the only remaining issue was his Japanese assistants. He gave no ground. When asked by Colonel Prior (both accuser and inquisitor) if he considered that "the Japs" were "trustworthy," Eastwood steadfastly maintained "I have had more faithful attendance with my Japs than ever I had with white men." Stunned, Prior pressed on:

Q. Captain Gaudin knew you were employing Japanese?
A. Oh, yes.
Q. Did he ever tell you you should not employ them?

A. No, he has never told me plainly that I should not.
Q. He has never shown you anything in the Regulations that you should not?
A. No, there is nothing in them about that.
Q. You have a copy?
A. There is nothing in the Regulations showing who I should employ.

Having failed to prove negligence, and snared by the lack of specific racial discrimination in their own regulations, the commission decided that "the evidence did not substantiate the charges" and adjourned. It was the first and last full scale inquiry into the competence and performance of a lightkeeper.[10]

A patronage system is only as secure as a party's grip on the levers of power. When the electorate pried the Conservatives' fingers loose in July 1896, a shock wave went through the public service. The ripples soon reached the lights. L.O. Demers, a transplanted Quebecker who kept a hotel, had hoarded two letters of recommendation from J.F.R. Prefontaine, the minister, attesting to how much he "contributed and worked for the party in Hochelaga" for twenty years against the day of the Grits' triumph. Surely the keepership of Race Rocks was a fitting reward. He wrote L. Gelinas, secretary of the Department of Public Works, pointing out, "[Eastwood] has never been in favour of the Liberal Administration and consequently is not entitled to any party favours," and enclosed the precious Prefontaine letters.

Fortunately for Eastwood, Demers either lacked sufficient political clout or settled for another plum. At any rate, the department knew that the testy keeper out at Race was not one to be trifled with. He remained on the station until retiring in 1919. But for decades to come, the winds of change in Canadian politics would buffet the keepers with as much relentless, unpredictable fury as the gales blowing up and down their coast.

Nanette was the last vessel to ram Race Rocks on a clear night. The light was easily visible for eighteen miles from the wheelhouse of any ship bound up the Straits toward Victoria. When fogbound, George Davies wound up a clockwork bell and ships' officers demanded strict silence aboard during their approach. They could hear it pealing clearly enough in good weather, but dreaded the high winds and heavy seas which muzzled the gong. In 1892 the department installed a steam plant and compressed air horns which blasted forth a longer, more powerful signal. This should have assured complete safety when fog rolled in within arm's length of the rails, yet over the years, ship after ship was taken captive by the merciless rip tide and driven aground. SS *Nicola Biddle* sank 5 January 1867; followed by *Swordfish*, 6 November 1877; SS *Rosedale*, 12 December 1882; *Barnard Castle*, 21 November 1886; SS *Tees* in 1896; and the *Prince Victor* in January 1901. Two Indians standing at Rocky Point on the storm-tossed night of 24 March 1911 witnessed the worst calamity. The ferry *Sechelt* had just cleared Victoria en route to Sooke. Heading into the teeth of the gale, her captain tried too late to turn his ship about. Her beam to the wind, *Sechelt* capsized and sank

"The most beautiful lighthouse tower on the Pacific Coast." Jim Ryan photo.

like a stone with all her crew and over fifty passengers entombed in their cabins.

As losses began to pile up everyone from Lloyds of London, the world's leading maritime insurers, to sea captains hanging about the waterfront, knew that something was amiss. Time and again ships' officers came ashore soaking wet, in lifeboats, to assail the marine agents and the commissioner of wrecks with charges that the horns at Race Rocks were quiet when they could scarcely see the bow from the wheelhouse just before they struck. And time and again department officials went to Race, seized the lightkeeper's logs, and learned, much to their chagrin, that the horns were blowing full blast, often for hours beforehand. Someone, it seemed, was lying. Opinion divided those who blamed inexperienced navigators or negligent lightkeepers. Whoever was at fault, the groundings and sinkings continued with sickening regularity around the light. As late as the 1920s sailors dreaded passing Race Rocks in fog as much as their grandfathers had feared the place before the tower was built.

In July 1923 the Furness liner *Siberian Prince* went aground. Though she was within a mile of the lighthouse in thick fog, no signal was heard before she crashed. Later that year the officers and men of the lighthouse tender *Berens* had the same eerie experience. It was clear weather and the keeper had seen the *Berens* approaching. He began making signals, consisting of four short blasts, for her to send a boat ashore. The *Berens*, with the marine agent aboard, steamed close by, hearing nothing. Obviously some mysterious action of wind and water created a "silent zone" which the horns could never penetrate.

On 2 November 1925 the Holland American liner *Eemdijk* approached to within a mile of the light. Hearing no signal, she ran up on the rocks on the same spot as the *Siberian Prince* before her. Two days later the salvage tug *Hope* became ensnarled in the *Eemdijk*'s lines and capsized, taking seven crewmen down with her.

On 4 December Mr. Logan, special officer and surveyor of the Salvage Association in London, wrote the Lighthouse Board in Ottawa, claiming, "It is the general opinion in shipping circles that this vessel, like the SS *Siberian Prince*, ran ashore owing to a 'silent zone'. . . on which the signal cannot be heard." The Board marked "No action" on this letter.

Colonel Wilby, the marine agent who had unknowingly sailed through the silent zone on the *Berens*, wrote the deputy minister to "respectfully suggest" that Race Rocks be the first West Coast light equipped with new radio beacons. In July 1927 the beacon went up on Race Rocks, filling the silent zone with its regular morse signal. In May 1929 the Hydrographic Survey ship *Lilloet* steamed out to Race Rocks to probe the mystery of the silent zone. Investigators concluded that the fog signal was deflected by the tower and surrounding rocks. The department surmounted the obstacles by mounting the horns in a separate tower. For more than a century the light and fog signals on Race Rocks saved hundreds of ships, but the surging current remains as deadly as ever. The lightkeeper's tattered logs catalogue strandings with an air of casual indifference:

1929 Nov 2—Str Cogdale touched Bentink Id. a.m. got off on her own power
Nov 7—Gasboat M2760 in trouble came into slip and away again 2:30 p.m.

1930 Mar 18—Motorboat Maple Leaf in trouble with boom off North Rock, p.m.

1931 Mar 3—A.M. str. James Griffiths grounded on Rosedale Reef 1 a.m. Floated off by Salvage King noon
Aug 30—3 young men in gas bt. from Port Angeles out of gas. Gave

them enough to reach Victoria

Sept 4—J. Bolney, 13 yr old boy from Metchosen lost in fog landed at lighthouse. Towed him to Pedder Bay

1934 May 6—Childar towed past in sinking condition

Dec 25—Ben Lawres passed badly damaged. No masts. Deck houses gone

1935 July 17—Maquinna collided with Elgar near Flatt

1936 Aug 25—Atlantic City struck rock off Race Rocks. Badly damaged. Salvage King out to tow her in

1937 Mar 19—Tug Storm King aground on North Rock for several hours. Left 11 a.m. unaided.

Ever since the war, radar has given ample warning of Race Rocks in any weather, but they still prove menacing, even to those who know the waters best. On 23 January 1950 lightkeeper Arthur Anderson bid his wife and two children good-bye and set out for supplies. On his way back he stopped at the leper colony on Bentinck Island. The storekeeper there offered to let him spend the night, as the white-capped sea was heaving under a rising wind. Anderson brushed his advice aside and launched his skiff.

When he hadn't returned by nightfall, Anderson's wife assumed he had stayed over. Next day she reported him missing. A pilot spotted his empty boat thrown up on the Port Angeles shore, but the lightkeeper disappeared without a trace.

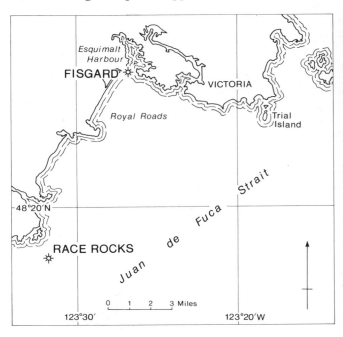

Sandheads

Fisgard and Race Rocks cast their beams over the waves just in time to guide the first great boom in marine traffic bound north for British Columbia. The mineral wealth, which Captain Richards noted had "so strangely been concealed," was quickly coming to light in the pans of prospectors who squatted along rivers and streams, grovelling for anything that glittered in the sludge. Between May and June 1858 ten thousand men went up the Fraser. Ships put out from San Francisco, loaded to their gunwales with a motley manifest of fortune seekers bound for Victoria and thence up the Fraser to the Cariboo, exploding the colony's population from two thousand to twenty thousand in two hectic years.

Though the mouth of the Fraser is sheltered compared to the mouth of the Columbia, gales blowing up the straits could whip the entrance into a frenzy which belied the *British Columbia Coast Pilot*'s boast that, "in its freedom from risk of life and shipwreck, it possesses infinite advantage over any other river on the coast."

The estuary posed an even greater threat in its infinitely shifting bed of silt, washed down from the tortured course of canyons upstream. Running aground in those days before depth sounders was the greatest hazard. A course which offered three or more fathoms below a vessel's keel might hold it fast a few months later. In the night, passengers and crew clung to their belongings and waited in mounting suspense as deck hands cast lead lines from the bow and shouted out the mark. In the dank fog it was enough of a problem to find the river's entrance, let alone a safe passage, and profits hung heavily upon making all speed in conveying passengers upstream and returning for more.

In May 1859 petitioners demanded the colony anchor a lightship at the Fraser's mouth. Sudden seasonal changes in the channel seemed to rule out a stationary beacon. Pleading lack of funds, the government in Victoria deferred action and the *Colonist*, conceding the necessity of "a light of some kind," recommended a lighthouse be built "near the Lone Tree."

Six years later Victoria purchased a New Westminster vessel, dubbed her *South Sand Heads*, and anchored her off the river's mouth. In spite of severe gales her crew kept her on station for the next fourteen years, until 1879, when an inspection found *South Sand Heads* "in such bad condition" that she was "no longer serviceable." The lightship ended her career as a fishpacking barge.

The North Sand Heads lighthouse which replaced her was a unique engineering feat. Adapting a technique of "wave-swept" construction, iron piles were screwed deep into the sand, braced with stringers, and topped off by an ornate hexagonal wooden tower which seemed, from a distance, to hover over the water. At the time of construction the queer structure stood one and a half miles south of the entrance with an elevation of fifty-two feet, showing a fixed white beacon visible for twelve miles on a clear night. In foggy weather keepers wound a bell outside which pealed every twenty seconds.

Two men kept North Sand Heads. Boredom in close quarters strains any relationship, and Sand Heads put men shoulder to shoulder for weeks on end, each adding secretly to his catalogue of the other's faults and flaws. And alcohol has often booked passage to Sand Heads with predictable results.

One April night in 1892 a breathless assistant keeper arrived at the customs shed in Vancouver harbour. He related to Captain Lewis of the *Quadra* all the abuses he had endured from his drunken partner until making good his escape. Waiting for his nemesis to fall asleep, he sneaked down the gangway and unslipped the rowboat. Suddenly the chief keeper appeared at an upper storey window, shaking his fist and ordering his man back with a string of curses. In his rage he hoisted a sandbag over the railing and heaved it down, missing the fugitive but breaking the boat's thwart. Seizing the oars, the assistant rowed non-stop to the harbour.

Captain Lewis sat the embittered assistant down and implored him to return to his post. No way. Exasperated, Lewis ordered up steam, sailed out to the station, took off the remaining keeper, and left two crewmen behind to relieve him.

Winters were the worst out on that mechanical stork, as the dogfish oil clotted and froze, sending the keepers "on a continuous trot" up and down the stairs to the lantern room toting sacks of heated scrap iron and hotwater bottles to pile around the reservoir. "At Race Rocks, if I am not mistaken they have a stove in the lantern room & I suppose they will be able to keep their oil in good running order," Sand Heads' weary keeper wrote the marine agent on Boxing Day 1884, "however we have done the best we could and have started in about three o'clock to prepare for lighting up."

Winter or summer, they kept constant watch. In August 1897 Hamilton Armour heard screams out in the dark, let down the station boat, rowed out, and hauled in two fishermen clinging to their overturned skiff. He wrote Gaudin advocating rocket apparatus be installed during the fishing season to summon larger vessels. Back in Ottawa Gourdeau, the deputy minister, scotched the plan, reckoning the cost much greater than the keeper estimated. Instead he would send out life buoys with light heaving lines—"all the apparatus that it would be profitable to keep at the station."

The *Quadra* anchored off Sand Heads in the spring of 1898 and her tars rowed over with James Gaudin. The agent hauled himself up the ladder, went in, and found the place "in a very good condition," but apparently deserted. Harvey, Armour's successor, lay in bed. When Gaudin shook him awake, he discovered the keeper was "in a poor state of health"—a casualty of constant campaigns against deadheads and flotsam fouled in the tower's girders. "He has been bedridden for the last six weeks and was in a very weak condition," the agent reported.

By 1905 steadily shifting sands had encroached upon the station, leaving a draft far too shallow for shipping. North Sand Heads stood a mile off the main channel. That March the department elected to acquire another lightship and fit her out at a cost of $10,000 to work in concert with North Sand Heads. In May the schooner *Mermaid* was purchased from the Victoria Sealing Company.

Built in Portsmouth in 1853, *Mermaid* served as an armed Coastguard cruiser and revenue cutter off the southwest English coast from 1856 to 1868, then was transferred to Hull and later to Harwich where she supervised the North Sea fishing fleet. In April 1893, under new owners, the *Mermaid* was labouring

Fog alarm machinery located in the hold of Sandheads *Lightship No. 16.* (*Thomas F. Bayard.*)

through a howling gale two hundred miles off Japan when her captain heard the watch call out "Whale ahead!" Running up on deck, he watched the leviathan rise up and charge full speed from a distance of fifty feet, striking with a crash that sent a shudder through the ship, "snapping two ribs off clean and turning the bowstem to one side like a rudder."

A Department of Marine notification dated 24 October 1905 announced the *Mermaid* in operation off the Sand Heads, describing her as a vessel "of wood, with two bare masts and no bowsprit, painted red with 'SAND HEADS' in white on the foremast head." The original fixed white light was retained and mounted on a mast thirty-six feet above her water line. The crew rang a fog bell every ten seconds. "Old North Sand Heads," the notice announced, "has been permanently discontinued."

Michael O'Brien, first skipper of the anchored *Mermaid*, was a veteran light-keeper of the U.S. Lighthouse Service. His stint on the ship bound for nowhere began with an experience all keepers dread: a surprise visit from the brass, Chief Engineer Anderson from Ottawa, who caught him completely off guard. "The ship was not only untidy—she was dirty," Colonel Anderson later wrote Gaudin from his suite at the Hotel Vancouver. "The keeper wants stirring up." Ever watchful of pennies, Anderson demanded to know, "How *can* he use 23 cases of oil per annum? I am afraid they must leak *somehow*."

In fact there was no end of leaks on the lightship, if not in the oil cans. Whenever gales proved too fierce to ride out, or if their chain tethers snapped, O'Brien and his one-man crew hoisted sail and fled for shelter. By December 1911 their foursail and jib were "very seedy," and O'Brien sent off measurements for replacements. "They are our Marine engines," he pointed out, but in their condition he didn't, "Trust her Not five Minutes in a heavy Wind." There was no shortage of heavy wind at the Fraser's mouth. One gale had recently shredded the jib, and *Sand Heads* ran hard aground, rupturing her seams which "Caused her To leak Badly and She leaks Very Badly at the present."

That June an unknown steamer came out of the fog with a scow in tow and rammed the lightship, shaking up her human cargo and staving in two starboard planks. O'Brien crawled through the stinking bilge to nail a copper sheet over the breach, then spent his watch at the pump, cursing the captain, until the gale subsided long enough for him to row across to Steveston to report the "Axident."

O'Brien's assistant jumped ship soon after. When the *Quadra* dropped off a replacement, he found O'Brien "a Very Sick Man," bedridden between stints at the pump, in a ship deteriorating as fast as her master. The channel was filling fast and if he couldn't anchor *Sand Heads* in deeper water he predicted, "She Will pound her Bottom out."

The tender *Leebro* towed the much-mauled hull into drydock in November 1911 for caulking. Back at her station she took on three feet of water her first night, "And it Took Three of us Two hours to pump her out—steady pumping," announced O'Brien. Within a week three inches of water came through her hull every hour, threatening to outpace the men spelling each other off doing knee-bends at the pump. O'Brien could actually see the water sluicing through her gaping seams. Incessant westerly winds and heavy swells had put her through a "severe test" and her master pronounced her "Not Sea Worthy." The next gale would doubtless send her down, and when it came the keeper planned "To slip and beach her." He dreaded the prospect of going down in deep water. "It Would Cost More than She Is Worth to get her up," he claimed, "And if She Was left here In Mid Channel She Would be a danger To the Trafic or pasing Steamers."

That scenario was enough to bring the superintendent of lights out from Victoria. Gordon Halkett went back with wet socks to confirm all O'Brien's fears. Even in fine weather an inch and a half of the Fraser River flowed into the hold. "The only safe course is to condemn the vessel and take her from the station," he recommended, "temporarily marking the position with a gas buoy."

They had to be quick about it. Within a week *Sand Heads'* passengers could *hear* water gurgling below them. They went down with pails of putty and copper sheeting. "She leaks like a basket yet," O'Brien warned. Now he was afraid to maroon his assistant on board when he rowed out with the mail. If a gale came up one man could never rig her alone and would have no lifeboat. By now the detested pump was good

Ex-sealer *Thomas F. Bayard* before and after becoming *Sandheads No. 16.*

only for exercise, excruciating workouts for an arthritic keeper who insisted he "Could not Throw Water enough to keep this Vessel free in a gale of Wind so Their will have to be something done with her Very soon."

The barely floating hulk was hauled away that summer and the old North Sand Heads tower was rekindled again until O'Brien took command of her replacement.

The *Thomas F. Bayard* was constructed in Brooklyn in 1880 as a pilot boat for the world's busiest harbour. Schooner-rigged, eighty-six feet long, her hull was constructed of solid oak and teak with copper sheathing. She was a fine, fast, and handsome vessel in her heyday when she shipped through Panama and ferried miners and freight to Nome at the height of the Klondike madness. Later she turned to sealing between Alaska and Monterey, shattering the long-standing record of eight days' sailing from the Unimak Pass to Cape Flattery. An international agreement reprieved the seals in 1911, and *Thomas F. Bayard* had a last fling trading out of Juneau along the coast until she came to a reluctant standstill in 1913 as *Sand Heads No. 16.*

Once the new lightship was on station the department set out with a derrick scow to dismantle North Sand Heads. The *Newington* landed a team of carpenters who were to free the frame tower from its pedestal for removal to Rose Spit on the east Queen Charlottes' shore. They soon found that the previous workmen had built so sturdily that the task defied all their wiles and experience. Finally Oscar "Long Bill" Hallgren, the *Newington*'s mate, clambered up and doused the woodwork with kerosene, struck a match, and found himself on the top floor of a bonfire. Dashing from one window to another, he finally jumped out over the flames into the sea and was pulled to safety by his guffawing mates.

Once the tower had burned out, the derrick barge strained for days on end to pull the piles, her decks flooding with each futile heave. In the end only one piling came up, six inches around with screw fins at the lower end. So well had the engineers built North Sand Heads that the braces came up as shiny as the day the nuts were tightened on their couplings.

Four months later O'Brien and his helper became captives on board a ship with a mind of her own. As if she remembered roving the coast with sails on her masts and foam flying in her wake, the lightship snapped her chains at the water line at 2:30 in the morning. Before her crew could make sail she "was pounding on the North Sands." When they finally rigged her, the wind was strong enough to wrench her free. O'Brien and crew "sailed her Arround the gulf Untill day break, Then squared away for English Bay," right past the incredulous crew of the *Leebro.* "The old Vessel Was bad enough," O'Brien concluded, "but This one Is Four Times Worse."

The water tank for the horns leaked but they could only keep watch and top it up as it was "impossibel" for two men to disconnect the pipes and upend it. Every day someone had to row for Steveston and fresh water. Heavy seas had wrenched steel plates off her bows, prying heavy screws clear through the planking, bow to stern. It was "quite impossibel" to swing the boats out "in any Ordinary Weather

Deck of Lightship *Sandheads No. 16.*

since the rails were half rotted away." She pitched and rolled so that it was equally "impossibel" to keep the mast-head beacon "elighted." "Conditions of This lightship is farr from being up To date," her captain warned. He had done his duty in reporting them and served notice that "if any reports Are handed in To you About the Fog Alarm...is Not in Operation Then you will kno The Cause." A month later he resigned.

That step seemed, at long last, to prod the department. By October shipwrights had crawled over and through her hull, stem to stern, to make her tight and seaworthy. Gaudin inspected her with O'Brien in drydock and wrote Anderson that *Sand Heads'* skipper wished to withdraw his resignation. O'Brien transferred to Triangle Island light where he would soon have ample reason to wish he were back on the *Bayard*.

Sand Heads No. 16 gave sterling service on her station for the next forty-two years. She underwent occasional refits to remove and replace steam boilers with air compressors for typhoon foghorns. Aluminum radar reflectors were installed on one of her sheetless

North Sandheads Lighthouse, 1879.

masts to give a bearing on screens seven miles away. Finally she was electrified. Her red and white alternating lights were visible eleven miles away at night. In daylight, with her brilliant red hull and billboard-size white lettering, she was a familiar facet of Vancouver's seascape. Altogether, *Sand Heads* underwent five overhauls, and coats of paint were laid on every summer as her keepers dangled over her side in bosun's chairs.

In 1948 she drove ashore on Westham Island and proceeded upriver to New Westminster for repairs. In November 1957 she was driven by another gale onto Point Roberts, and the department withdrew her from service.

Sand Heads evaded the wreckers and served a brief stint as a scow, back in once familiar northern waters before J. Parke-MacKenzie bought the hull, the oldest afloat on the Pacific Coast, and moored it in North Vancouver. But her career was far from finished. The Maritime Museum of Vancouver then acquired the ancient hull, hoping to restore it as an exhibit.

Reassured by a stone jetty which, combined with periodic dredging holds the main channel in place, the Department of Transport raised a second fixed station at Sand Heads in 1960, a thirty-four by forty-six foot square building with a rotating beacon and diaphone horns. Sand Heads remains a rotational "crib" station where two men live together again in close quarters. Television and shore communication reduce their boredom, but they still add up the days, and everyone at Sand Heads wakes excited on the sixteenth, when relief keepers are on the way from Steveston.

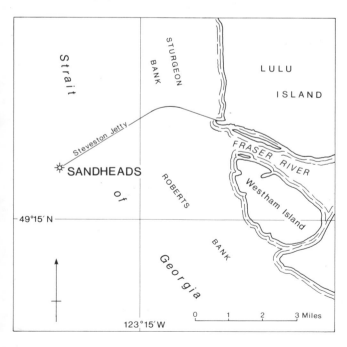

2 Safe Harbours

When they took over the Imperial lights from the colony, officials in the Marine and Fisheries Department faced an immediate challenge: to make the province's principal harbours—Victoria, Vancouver, Nanaimo, and Port Alberni—safe for the growing volume of regular marine traffic. Commercial shipping was mushrooming as more stable commodities—coal and lumber—displaced the gold and fur harvest to lay down a solid economic foundation for the fledgling province. In 1869 forty-five vessels shipped out of Burrard Inlet, their holds and decks loaded with fir and cedar. Over 35 thousand tons of coal left Nanaimo bound for California.

It was still the age of sail. Schooners and sloops rode at anchor beside the steamers which would take some forty more years to eclipse them. Their crews muttered about the ugliness of all that iron and smoke, but steamers like the *Enterprise, Eliza Anderson, Olympia,* and *Wilson G. Hunt* were already carrying passengers, mail, and freight to and from Victoria and American ports.

Victoria remained the commercial hub, visited by 652 ships in 1870, but Burrard Inlet stood poised to usurp a role that had been promised to Esquimalt. If the Canadian Pacific Railway's legion of planners had had their way, Esquimalt, or even Port Alberni, might well have become a booming metropolitan port, leaving Vancouver a backwater company town. In their original scheme, surveyors laid track across their maps to the Chilcotin, then followed the Homathko River down to tidewater in Bute Inlet. There they proposed bolting together monstrous iron bridges to span Seymour Narrows and reach Vancouver Island. Under one scheme, Barkley Sound, at the head of the snake-like Alberni Canal, would be the leading port of entry, two days, maybe three, closer to the Orient than Burrard Inlet.

A light on Cape Beale at the southern entrance to Barkley Sound would attract more shipping than Alcatraz, as Canada's Pacific gateway would one day eclipse San Francisco. But the lighthouse was destined to be the only concrete achievement. The plans lie curled and yellowing somewhere in the CPR archives, curios of a grandiose scheme tempered by two formidable realities: the precipitous bulk of Mount Waddington at the head of Bute Inlet and the murderous foul ground in Barkley Sound.

In 1872, with ink barely dry on the new province's confederation papers, the MacDonald government sent Hector L. Langevin, minister of public works, out west to survey British Columbia's requirements and priorities. It was a long list. The former colony was surly and suspicious, like a reluctant bride discovering her suitor is really a fawning habitué of Bay Street boardrooms who might rate a rich dowry higher than her spectacular looks. Perhaps the national railroad was merely a hollow promise made in the heat of their whirlwind courtship.

Commercial interests, always fearful of losing trade and traffic to the detested Yankees of Seattle and San Francisco, clamoured for port improvements. With the Vancouver Island rail link on the drawing boards, Langevin could hardly argue against the Cape Beale light. Not to be outdone, boosters from Victoria,

Vancouver, and Nanaimo drew him aside with demands of their own: lighthouses at Point Grey, Burrard Inlet's south shore, and Turn Point on Stewart Island in the Gulf of Georgia; a beacon in Victoria's Inner Harbour, and yet another on Entrance Island off Nanaimo. Langevin packed their petitions into his bulging carpetbag, and headed back to Ottawa. With the CPR signalling "full ahead," the cabinet quickly approved the harbour lights.

Cape Beale Lightstation 1981. Jim Ryan photo.

Cape Beale

In the autumn of 1872 the Canadian government steamer *Sir James Douglas* left Victoria with a surveyor aboard to select a likely site for the harbour light at Barkley Sound. Arriving off the entrance, Mr. Pearce embarked with a party of civil engineers and a construction crew in a workboat, and made several fruitless attempts to land beneath the forbidding cliffs of Cape Beale. Frustrated by the heavy sea, they clambered back aboard the steamer and proceeded to the tiny village at Bamfield. They attempted to flail their way overland to the Cape, but were stopped by impenetrable salal and deadfalls. The *Douglas* returned to Victoria, defeated, on 5 November. On 3 June the next year HMS *Tenedos* succeeded in landing the persistent Pearce and the Lieutenant Governor on a peninsula which they selected as the site for Cape Beale light.

First called Punta de Alegria by Lieutenant Eliza in 1791, the headland was renamed by Captain Barkley in 1781, in memory of John Beale, purser of the *Imperial Eagle*. Beale, the *Eagle*'s second mate, and an entire boat's crew, were killed in a skirmish with Indians when they went ashore near Destruction Island that year.

Building a lighthouse on the Cape was the most trying project yet undertaken by the department in British Columbia. Tenders specifying that all construction was to be of wood, "severely anchored" against hundred knot winds, were awarded to the firm of Hayward and Jenkinson. The plans portrayed a tower twenty feet square at the base, thirty-one feet high, with the light standing 167 feet above high tide. Materials and men sailed with Captain Spring aboard the schooner *Surprise* and anchored in Dodger Cove, six miles of tangled rain forest away from the site. All equipment, including seven tons of lantern and machinery, made their way to the cleared station on the backs of local Indians.

Little is known about Robert Westmoreland, first keeper at Cape Beale, aside from the fact he was a "giant killer," whose fearless revelations of corruption brought down a marine agent, but also cost the keeper his job.

For the first months after Confederation the surveyor-general administered marine policy until the fledgling Department of Marine and Fisheries assumed control in 1872. Captain James Cooper won the appointment as first marine agent. Cooper had been something of a political spitfire under the colonial regime. His deep dislike of the Hudson's Bay Company's monopoly had developed into a keen hatred of Governor Douglas. His animosity was so intense that he had even

The first *James Douglas*, an early lighthouse tender commanded by Capt. James Gaudin.

left his Sooke homestead to sail to England in 1857 to testify before a Commons Select Committee investigating HBC misdealings. Much to Douglas' dismay, Cooper used his influence there with Lord Lytton to secure the office of harbour-master at Esquimalt—a timely appointment since Cooper was teetering on the brink of bankruptcy.

"Mr. Cooper's office is a sinecure," Douglas wrote the colonial secretary in disgust, "there is literally nothing for him to do, the entering and clearing of vessels being effected at the Custom House. His services would be no acquisition in any other Department and his pecuniary embarrassments present an obstacle to his being appointed as a collector of revenue."[1]

Once having wormed his way into colonial upper crust, Cooper used his "sinecure" as a springboard to win election to the legislature as a "reformer." Governor Douglas, barely able to stand the sight of the man, transferred Cooper to New Westminster. Cooper resigned and ploughed his eighteen months' salary in lieu of office into the Beehive Hotel in Victoria.

By 1872, when Cooper wove his way back into the public service, his arch-enemy Douglas was gone. But the governor's earlier warnings about Cooper's trustworthiness were soon borne out. In his new post as marine agent he took charge of the two existing lights, Fisgard and Race Rocks, presiding over the new government's policy of reducing wages and eliminating colonial fringe benefits. He also superintended the construction of the new light at Cape Beale where, in a move he must have rued forever after, he appointed Robert Westmoreland at a salary of $700.

Westmoreland kept a careful tally of his stores when they arrived, and soon noted discrepancies between bills of lading and what came ashore from the *Sir James Douglas'* hold. He began to speculate loud and long, to all who would listen, about the real fate of coal and oil destined for Cape Beale. Westmoreland's rash rumours ultimately reached Cooper in Victoria. In 1875 the agent brazenly sued the lightkeeper for slander on four charges alleging misappropriation of stores. He won a settlement of $500.

It was a hollow triumph. Clerks soon set off on a paper chase and uncovered damaging evidence of Cooper's hands in the public till. The evidence underlying Westmoreland's impotent mouthings was so compelling that the agent appeared in Municipal Court in Victoria in October 1877 to answer charges of obtaining money under false pretenses. Mindful of Cooper's stature, Magistrate A.F. Pemberton granted bail and remanded his case to the Supreme Court of British Columbia.

He never appeared. Cooper skipped bail and fled the country, a futile and failed figure. It seems no great effort was made to track down the wayward marine agent; his appointment was quietly cancelled by an Order in Council in June 1879, "on evidence that the Agent had been guilty of fraud in the transaction of Departmental business."[2] At Race Rocks, Thomas Argyle must have gloated over the fate of the official who had been so indifferent to his troubles.

If James Cooper, somewhere on the lam south of the border, betrayed all the worst features of the Victorian bureaucrat, his successor, Captain F. Revely, gave some comfort in his almost calculated obscurity. He was followed by an equally inconspicuous man, Herbert G. Lewis. Even so, a cloud hovered over the ornate facade on Wharf Street which housed the marine office; a cloud that was not dispelled until well into the term of Lewis' successor.

When a twenty-eight-year-old chief officer shouldered his kit bag and walked down the gangplank of the HBC ship *Prince of Wales* one summer afternoon in 1865, ten years before Cooper's disgrace, no one could have foreseen that this young seafarer would eventually transform the waterborne commerce of British

Columbia. A peerless master mariner, shrewd bureaucratic infighter, and paternalistic protector of the men and women on the lights who became his wards, Captain James Gaudin singlehandedly resurrected the Department of Marine and Fisheries' dispirited western service, and built it into one of Victoria's proudest institutions.

Portraits of Gaudin show him as a ruggedly handsome full-bearded officer, resplendent in blue serge and brass buttons, who might have walked off the pages of Conrad. He cut quite a figure, the "rollicking sailor with stories of far distant ports," and soon made himself "extremely popular. . . with the belles of the time." Once word spread that Gaudin was in port there was no end of embossed invitations to high teas, picnics, and glittering balls, with much flirting behind fans on clematis-shrouded verandas as Victoria's matrons jockeyed to land a most eligible bachelor for their "belles.

Agnes Caulfield Anderson won out in February 1873 and spent her honeymoon and early married life aboard *Lady Lampton*, somewhere between Victoria and the Gaudin ancestral estate on the Isle of Jersey. In the late seventies he left her ashore to scout property, and bought a spectacular tract on Craigflower Road where Gaudin built Illa Villa. He spent his shore time laying out an old world garden "running riot with roses and masses of wild sweet peas."

But the gardener still harboured a dream of being master of his own ship. In July 1878, with James Cooper on the run in the States, the *Colonist*'s attention

Cape Beale Lightstation 1917.

was turned to happier matters: "[Gaudin's] numerous friends. . . will be pleased to learn that he has become the owner of a smart Clipper which is loading for this port in London." When the *Rover of the Seas* slipped around Race Rocks with Gaudin at her wheel that fall, reporters were waiting. He must be "well proud" of this "trim looking vessel," they wrote, and of the "excellent condition in which she came into port" with a cargo of gunpowder "in as good a state as when it was placed on board."

Every sea captain has two loves in his life. Gaudin's affair with his gamine new mistress lasted ten years, an anxious decade for Agnes and their two daughters as they waited every afternoon for news of the *Rover*. In 1884 the wayward husband "was persuaded" to forgo the open seas for the post of Victoria harbour pilot. Soon after he joined Marine and Fisheries as master of the *Sir James Douglas.*

Eight years later, in 1892, having relinquished command of the new tender *Quadra*, he traded the wheelhouse for a land-locked view of Wharf Street in that besieged marine agency.He was commissioner of wrecks, examiner of masters and mates, and marine agent, taking command of a far-flung crew of lighthouse keepers, a command he would hold for two distinguished decades. "When he took office there were very few lights along the coast, or any sort of marks," the *Colonist* reminded its readers in an obituary in 1913. "Knowing the coast as well as he did—it is largely on his recommendations that the aids to navigation which make this one of the safest coasts in the world to navigate were installed."

It was the last time B.C. keepers would shed tears at the demise of an agent. After James Gaudin came the autocratic Robertson, another ship's captain, then an unlikely succession of army officers—the Colonels, Wilby and Dixon—who imposed their brand of martial law on the lights. None sank as low as Cooper, but neither did they emulate the humanity of Gaudin.

The enlightened years under Gaudin were still in the future in 1875 when Cape Beale lightkeeper Robert Westmoreland yanked the thread that unravelled Cooper's stormy career, and humanity was not the order of the day. Westmoreland's reward for exposing Cooper's corruption was to be summarily dismissed. His replacement, Emmanuel Cox, had served as an overseer on Lord Hamilton's estates in county Cork, Ireland, patrolling on horseback, checking the sloth of his tenants and ferreting out poachers. Frances Cox's parents had had high hopes for her—including marriage to Lord Hamilton's son and heir—but there was no thwarting her infatuation for the dashing Emmanuel. She "lost caste" by marrying him. "But she took care to bring us up so there was none of that," her daughters recalled. "She disliked it very much—class distinction. She was very much afraid of it."[3]

Emigration was the surest escape from the shackles of class, so the Coxes, with their infant son and two daughters, joined the stream seeping out of Ireland in the 1860s. They came first to Marysville in California. When he heard that Vancouver Island was like another Ireland, however, Cox booked passage on the *Prince*

Albert for Esquimalt. He soon found work as an agricultural labourer in the newly cleared fields around Cedar Hill and Mount Tolmie, scratching out a meagre living and dreaming the dream of all immigrants: to make something more of himself.

The Governor General of Canada, Lord Dufferin, and Lady Dufferin, the daughter of Lord Hamilton, visited Victoria amid much fanfare in 1874. Lady Dufferin was anxious to seek out her old friends, but when she found them she was appalled to see that Emmanuel had sunk to a level little better than her father's tenants. She urged her husband to exert his influence to find them something—anything— better in the government service. As a result, Emmanuel Cox was appointed lighthouse keeper at Berens Island in Victoria harbour.

The Coxes had five children and the pay at Berens was poor so Emmanuel applied for a promotion. His efforts were soon rewarded. On Christmas Eve

Captain James Gaudin, much beloved Marine Agent 1892-1911, who presided over a golden age on west coast lights.

1877 the family received confirmation of their move "to the end of God's reach": Cape Beale. The ship deposited them, with their effects, at Dodger's Cove. They stayed there a week with a storekeeper, the only white man in the settlement, waiting for foul weather to break so they could land at the lighthouse. Finally they pushed off in five dugout canoes, each manned by three Indians. In the course of the journey a pod of killer whales terrified them as their huge dorsal fins sliced through the waves between the canoes.

Once in the shallows, the crewmen leapt out and carried all the Coxes in turn onto dry land. Only five at the time, Pattie Cox would never forget that trip ashore aboard "Whiskey Charlie," who shouted, "Hang on, hang on!" above howls of laughter. Emmanuel, a strapping two-hundred pounder, needed two Indian steeds to carry him through the surf. "Whiskey Charlie" and his mates waded back to unload the Coxes' belongings and hauled them up the cliffs.

The toil and dedication of the Barkley Sound tribesmen, who had built the station, was always crucial to Cox and those who followed him. John Mack was nominally in charge of providing assistance. For a fee of five dollars per month he kept constant watch for a Union Jack to summon him from Dodger's Cove if the

light failed or if its occupants were in distress. In response to the flag snapping in
the breeze, Mack would immediately paddle over to the station. He also delivered
mail and supplies to the lighthouse for more than fifty years.

On one occasion when Emmanuel was off the station, the lens clockwork
broke. Frances ran up the flag to summon John Mack. She gave him some
provisions and a message to the marine agent and he set off alone on the eighty-
five mile trip down the coast to Victoria. Two days and nights later Mack rounded
Race Rocks into the harbour, scrambled ashore, delivered the letter, and returned
with his canoe, replacement parts, and Emmanuel Cox aboard the *Sir James
Douglas*.

Manpower always filled the breach when machinery failed. On another occasion
when Cox was absent, the rotating mechanism gave out. For ten endless nights
the family took turns up in the tower, cranking the lens by hand at a constant
speed to time its flashes. Frances and the two girls took the early shift and the
older son, Gus, relieved them from midnight to daybreak.

In 1890 Pattie Cox was manning the station when she spied a fully rigged ship
lying becalmed near the breakers. She immediately wired Victoria to send up a
tug before the *Old Kensington* drifted onto the rocks. The vessel had no agent in
Victoria, so no towboat would sail without a guarantee of $500. Pattie wired back
that she had the money in her savings account and would personally guarantee
the costs. A tug arrived next day and hauled the schooner out of its doldrums.
Before cutting her loose, the tug's master informed her captain that they owed
their rescue to the lightkeeper's daughter. A year later a parcel arrived from a
Chinese port, sent by the *Old Kensington*'s captain, which contained a silk shawl,
a daguerreotype of his ship under full sail, and five pounds of tea. In 1957 Pattie
proudly showed the faded photograph to George Nicholson of the *Victoria Colonist*.

Twice a year the *Douglas* landed provisions at Cape Beale—the Coxes' only
scheduled contact with "civilized" outsiders. Transportation to and from Victoria
for shopping sprees, leave, or personal business was always haphazard. Captain
Victor Jacobson of the sailing schooner *Minnie* once landed his wife at Cape
Beale to stay with the Coxes while he went on to the killing grounds. Upon his
return, Pattie and sister Annie leaped at his invitation to accompany him to
Victoria, hoping to come back on the next tender.

The *Douglas* was out of commission. Faced with a wait of weeks, even months,
the girls elected to travel back by canoe with Gaelic Dick, an Indian, and his wife,
homeward bound after a summer of hop-picking in the United States. The journey
took four days. "You couldn't sit any way but tailwise," Annie recalled, seventy
years later. "When we did stand up to get out of the canoe, we couldn't walk."
Every night the girls helped to haul the canoe ashore, built a fire, and improvised
a meal from their meagre provisions and whatever fish luck brought them. They
washed it down with scalding tea, and slept wrapped in blankets on mattresses of
moss under the trees.

As they neared the Nitinat River, Gaelic Dick became noticeably agitated.

Finally he confided that he feared for his life among the Nitinats, having eloped with his wife without their chief's consent. They had recently killed a friend for a similar indiscretion. Pitching camp, he warned them to hide if any "delate mesatchie tillikum"—very wicked friends—appeared. After a sleepless night they stealthily launched the canoe before daybreak and headed home.

As the only sentinels on the West Coast, the Coxes were often forced to share their home and provisions with luckless shipwrecked sailors. On the night of 26 July 1879 the *Becherdass-Ambiadass* was bound from Shanghai to Port Moody to take on lumber. A capricious shift in wind and a curtain of fog conspired to drive the ship onto the rocks off Pachena Point. Luckily, a huge swell hoisted her over the reef and deposited the stricken ship in a small cove. As water gushed into the broken hold her crew took to their boats and reached the shore safely.

At daybreak Indians picked up the mate in a canoe and landed him at the lighthouse. Cox paddled him over to Dodger's Cove to enlist help from Captain Spring of the *Favourite*. He counselled Spring to dispatch Indians to Victoria to see the ship's agents "for assistance to take the necessary steps." "He led the mate and me to suppose it would be done," Cox noted in his log, "but I know from a fact, he did not do it." Cox paddled back to the wreck and returned home with the captain's two children.

A year later the *Glen Fruin*, her hold crammed with Australian coal, sprang a leak in mid-ocean. Her crew pumped feverishly for several weeks as the schooner, minus her foretop-gallant and jib-boom, limped toward the mouth of the Columbia. As if he had not expended enough effort to keep his crippled vessel afloat, Captain Lang stubbornly refused any offer of a tow. A sudden gale blew *Glen Fruin* steadily north into Barkley Sound. Finally conceding defeat, the crew abandoned ship on 8 December. Reaching deserted Village (Effingham) Island in their lifeboats, they subsisted for several days on dried fish they found in an Indian smokehouse and on some goats belonging to a priest. They finally tramped to Cape Beale.

Cox noted in his log on 13 December, "Captain Lang and 4 seamen from bark Glen Fruin of Greenock at 6 of pm. All in an exhausted state, wet, cold and hungry. Capt. Lang left 8 men at Dodger Cove until weather moderated sufficiently to get them here...." The remaining crew straggled in three days later and immediately fell upon the Coxes' provisions. Grateful for their sanctuary, the sailors set to work with axes and saws to split a winter's supply of firewood, and pitched in with the daily chores, painting, polishing, making repairs. One seaman presented Frances with a handwoven rug mat. Two weeks later they set sail to Victoria with Captain Spring aboard the *Favourite*.

Of all the incidents around and about Cape Beale during the Coxes' tenure, the case of the *Dunbarton* was the most bizarre. Her captain committed the frequent, often fatal, blunder of overshooting Cape Flattery in fog and found himself off Barkley Sound, with Juan de Fuca Strait nowhere in sight, when it cleared. Thinking fast, he dropped anchor and asked the curious Indians who came out, to take him to the lighthouse. Cox explained to the distraught captain that it would be foolhardy to try turning his ship about in that foul ground. Weeks might pass before a tug could come from Victoria. Meantime, he warned, if the weather broke, the ship would certainly be ground to pieces.

The chief of the tribe interrupted. Using Cox as an interpreter, he offered to pilot the ship safely out to sea on condition that he have complete charge, brooking no interference from captain or crew. The chief had good reason for insisting upon a free hand on the tiller. Cox explained that years ago an American schooner had found itself in similar dire straits and had agreed to the same solution. Once aboard, however, the captain disputed the course chosen by the Indians. In the course of the ensuing argument the schooner ran aground. Furious, the crew hurled the Indians over the side without their canoes. Two drowned. The captain and crew took to their boats and were never seen again. The Indians consoled themselves by looting the wreck.

Taken aback by such an outlandish proposition, and doubtless expecting a similar fate, the *Dunbarton*'s captain balked, but later accepted the offer under Cox's insistence. Next day the Coxes watched a fully-rigged three-masted ship unfurl her sail with an Indian chief at the helm. After steering the vessel well out to sea and safety, the Indians returned shouting their chief's new title, "Hyas-ship-tyee!"—big ship chief—in triumph.

For the Cox girls, Cape Beale was a world removed from the safe, sober, and stultifying existence of other Victorian girls which so disgusted their contemporary, Emily Carr. They were far more at home in canoes than carriages, and supplemented provisions with salmon caught on lines tied to their paddles. Fashion was dictated by the weather rather than by designers in Paris and New York. While their peers sat sipping tea in parlours, Annie and Pattie squatted on dirt floors in longhouses, swaying to the beat of drums at potlatches. Both were crack shots and entertained themselves hunting raccoons and cougars. Pattie once surprised a cougar on the trail. Instead of fleeing, the enraged cat charged her dog. He ran to his mistress, bowling her over. Firing into the snarling mass of flying fur, she killed the cougar with a single shot. Emmanuel Cox was so proud that he sent a pair of claws off to a Victoria jeweller who fashioned them into a gold brooch for her. Looking back eighty years, Pattie Cox remembered it as "an ideal life. We . . . just lived our life apart from everybody."

Frances taught them until their early teens, then sent them down to Victoria, under the stern vigilance of Reverend Bartholomew Chantreau, to be "finished." Determined to "civilize" his wards, he punished them severely for the slightest misdeed. Three years at Bishop Cridge's private school were three years too many. They came home and Frances resumed their schooling. "She never failed on that," the sisters claimed, "with the happy result that we can go anywhere—always have been able to do it—and know how to behave."

As for their mother, Frances seldom saw another white woman for eighteen years, aside from a mysterious girl captured as an infant by Indians after they had

plundered a ship twenty years before. Yet her daughters never heard her complain. And if *they* did, she admonished them: "Oh dear, do be quiet. Everything's all right." She spent summers on hands and knees in the gardens, autumns at a steaming canning cauldron, and whiled away the long winters with needlework and embroidery. Annie marvelled at her mother's ability to adapt to isolation and enjoy it: "Oh, she was a wonderful person, really, after the life she was brought up to . . . to go down there and live absolutely alone except for the Indians."

Top: Bamfield in 1910 showing cable station. Bottom: Lighthouse tender *Estevan* unloading supplies at Cape Beale.

On the morning of 16 May 1894 Frances Cox hoisted the Union Jack and summoned John Mack for his saddest mission yet. Arriving with his aged father Nespus, he learned that his old friend Emmanuel had suffered a heart seizure in the night and died. Gus, Pattie, and Annie were all married by this time, and lived in Port Alberni. The telegraph line was down and the grieving widow was desperate to get news to them. Taking a letter, Mack shoved off and paddled furiously forty miles up the Alberni Canal, pounded on Pattie's door at 2:00 a.m., and rowed back to the station with her and her son Tom. Pattie managed to send a message through to Victoria. The lighthouse tender *Quadra* came and took Cox's body to Port Alberni for burial. When the family offered John Mack "chickamum" —payment for his services—he was sorely offended and sulked for weeks after, muttering "kahta-mika-tum-tum," meaning "how would you feel?"

Frances immediately wrote William Smith, the deputy minister in Ottawa, advising him that Emmanuel had died "of Old Standing 'Breast-Pang'." She implored him to "kindly consider [her] trouble" and appoint her lightkeeper. Colonel William Anderson, chief engineer and chairman of the Lighthouse Board, endorsed her scheme, noting that Captain Gaudin considered her "an able and energetic woman." Owing to her husband's heart condition she had long ago assumed "the greater part of the work. . . maintaining the light" with her daughters' help. If she were appointed, he recommended that one of her sons-in-law, or another man, be there as her assistant.

Alexander Haslam, MP for Nanaimo, also wrote supporting the widow Cox, but Gaudin replied that, "in view of the importance of the light," he could not recommend her and enclosed forms for Haslam to nominate a successor. Annie's

Lighthouse engine rooms often bore signs of overzealous care. This one at Cape Beale sports a gleaming polka-dot floor.

husband was appointed but resigned in early October. On 1 November the *Quadra* came to take Frances away. It was a difficult, despairing trip. "Poor old lady," Gaudin wrote Anderson after they had docked at Alberni, "she was sorry to leave her home of the last 18 years." The seas were so wild that they narrowly escaped drowning when the workboat swamped. All Frances' belongings were soaked. She had had no opportunity to make arrangements in Alberni, so her sodden provisions sat for three weeks, sprouting mildew in a warehouse. "I sustained what was to me a very heavy loss on that account," she complained to the minister, asking him as well to bring his "powerful influence " to bear upon obtaining her husband's pension.

The fifty-eight-year-old widow desperately needed some means of support. James Gaudin, always mindful of her husband's "long service under the government," wrote Haslam again. While acknowledging that she had no legal claim, he affirmed that "it would be an act of charity if something could be done for her in her helpless condition." Besides, Emmanuel had been paying into the superannuation fund for twenty years. But there were no pensions provided for lightkeepers' wives and assistants. Frances was left to make a living as best she could, alone. "She never got any of it," her daughter recalled.[4]

Cape Beale attracted worldwide attention in the winter of 1906 as a result of the unparalleled heroism of Minnie Patterson, "Canada's very own Grace Darling." (Grace Darling, daughter of the keeper of England's Longstone Light, achieved fame for her role in rescuing crewmen of the steamer *Forfashire* in 1838.) On 6 December Tom Patterson knew from hard experience that foul weather was brewing. He spent the morning up in the tower polishing the Fresnel lens, topping up fuel oil, and trimming the wicks. After cranking up the counter-weighted clockwork which rotated the beacon, he walked back home at sundown to sit and watch the night through.

Sure enough, it was a gale, with eighty-knot winds battering the tower. Each thundering swell, like a wall of green glass frosted with snow, came crashing into the rocks and lashed the beacon with spray. The wind bulged the windows inward. Through it all, Tom sat squinting out to sea, drawing on his pipe and sipping tea. As the sun rose, his practiced eye picked out a ship offshore. He awakened Minnie and they took turns at the telescope as the devastated bark drifted slowly into focus, decks awash, masts and rigging dangling over the side. The lens also framed a group of seamen clinging to the mizzenmast's stump. Tom's telegraph key lay dead and useless; the winds had toppled trees and snapped the line to Bamfield.

Out there on board the *Coloma*, Captain Allison and his ten-man crew were "deliberately and calmly contemplating the end." Since 3:00 a.m. they had been clinging to the mizzen rigging, watching their 168-foot ship disintegrate beneath them. Her lifeboats were long gone, and a feeble attempt to lash a raft together from a spanker boom and other debris had failed. Fearing panic among the crew after this final, feckless attempt to abandon ship, Allison made his way to his cabin and returned clutching a loaded revolver. He had sailed only two days with them "but they were all brave men," he claimed. "They looked death in the face. At one time we didn't expect to live another 15 seconds."

Suddenly Minnie remembered that the *Quadra* rode at anchor off Bamfield Creek six miles away. Tom was determined to stand by. "I guess you better go, Minnie," he said. "Maybe I can do something down on the rocks, and you can't."[5] She pulled on a jersey and cap, thrust her feet into Tom's slippers, slipped out the back door into the screeching squall, and ran down the tramway. High tide swept across the slender neck of sand joining the station to the mainland. Rather than waste time launching their skiff, she plunged into the frigid, waist-deep water and waded fifty yards across to the end of the telegraph trail. Rain and hail fell in a staccato torrent in the pre-dawn.

Once on the slash of a track she ran over the level and downhill stretches, catching her burning breath as best she could, labouring up the three-hundred foot incline. Winter winds and rain had mangled the trail. Sometimes she could find her bearings only by threading the fallen telegraph wire through her fingers as she sank knee-deep in the forest muck and the salt marshes of Mud Bay. She fell time and again on the greasy corduroy road, and finally emerged into the feeble daylight to slog across Long (Topaltos) Beach. Then back into the forest for the last, the worst stretch, "dark at dawn and twilight at noon"—the same twisted jungle barrier which had barred the way for Pearce and his cursing team of surveyors thirty-eight years before.

At last, after three miles' clawing over and under fallen trees, up and down moss-carpeted rock faces, she stood, exhausted and disheveled and bruised, at the head of Bamfield Creek (Inlet) where a rowboat was kept, her breath coming in long tortured sobs. The boat was gone. The swollen tide left only a narrow sliver of sand on either side of the inlet, and this was made an obstacle course by overhanging trees and treacherous rocks, slippery with garlands of seaweed. Minnie started running.

Wherever her way was blocked she waded or went around, depending how deep the water, crawling under the overhangs and through the thick, grudging salal. Finally, after zig-zagging another two and a half miles up the creek, she stumbled up the steps to the McKays' house, pushed in, and cried, "Barque ashore!" Annie McKay (the former Annie Cox) wasted no time. Together they bailed out a skiff, dragged it to the water, and rowed towards the *Quadra*.

Captain Hackett had just lowered a yawl and was rowing ashore himself when he saw the two women coming through the ragged curtain of rain. Ten minutes later the *Quadra* weighed anchor and was underway—four hours after Minnie had left home.

The two women rowed back to the landing and climbed up to the cable station. Shocked by Minnie's appearance, telegraph operators Topping and McIntyre pulled off their headsets, cut off transmissions in mid-sentence, dragged out a cot and blankets, and put the kettle on. Minnie laughed off their concern. "If they've

The 168-foot bark *Coloma* foundering off Cape Beale, 6 December, 1906.

struck, Tommy'll do what he can and if they haven't, the Quadra will get them," she said. She gulped down a cup of tea, then declared, "Now I must get back to my baby." Astonished, the operators tried to talk her into resting awhile, but since the baby was not yet weaned, the mother was adamant. Topping and McIntyre convinced her to take them along.

This time they rowed up the inlet. Though she never betrayed it, Minnie sat in agony in the skiff, her legs and stomach knotted with cramps. "I almost had to let them help me before we got there," she later confessed. "I got so cold in the boat that I got the cramps in my legs and sometimes it seemed as though they just wouldn't move another step and on Long Beach one of them just crumpled up under me. I told the boys I stumbled, and I didn't dare to stop because I couldn't ever have started again." She laughed and urged the "boys" on faster as they slogged back home through the woods and rain.

Captain Hackett made all steam for Cape Beale, arriving as the *Coloma* began to break up. "The bow was open," he recalled, "the seams split so wide that lumber from the cargo was floating out stick by stick. Bulwarks were gone and the deck . . . was flush with the high running seas which surged over it and battered against the poop, throwing clouds of spray over the shivering crew."[6] The *Quadra* set her longboat over the side into the heavy swell and it hove to alongside, put a line aboard, and took the men off. No sooner did they reach the *Quadra* than the *Coloma* struck the reef.

The saga of Minnie Patterson was rich meat for newspaper editors and quickly captured the public's imagination. The *Toronto Globe*'s editor called upon the dominion government to present her with a valuable piece of silver plate for her heroism. "Yes," declared the editor of her hometown paper, the *Port Dover Maple Leaf*, "put a thousand dollars in gold on that plate! It could be easily raised, and more too from admiring friends."

Captain Davies of the Seattle branch of the Seamen's Union of the Pacific wrote Gaudin in Victoria, anxious for details of Minnie's exploit, and asked for a photograph of Cape Beale. "I think Mrs. Patterson is one of the last persons in the world to think she did a heroic action," the agent replied, "but I can tell you she is one of the best and grittiest little women ever I met." The union presented her with a framed citation as a measure of "her sterling worth as the highest type of womanhood, deeply appreciating her unselfish sacrifices in behalf of those 'who go down to the sea in ships'."

A week later the *Seattle Times* dispatched a reporter and photographer to Bamfield. They met Tom Patterson who had come to town to load up his skiff with "Christmas cheer." Tom rowed down the inlet into the Sound and rounded the Cape to the station, hugging the shore all the way. It was a calm day on the coast for that time of year. Even so, the visitors were overawed at the size of the swells rearing up around them. When they arrived off the gap—"twenty-five feet of daylight and spray between the jagged rocks"—they crouched waiting for the right wave to propel them through. "It seemed all day," the reporter recalled. "Finally he saw it and with a shout to us to pull, we shot through the flying spray, past the rocks, into a quiet inland lake formed by the tide."

The shaken passengers climbed up the three-hundred foot tramway to the house. The journalist was obviously impressed and infatuated with his vivacious heroine. She was good copy, to say the least. He marvelled that, with her braided hair and her "unfailing high spirits and good nature," she struck him as "more of a girl than most young women of twenty," though she was the mother of five and had been married thirteen years.

They brought along a purse with a gold locket containing a cheque for $315.15 from the women of Vancouver and Victoria, a silver tea set from the officers and crew of the coastal steamer *Queen City*, and some personal gifts including a new pair of slippers for Tom. Laughing, she brought out what remained of the original pair. "I told Tommy," she joked, holding them up, "that if going over the trail is worth all this money, I had better do it every time it storms so we can retire and get away from here."

While the camera clicked away and the acrid fumes of flash powder filled her parlour, Minnie told of her life on the lights. "It wouldn't be so bad here if it wasn't for the storms," she confessed, gazing wistfully down at the surf sweeping the rocks. "The spray flies right over the house and the salt gets so thick on the windows you can't see out. There isn't a window on the house facing the sea that can be opened. . . the wind would shake an ordinary window to pieces in a night."

And what of the wrecks? "They're terrible, and we have seen so many in the eleven years we have been here," she said. "It's an awful coast and it's a wonder there aren't more of the poor fellows killed." They were a sad claim to fame, an awful price for celebrity. She would "rather not have the money and the nice things that have been said about me than to have had the wrecks."[7]

On 31 December James Gaudin received a cable from Ottawa asking if Minnie would prefer a gold medal or a piece of silver plate with her reward of fifty dollars, or if she would rather have seventy-five dollars in cash. Gaudin passed on the message, hoping she would "not think it presumption" on his part to suggest that the medal and plate, "duly inscribed," would allow her great-grandchildren to "be kept in mind" of her "heroic deed."

Minnie settled for the medal and plate. But no amount of gold, silver, or cold cash could mend her constitution, shattered somewhere on the trail to Bamfield. In her weakened condition she contracted tuberculosis and died five years later.

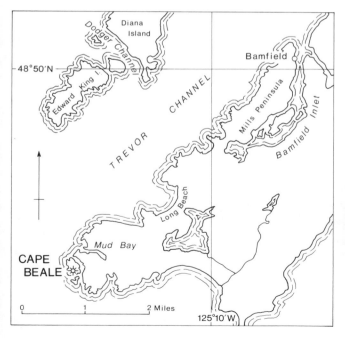

Cape Beale light tower 1978.

Point Atkinson

The Department of Marine and Fisheries first selected Passage Island over Point Grey as the site for Vancouver's light, but changed its mind again when James Cooper wrote the deputy minister that Point Atkinson, on the north shore at the mouth of Burrard Inlet, was a superior location which "would lead directly in and out of Burrard Inlet."

The beacon at Point Atkinson is one of Canada's most familiar lighthouses. Its tower is synonymous with Vancouver for foreign seamen and residents alike. Balancing their tripods precariously upon the Lighthouse Viewpoint, or on rocks along the shore, photographers have, over a century, exposed miles of film to capture one of the country's most spectacular seascapes. The people of West Vancouver have a nearly mystical attachment to "their" lighthouse, and to the 185-acre park around it which contains the last stand of virgin coastal timber to be found in that part of the province. Captain Vancouver was no less impressed by the towering stands of fir and cedar when he rowed past the point on 4 July 1792 in the *Discovery*'s yawl and named it for "a particular friend."

In 1872 the Marine Department awarded a contract to Arthur Finney for the sum of $4250 to build the light. In May 1874 Finney and his construction crew sailed from Nanaimo on the steam yacht *Leviathan*; on 10 June he returned and informed the *Nanaimo Free Press* that the project was complete. However, Stone-Chance sent out the wrong light from Birmingham and a replacement did not arrive until 14 January 1875. Three months later, on 17 March, Edwin Woodward and his wife, the first white woman in West Vancouver, landed at the station. The original light shone from a wooden tower on the roof of their dwelling, ninety-five feet above the sea, visible fourteen miles away on a clear night.

Edwin and Ann Woodward, first keepers of Point Atkinson Light.

On 25 April 1876 Edwin delivered his third child, James Atkinson Woodward, the first white child born in West Vancouver. When James went off his mother's milk, a cow was brought over by tugboat. The crew tied a line to her horns and unceremoniously dumped her overboard. Woodward reeled her ashore and hacked a trail up to the house. Strange as it may seem today with its four thousand annual visitors, Point Atkinson proved too isolated for Ann Woodward. There was only a sawmill at the foot of Hastings Street and an Indian village at Kitsilano. They packed up after five years to go farming in Ontario. James later opened a general store in Plenty, Saskatchewan. The Weldwoods, who succeeded them, purchased their cow for a sixpence but stayed less than a year.

1910 postcard showing original wooden tower at Point Atkinson.

In the autumn of 1880 Walter Erwin landed at Point Atkinson. For the next three decades the Erwins would become synonymous with the lighthouse in the public mind. Erwin, a Moodyville resident, had been recommended by T.R. McInnis, MP for New Westminster. His name appears on a list of the sixteen original homesteaders of West Vancouver. He pre-empted a large area near the lighthouse, known today as Cypress Park, one of the most exclusive neighbourhoods on the West Coast. The Erwins also figured in Nora M. Duncan's epic poem "The Heroine of Moodyville," fourteen stirring purple stanzas which relate how a Gastown nurse braved a gale to treat Erwin's wife. Duncan provided a prime example of how a lighthouse can fire a poet's imagination. First the nurse begs the "hoary captains" moored in the harbour to take her over. No way.

> Their captains scan the frowning heav'ns
> 'Tis fools push off tonight!
> We cannot face those surging seas
> that beat in monstrous might
> Upon the cliffs and rockbound coast
> of Atkinson's great light.

So she turns instead to a "Squamish son" who "fears not the leaping wave." To make the story mercifully short, they "pass from foaming crest to foaming crest tossed high," to Caulfeild Cove where

> The keeper waits with fearful heart
> to guide them carefully
> O'er roughened trail; by thicket deep,
> by darkling forest tree-
> Until with weary gratefulness
> the lighthouse door they see.
>
> Thus soon our Mistress Patterson
> above the sufferer bends
> And by her touch and healing grace
> soft, restful slumber lends,
> As from her heart Doxology
> unto her God ascends![1]

So even in their sickness, lightkeepers held romantic appeal, but there would be no better measure of the wide gulf between romance and reality on the lights than the medical problems which later beset Walter Erwin—all of them work-related.

T.A. Fullerton, superintendent of Canadian Pacific Steamships, contacted the port warden of Vancouver in August 1889, insisting that he inform the minister of Marine straightaway that "the shipping interests of the port" required protection from fog while entering and leaving the harbour. "Should any accident occur to any of the Steamers in the Narrows," he warned, "it would be a serious matter to a young town like Vancouver." At the very least the department should install a fog alarm at Point Atkinson and build another manned lighthouse on Brockton Point, at the entrance to the inner harbour.

The CPR seldom had to wait long for Ottawa to do its bidding. Within a matter of months a new fog alarm went up on the shore line, three hundred yards west of the tower. The earliest horn, the "Scotch siren," was driven by steam pressure of at least fifty pounds, which spun a rotating drum—much like a giant kazoo. In 1902 J.P. Northey, a Toronto manufacturer, replaced the drum with a high velocity pulsating piston, a much more efficient design which he christened the diaphone. Northey's invention placed Canada at the forefront in lighthouse technology; a role abdicated only in the 1970s.

The arrival of a fog horn on a station entailed a revolutionary transformation of the keeper's responsibilities. Before, the sounding of the horn was the prerogative of ships' captains. Steaming toward the harbour through fog, the captain gave the order to sound three rapid blasts of his ship's horn. When they heard this signal, Erwin and his fellow keepers would carry a hand-horn outside. This horn was a system of twin bellows, worked by wrenching a handle back and forth. Lightkeepers would pump away at prescribed intervals until signalled by the vessel to stop.

Once the steam plant was built, however, ships' masters no longer initiated the signal. It was up to the keeper to shovel coal and raise steam whenever fog or smoke advanced to within four miles during squalls, heavy rain, or snowstorms. "At all times, night and day. . . a careful watch on the weather is to be maintained," Erwin was instructed, "and on no account whatever is this regulation to be broken, even during prevailing clear weather." The horn, sitting in its lair down below, was a mechanical tyrant.[2]

Once a month he had to open the boiler, crawl into its damp innards, hammer off any deposits on the walls, and hose it out. When the plant was in operation he was compelled to stay inside, in that ear-splitting din of hissing steam and flapping belts, with the bellowing horn rattling tools on their racks. Erwin could be relieved "for meals &c" only by another competent hand. When thick weather finally cleared (in 1896 he logged 1450 hours of it), he had to shut the plant down, rub down all the machinery, sweep up coal dust, dump clinkers out of the grates, then polish lubricators, flywheel rims, and all the other brasswork before locking the doors and trudging up to the house to watch for more fog. In clear weather he packed sacks of coal and hauled water for the boiler. In February 1897 Erwin exhausted his annual coal supply and began cutting trees for fuel. All too often it was an exercise in frustration when the fog stopped by long enough to exhaust his entire supply of split kindling, then capriciously moved on.

The department laid claim to the "whole time of the keeper." If there was any time left after tending the tower and fog alarm building, keepers had to "keep their lanterns, lighthouses, dwelling houses and outbuildings clean and tidy and in good repair," and "also keep the surroundings of their stations in a state to reflect credit on the Government and be a model to the neighbourhood."[3]

All this in return for free rent and $700 a year. The pay was barely enough with only a light to keep; the fog alarm soon altered that. In November 1888 the department granted Erwin an increase of $300 to hire an assistant. "I could not get an Engineer who holds a certificate for less than $1,200 a year," he replied. The best deal he could strike was with Thomas Grafton, a young man who held no certificate, for $600. "It would be impossible to get any man in this country for less," he explained. So the foghorn cut Walter Erwin's pay by over half. By March 1890, having tried the arrangement for a year, he asked for a raise of $200 since he could no longer meet his own expenses. "I think this man gets enough," William Smith, the deputy minister, decided. After all, it was a "nice station" and Erwin wasn't even a mechanic.[4]

On the night of 19 December 1903 the CPR steamer *Princess Royal* ran aground two miles east of the light. Her captain saddled Erwin with the blame, charging publicly that the horn was silent. James Gaudin immediately examined Erwin's log which clearly showed the horn in operation. He wrote Ottawa branding the captain's charge a clumsy lie "for if he was in any doubt, the whole Gulf of Georgia was straight in front of him." Obviously the skipper ought to have run "a few extra minutes before turning." It was the only charge of incompetence ever leveled at Walter Erwin.

By 1905 work, weather, and age had taken their toil. Arthritis, always a problem for lightkeepers, was winding its way through Erwin's frame. R.G. McPherson, MP for Vancouver, asked the department if his constituent might be pensioned at an amount approximating his regular salary since he was "a bit broken down now." The accountant for the Marine Department replied that he was entitled to only $250 per annum from the superannuation fund.

Later that year Erwin fell down the tower ladder, bruising his leg on the stairs. The constant pangs of arthritis overlapped this new damage, and in the end he became lame and could only hobble about the station. His doctor attributed Erwin's condition to rheumatism and packed him off to soak in Harrison Hot Springs. He returned in worse condition and learned from specialists that he had received the wrong treatment. Instead, they removed a portion of "deceased bone" in his leg.

All this took fourteen months. For the whole time he had to hire a second assistant, which ate up all his wages. Now he was heavily in debt to two doctors. "It will take me a long time to pay it up if I have to bear it myself," he informed Gaudin and he plaintively appealed for some compensation. "As you are aware, the injury in question occurred to me while in the performance of my duties," he pointed out, asking the department to pay his expenses in full, in consideration of his twenty-six years' service during which he had not taken a day off and always had earned the "satisfaction of the Department."[5]

James Gaudin pressed ahead with Erwin's case. By February 1907, however, no reply had arrived from Ottawa and he advised Erwin to ask some of his friends to use their influence with McPherson to bring political pressure to bear on William Templeman, acting minister of Marine and Fisheries. The crippled keeper

Concrete light tower at Point Atkinson 1925.

took Gaudin's letter downtown to J.A. Russell, a Vancouver lawyer and prominent Liberal, who wrote McPherson, "It has been pretty hard on the old gentleman, and at present he is badly in the hole." McPherson, in his turn, told Templeman "it would be an act of Christian charity" to pay Erwin, and predicted he would have no difficulty "getting the House to pass the estimate."

The difficulty, however, lay with the department. It would be a nasty precedent indeed, one sure to bring all sorts of lightkeepers from both coasts hobbling forward with compensation claims. Exasperated by such stingy logic, McPherson told Colonel Gourdeau, Templeman's deputy, to draft a memo, for the minister's signature, which would grant two years' leave of absence with pay in response to an "absolutely meritorious case." "I would like to have that done before I went west," he instructed. Templeman balked. However disguised, it would amount to payment for injury on the job.[6]

By May 1909 Erwin had had enough physical toil and bureaucratic stonewalling. He decided to resign—reluctantly, since his relationship with the department had "always been of the most friendly nature." He asked how much of a pension, if any, he might expect. It took over a year for an answer to come: $33 a month. As a parting gesture he recommended his assistant of over twenty years, T.D. Grafton, be appointed in his place.

In March 1911 at a ceremony on the steps of City Hall, Vancouver's mayor paid glowing tribute to the man who had held what was otherwise one of the most unrewarding jobs in the city's history. Observing that, from his vantage point on the rock overlooking the harbour's mouth, Walter Erwin had witnessed "a great wave of progress" sweep over the city, "transforming what once was a tract of virgin forest land into thriving city," the mayor described how he had single-handedly "performed a great and useful service in safeguarding vessels from shipwreck. . . no matter how the elements may rage on the stormbeaten coast."

His Worship then bestowed the Imperial Service Medal on behalf of King George V in accordance with the request of "the Hon. Mr. Templeman, Minister of Marine and Fisheries for the Dominion Government." One wonders what Erwin was thinking, or what he might have said if the minister had found the time to make the presentation in person.

Erwin died 15 August 1921. His widow, Rhoda, who was left penniless, thought she deserved to inherit his pension as payment for all the long nights she had kept watch and wound the light while her husband slept. A medal, after all, was no currency. Sympathizers sent a copy of the mayor's 1911 proclamation to the minister, followed by repeated and fruitless appeals. As late as 1927 they informed the department she was in "infirm health, and it would be a great boon to her." But no "boon" was forthcoming from a cost-conscious Department of Marine and Fisheries.[7]

Counting the twenty years he put in as Erwin's assistant, Thomas Grafton could boast of the longest service of any lightkeeper by 1934, his last year at Point Atkinson. He officially took over from his old friend on April Fools' Day 1910.

On the night of May 23 he witnessed "a total eclipse of the moon and a good view of Halley's comet and tail." Astrologers as far back as Aristotle would shudder at the import of such a celestial coincidence, but for twenty-four years fate seemed to look kindly on the Graftons' tenure at Point Atkinson.

"Real" West Vancouverites, the declining handful whose roots go back "before the bridge"—before the sleepy seaside resorts of Hollyburn, Dundarave, and Caulfeild were transformed into swank suburbia and a lush Indian reserve was paved over with Canada's first shopping mall—still recall the Graftons with much affection. More than anything else, the lighthouse and its keeper gave them a sense of place and permanence in the world before succeeding waves of affluent immigrants from Toronto, Montreal, Edmonton, and Iran swamped them.

In those days, one had to hike into Lighthouse Park instead of parking a car and strolling down the road and clear trails with a case of beer and a "ghetto blaster." Bear, deer, and cougar still held sway in the forest which has long since been given over to dogs. Grafton hacked out the first trail to Caulfeild. When the sea was rough, his wife tended the light while he carried their supplies over this trail on his back, detouring to deliver neighbours' mail as he went, always a welcome visitor in wood-warmed kitchens with his bottomless pocket of candy for the children.

Theirs was a life which, more than any others on the lights, gave some substance to all the idyllic notions about lightkeeping: they were isolated, but with neighbours at arm's distance and with ready access to a budding metropolis. The best of both worlds. It seems the only problem confronting Thomas Grafton was finding a reliable assistant at the meagre wages afforded by the department. One of his first assistants doubled as a school teacher for Grafton's four sons before he quit, complaining bitterly to the agent that he had been underpaid. Another assistant resigned 4 October 1913 and Grafton hired a replacement two days later. Tom woke at one next morning and couldn't see the beam flashing in his bedroom. Pulling on his clothes, he hastened to "run up to tower, started light revolving, then looked for man." Grafton reported, "[I] found him asleep in fog alarm, woke him and told him that would not do sleeping on his watch when he told me to go to Hell and blackguarded me with foul talks. I told him to get out of the fog alarm and as soon as it got daylight to leave the station, he left 6:30 a.m. for Caulfeilds to catch a boat to town."

The year he took over, the entire station was transformed. The old dwelling and tower were torn down. Colonel Anderson seized upon the publicly accessible site to show off his latest concrete design—a hexagonal tower embraced by six buttresses—an adroit combination of aesthetics and function which always evokes a chorus of "oohs" and "ahhs" and "far outs" from those who climb the Lighthouse Viewpoint and see it for the first time soaring up from below. The steam engines were thrown piece by piece into the chuck and a new fog alarm building was constructed to house internal combustion engines, air compressors, and diaphones. The new house was a rambling duplex adorned with gingerbread fretwork and a

Point Atkinson from sea 1925.

wide, open porch fronting a lawn at the foot of the rock. There was shelter at last from the relentless southeast wind. For those who trekked to see the new station the Graftons' fortune must have seemed like a dream come true in someone else's life. Their enthusiasm and contentment were contagious as the keepers showed visitors around their lush, spotless, freshly painted paradise.

It was shelter, too, from the gathering storm of the Great Depression, when the downtrodden and jobless stood dazed and mute in breadlines stretching around the corner on Granville Street, watched by fidgetting plainclothesmen and beat cops who were finally set upon them, running amok with a club-swinging vengeance outside the Post Office in the summer of 1938.

Opening Grafton's log books at the very desk where he sat down to write them fifty years ago, one is struck by his obsessive vigilance and attention to detail. He observed every shift in the weather, each patch of haze or smothering mantle of fog as it came and went. He logged the hour, to the minute, when he fired up the horns and shut them down, and dutifully recorded the performance of his plant and equipment, documenting the hours he spent wiping down soot after flare-ups in the tower, topping up the mercury, polishing the new lens. The schizoid personality of his engines—willing slaves or cranky malingerers—emerges as if they still droned away in the background. Every item, from postage stamps and pushbrooms to cotter pins, is duly entered and accounted for. The lighthouse tender *Estevan* comes and goes, and an endless cavalcade of steamers parades by, bound to and from every corner of the globe.

On the morning of 11 January 1933, the day his luck changed, Tom Grafton wrote

> Started calm & hazy S. shore lights in plain sight till daylight cloudy 8-0 a.m. haze drifted out from bay calm & cloudy all day 8 p.m. started light rain & light E wind S. shore lights in plain sight till. . .

Then Grafton's heavy-handed script gives way abruptly to his son Lawrence's

> . . . midnight 12 Started light E. wind S. shore in sight till 4 a.m. Then hazy on S. shore till noon Light W air till 6 p.m. Hazy in Bay, drifting out to Pt. Grey Str. whistling in Bay at 9:50 p.m. 9:50 p.m. started alarm. 11:00 p.m. compressor belt broke throwing keeper into flywheel. . . [8]

After his mauling (one wonders how long he lay on the engineroom floor before his family found him, or if he crawled back to the house), Grafton disappeared from his log for six months. By 30 June he had recovered enough to write—and to row.

Residents along the Caulfeild shore had long grown accustomed to the lightkeeper's unorthodox if deadly effective method of fishing for bait. When they heard muted explosions and saw the water belch up, they knew Grafton would be back in a matter of minutes to scoop up the stunned and quivering herring. By this time he was an expert at capping dynamite charges. The coho were running up the Capilano, and Grafton was out there on the morning of 6 October. According to his son Lawrence's log, his last day

> started calm with light haze in bay. Pt. Grey showing all morning dimly. Lightkeeper was killed instantly sometime before 6 a.m. from a dynamite blast which exploded accidently in his hand. The body was recovered at 7:15 a.m. by his youngest son, drifting in the submerged boat about 200 yards off the point. Light W. wind during the day. Then calm with light fog drifting out of bay from 9:30 p.m. till midnight. S. shore lights in sight till midnight. Partly cloudy. [9]

All that day and the next and for weeks after, neighbours and friends came through the forest and crowded into the Graftons' parlour to share their grief. On 8 October "Inspector Halkett paid a visit and expressed the Department's sympathy." It was like shellshock, as if, with Grafton, they had been blasted out of their somnolent past and present. The shock that was felt throughout the sleepy little communities of the north shore went beyond that of a single death in the family. It was as if all knew that, with Thomas Grafton's death, an era had ended and a greater explosion of urban expansion would soon blast away forever the peaceful and independent country life he had so memorably characterized.

Lawrence Grafton wrote Colonel Wilby, the marine agent in Victoria, the day his father died, advising, "[I] would appreciate your co-operation in securing the lightkeeper's job at this station." He added that he was engaged to be married and, for good measure, that his brother "was killed in action at the front—aged seventeen." He was suddenly head of a family of seven with no means of supporting them. The same day mourners from Caulfeild handed him a petition with twelve signatures, asking Wilby to appoint Lawrence in his father's place. "The family have been for years well and favourably known to all the old residents of Caulfeild," they explained. "The lighthouse has been their family home for many years. . . . We are convinced that he could fill the post with fidelity and competence and that your department would be well served by him."[10]

Still, a station like Point Atkinson was too tempting a plum, however much West Vancouverites might sympathize with the Graftons. C.R.C. Broderick, a master mariner from Dundarave, wanted it badly. He wrote Hawken, the deputy minister in Ottawa, thanking him "for the kind interest you have already taken on my behalf" and asked for the keepership as an additional favour. "I do not take any wines or spirits but smoke a little," he allowed, "& would be glad to get a permanent position in full charge of lighthouse."

But sympathy and patronage gave way before Wilby's priorities. He had a station on the Inside Passage, Sisters Island, which was little more than a dwelling clinging limpetlike to a barren wave-swept rock. As a matter of policy agents had always moved men off Sisters as quickly as possible. Another keeper's death or resignation offered the only opportunity to set all the chess pieces in motion and Wilby wanted to move Ernest Dawe from Ballenas Island to Point Atkinson, making way for a keeper named Dare from Sisters. He explained his dilemma to Hawken, enclosing the Caulfeild petition and conceding, "Mr. Grafton's son is of good character, knows the work, is in his twenty-first year, and single."

Hawken weighed the alternatives, then chose: Ernie Dawe would go to Point Atkinson. He had children of school age and had given "excellent service." The Graftons were doubtless desolated at the prospect of being harried out of the only home they had known. Lawrence ran the station until 6 June 1935, a day which "started calm and clear overhead. Clear. Mr. Dawe took over duties of keeper from L.W. Grafton" and ended the forty-seven year tenure of the Graftons. Their last year had been a nightmare and it showed. "Mr. Dawe took over a shit house today from L.W. Grafton," the new keeper fumed in the log as soon as the old ones had tearfully headed up the trail. "This is the dirtiest lighthouse or Junk Pile in the lighthouse service."[11]

On 28 September Dawe stood by in the radio room as technicians threw the switch which heralded Point Atkinson's entry into a new world of navigation technology. A radio beacon broadcast a signal, synchronized with the fog horns, which sliced through the fog and enabled vessels with receivers to pick up Point Atkinson well beyond the range of its light and horns.

Point Atkinson became a beehive in the war. Estevan Point lighthouse, midway up the west coast of Vancouver Island, was shelled in June 1942. Conscription, an issue which spawned more conflict than any other in Canadian history, came into force soon after. Pearl Harbour and its aftermath had already created a wave of racism and war hysteria which immediately swept the Japanese community over the mountains to inland detention camps.

Searchlights and cannon were installed at Point Atkinson, Stanley Park, Narrows North, and Point Grey. By 1942, 720 conscripts—"McKenzies Commandos" or "Zombies" as they were labelled with a mixture of disdain and derision—stood poised, according to reporters, passing "endless hours rehearsing for the few minutes of intense excitement they hope will come their way some day." Eighty were billeted in new cedar barracks hastily thrown up in the forest behind the Point Atkinson station. Labourers constructed a huge concrete bunker with sliding steel doors for a searchlight, and bolted a Mark I eighteen-pound cannon onto a pivot supported by a concrete base in front of the radio room.

An imaginary examination line stretched across the harbour from the lighthouse to Point Grey on the south shore, like a bit in the harbour's mouth. Any ships entering the harbour were to identify themselves to one of the two naval patrol vessels patrolling just outside. If they failed or forgot, gunners fired a round across their bow; if the ship continued, the gunners would sink them.

The only casualties came from hand to hand encounters on makeshift playing fields or from grappling with the celebrated painted ladies of Union Street. "Well, Doc," one casualty on sick parade sheepishly explained when pressed for more information about the enemy, "it's like this: when you cut yourself with a saw, can you tell what tooth on the blade done it?"[12]

Point Atkinson came under fire when an instructor closed the breech on a live shell at Narrows North and accidently sent a twelve-pound shell past the lighthouse. The defenders did manage to sink one vessel, though they seldom boasted of it.

Ken "Gunfire" Brown loved to put his battery at Narrows North to use and would often fire warning shots at the slightest provocation, thirty-one in his first month. The barrage kept the fishermen in line when they might otherwise be too casual about regulations. One night an examination boat lying off Point Atkinson radioed that a fishboat had slipped by. Brown and his crew ran for their helmets and gear, slid a shell into the breech, and pulled the lanyard. The fishboat stopped. But the armour piercing shell kept right on, skipping across the smooth water, and went in, then out below the waterline of a 9600-ton freighter *Fort Rae*, just

Gordon Odlum, veteran lightkeeper.

launched from Burrard Dry Docks and making her first speed trials. The crew apparently never even knew they were hit, but the *Fort Rae* began to settle as they steered her back toward the harbour. Her captain ran her aground at the foot of Lions Gate.

The barracks still stand in the park, having long since been converted to such peaceful purposes as a nature house and summertime gymnasiums. The searchlight bunker is a gallery for graffitti now. There was a bonus for Dawe in all of it, however, and for every keeper who came after. Aside from saving money by lining up with the khaki-clad gunners at chow time, the army left him a road cleared through the park. The old lighthouse trail, cut and cleared with so much effort by Erwin and Grafton, now forms part of Lighthouse Park's network of nature trails.

During another war scare in the early 1960s the department instructed Gordon Odlum to stock the concrete blockhouse which had been built to house generators for the searchlights. In the event of the unthinkable, he and his assistant were to leave their families behind and take shelter inside, emerging at intervals to give "reports." Odlum told them, "If me and my assistant had to live in that shelter, it would surely end up in an explosion that would dwarf the atomic one."

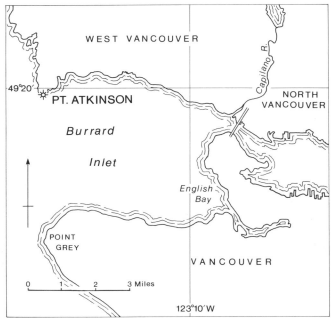

Inside the tower,
Point Atkinson.

Prospect Point

Vancouver's inner harbour stretches from Prospect Point, tucked against the bluffs of Stanley Park at the south end of Lions Gate Bridge three sea-miles east of Point Atkinson, up Burrard Inlet, to the logjams east of Coquitlam. Once past Point Atkinson, vessels would drop anchor along the north shore, west of an imaginary line across Burrard Inlet from Dundarave to Jericho Beach, to wait for daylight and a pilot to come out from Caulfeild before threading the needle between Prospect Point and the mouth of the Capilano River. In the days before the Capilano was throttled by the Cleveland Dam it could be a surging torrent, particularly in spring when the melting snow pack fed into its canyons. This presented a further challenge to masters who had safely made their way into Juan de Fuca and cleared the Strait of Georgia and Point Atkinson: a swirling current of fresh water far less buoyant than the sea.

South of the Prospect Point turn was another hazard. Both the *Chilco* and SS *Niagara* were casualties of a quirk of sound in the Narrows. Before radar, navigation in fog depended upon a trained ear and a stopwatch to time the intervals between a blast on a ship's horn and its echo. The cliffs just north of Siwash Rock gave a similar response to those above Prospect Point, and both vessels ran aground a mile short of the turn.

Only months before the light was erected, Prospect Point earned the dubious distinction of claiming the first steamship to ply the waters of British Columbia. The *Beaver* was built with steam sidewheels driven by two thirty-five horsepower engines, and sailed out from Britain as a brigantine in 1835. An ungainly precursor of the modern age, she ferried colonial bureaucrats and Admiralty surveyors on inspection tours, and brought the cream of society up the Fraser to proclaim the formation of the Colony of British Columbia. She was moored in the harbour when the first transcontinental steam locomotive puffed into Vancouver, and was

Prospect Point Lighthouse in 1926, showing signal station atop cliff.

a familiar, if perplexing, sight for sailors from around the world. The *Beaver* waddled, wheezed, and thrashed her way disdainfully past their stately becalmed barks like a lowly scullery maid at a tea party. In July 1888 her crew, drunk, ran the steamer aground on the Point. Souvenir hunters picked her bones clean over the next fifteen years.

The light was established that fall, a fixed white beacon only thirty-one feet above high water. A mechanical fog bell hung from its front gable and rang once every twenty seconds in fog. A notice to mariners advised officers "In entering the harbour when light is visible, all dangers on starboard side are cleared."

Visitors to Stanley Park, who lean over the parapet at Prospect Point and see the light, marvel at the thought of anyone living in such cramped conditions. So did James Gaudin when he first inspected them in March 1889. The marine agent reported that John Grove, Prospect's first and only keeper, kept it in "very fair condition," though the whole family was sick when he arrived—John and his wife "suffering from grippe and their two children were down with measles."

"There are only two living rooms at this station," he noted, "and the condition of these people can be imagined." And worse, water flowed "in and out of the cellar with the tide." Gaudin immediately ordered six barrels of cement so Grove could fill the cracks and pour a concrete floor "at his leisure" and when the tide allowed. He also ordered a boat, and laid plans for a boat house.[1]

As the Groves' boys grew older, Gaudin sympathized with the parents. After his annual inspection in March 1901, he again pronounced the station "in good working order and condition," but added, "It is hard work to keep the interior of the dwelling as it should be." Mrs. Grove "evidently does her best," he wrote, "but it is difficult for her to keep the place as tidy as she would wish with the whole family living in one room." Their older son was ten. Whether Grove needed to take his visitor aside to explain matters or not, Gaudin pleaded with Ottawa to grant $300 "for their comfort and decency's sake to add at least another room to the east side of the dwelling."

The agent shared the keepers' excitement when he arrived to find them moving their furniture into "the new cottage" in April 1904. Grove had secured the use of two acres from the Stanley Park Board, and asked if the department would provide him with $65 worth of lumber to build a "cow house." "It must be admitted that this stable is entirely for his own use," Gaudin allowed, "but as he is only in receipt of a monthly salary of $25.00, the supply . . . will be a great help to him."

Although John Grove was one of the lowest paid workers in Vancouver, he had his housing free, an ample supply of fresh water and firewood nearby, and one of the heaviest salmon runs in the world at his doorstep. And even if they would often have to sleep in daytime shifts thanks to the fog bell which must be wound every half hour, any keeper on the coast those days would willingly have traded places. All that changed in 1910.

The waters in front of Grove were rapidly becoming one of the busiest two-way streets in the world. Ships coming had no inkling of ships going until they rounded Prospect Point. The possibility of collisions loomed large. Some system of ship traffic control must be imposed to avoid certain tragedy. Both Prospect Point and Brockton Point around the corner had already become de facto lifesaving stations, owing to their keepers' vigilance and willingness to go out after boaters in distress. "And in that respect," Gaudin informed Colonel Anderson in the winter of 1909, "they have been instrumental in saving many lives from drowning in boating accidents." When the *Princess Victoria* rammed the tug *Chehalis* in July 1906, William Jones, lightkeeper at Brockton Point, rowed out to save the *Chehalis'* engineer who was thrown overboard by the impact. However, a keeper would be powerless to cope with the disaster of much larger proportions if two steamers met head on with no time to alter course.

Semaphore was the solution. Signal masts would be erected at both stations and the keepers would be charged with hoisting flags to report ship movements at all hours. At Prospect the mast was erected at the top of the bluff, 150 feet above the light. In February 1910 Grove observed, "If it was at the Light House it would be posable [sic] to operate it with one assistant, but as it is so far away, it will need two men to carry out the duties in a proper manner.... P.S.," he added, "the lowest wages paid for the same class of work [the CPR's signalmen] in Vancouver is $62.00 a month." Clearly, Grove's $25 a month would never stretch far enough.[2]

Gaudin had already recommended a raise of $10 a month for Grove and now hastened to advise that amount would not "warrant an efficient service." "The cost of living is daily increasing," the agent complained, "and the Civic authorities ...in Vancouver have increased the wages of their labourers from $2.00 to $2.50 for an eight hour day service." This was twice Grove's wage and Gaudin hoped Anderson could appreciate his difficulty. "I am of the opinion that $500.00 per annum would not be an extravagant estimate for operating the semaphore signals at this point," he concluded, since the service would "require the constant attention of one man stationed on the bluff both day and night." Hardly extravagant indeed. In fact, if Grove hired two assistants at the CPR rate of $62, he would fall more than $80 behind every month, paying out twice as much as he earned. Even the celebrated niggardliness of the Department of Marine and Fisheries could not withstand such simple arithmetic, and an Order in Council allowed Grove $55 per month to pay the operator, "provided he employs competent men."

But it was never enough. John Grove taxed his imagination and ingenuity over the next fifteen years to make ends meet. That first semaphore summer he set up a clandestine lemonade stand on the bluffs and did a thriving trade with the tourists until the park board complained. Lightkeeper Jones at Brockton Point seems to have made even more work for Grove and his assistants by shirking his end of the work. The Prospect Point station reported all ships bound in; Brockton Point was charged with signalling all outbound traffic. But in March 1913 (by Grove's reckoning) Jones failed to report 124 boats and missed 96 more the first ten days of April.

In mid-August 1916 Jones rang over to the semaphore station and said, "I have no man tonight so you go to bed as I am going to bed." Grove's assistant pleaded with him to stay up or Grove would sack him. "I don't care a dam for Grove & tell him I said so, also don't ring again tonight as I don't intend to answer," Jones snorted. Next day Grove sent a letter from his assistant off to Victoria. "I would take no notice of it if it was the first time it had happened," he confided, "but it has been going on for years."[3] If Jones was not up to his job then Grove definitely needed another assistant. He proposed to engage his daughter-in-law. Robertson, Gaudin's replacement as marine agent, sought permission from Ottawa but the deputy minister turned him down, quoting the 1911 Order in Council specifying "competent *men*" for the post. Grove replied that he regretted the department's decision. "I am getting better service [from my son's wife] than I ever got from single men," he claimed, "but as orders are orders, I will try and get another man." It wouldn't be easy—not when most competent men were away at war in

Prospect Point Light with Empress liner outbound. Note stairs to signal station.

Europe and those who remained could "find work with good pay, with Saturday halfternoon [sic] and Sunday off."[4] In May 1918 the semaphore service at Brockton Point was discontinued, doubling Grove's workload at Prospect Point.

If it was hard to lure men away from a five-and-a-half-day work week in 1916 for lower wages, it was a practical impossibility to attract them with $65 a month when the vicious post-war inflation set in. In February 1920 Grove announced, "[I] just had a good man leave to take a place where he gets $110 a month." Colonel Wilby, the agent in Victoria, advised Ottawa that "the approximate wage for a similar class of work" was $125 and recommended an increase to at least $90. He reviewed the performance of the signal station, declaring it had been "very well carried out," and adding, "Mariners for this reason have to depend very much on these signals." In addition to hoisting the flags day and night in all weather, the lightkeeper and his assistants had kept a careful log of all ship traffic. For ten years they furnished this information daily to the Vancouver harbourmaster so ships' agents might follow their vessels' movements in and out of the harbour with great precision. "Incompetency in this work will only tend to discourage mariners from paying attention to these signals," he warned, "and should this inattention. . .creep in, we might just as well do away with the signals altogether."

Hawken replied, "The work in the operation of these signals is so light that there is some hesitation in increasing the wages." Seemingly forgetting his earlier refusal to hire Grove's daughter-in-law, he suggested, "Members of the lightkeeper's family could discharge the duties without grave interference with whatever other duties they may have to perform."

The signal station up above had loomed over Grove's life and work for a decade and a half, requiring thousands of trips in the dark and wet up that perilous bluff. He always had to pay the discrepancy between a living wage and the pittance budgetted for an assistant out of his own pocket, or clamber up the 160 steps to run the flags himself. Then in 1926 came the ultimate indignity. In January Wilby informed him that the entire lightstation would be electrified within a week. "I am further instructed by the Department that when this work is completed, the Prospect Point Light and Fog Alarm Station will be operated from the Prospect Point Signal Station and that your services will no longer be required," the agent wrote. The signal station which had cost Grove so much time, effort, and money won out in the end. It cost him his job. There was only one consolation: "If it is your desire to remain on in your present dwelling," Wilby wrote, "I am prepared, in view of your long, faithful and satisfactory service, to recommend to the Department that this privilege be granted to you."

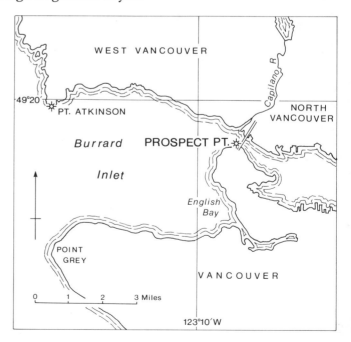

Brockton Point

Prospect Point was truly unique among all the West Coast lights since it was effective only for one-way traffic. Obscured by the lush peninsula named for Lord Stanley, it was of no use whatever to ships gathering speed and heading seaward from the inner harbour with their hatches battened over full cargoes. In 1890 the department built a station at Brockton Point, two kilometers east of Prospect Point. Brockton marked the abrupt turn into Coal Harbour for inbound ships, and drew outbound vessels toward First Narrows.

The first light was a ramshackle affair with red and white lanterns mounted on a mast. No dwelling had been provided so Brockton's first keeper, a testy Welshman named "Captain" W.D. Jones, built his own shack "chiefly of driftwood picked up in Burrard Inlet." In March 1901 James Gaudin reported, "The dwelling has to a certain extent been neglected," owing to the department's indecision about building a new one. They had waffled for two years while Jones hammered his eyesore together. In 1901 there was a compelling reason to build a "decent looking house at this point," which Gaudin described as "one of the loveliest spots in Stanley Park." "I would most respectfully submit that something be done to this station before the visit of the Duke of Cornwall and York to Stanley Park," he recommended.[1] There was nothing like a regal visit to bring out the Potemkin in Chief Engineer William Anderson, and a new dwelling stood on the site a year later. Jones, "a builder by trade," superintended construction of the latest "architectural adornment" in Stanley Park, the *Vancouver Province* reported.

In April William Jones returned his rude hut to the waters of Burrard Inlet and was "greatly improving the reserve in his charge." A new fixed white light, with a red sector pointing out the Burnaby Shoal, was mounted in a bay window off

Jones' bedroom. A separate bell tower went up on the extremity of the point. Brockton Point was the only light in Canada with a bath, "a fact of which Mr. Jones is justly proud," said the *Province*.[2]

Gaudin included a bill for fifty dollars, with his glowing report of the new house, to replace the boat's ways which had been honeycombed by teredo worms and carried off in a winter gale. "Lifesaving apparatus have been supplied to this station on account of boating accidents having occurred in this vicinity," he reported. A new boathouse was desperately needed so a boat could be launched as quickly as possible. "Mr. Jones having rescued several persons out of the water during the last few years."

One day in June 1905 Jones heard screams while he was sitting at dinner. He tossed his napkin aside, bolted for his boat, and rowed out to a man thrashing in the water. He arrived at the same time as a yacht, and "with another man pulled him out of the water and then transferred him on board the yacht, and tried to restore animation until the Doctor came. . . . Had he not died of the shock," Jones opined, "we would have saved him . . . this makes the ninth rescue for me since I have been here."[3]

Since most of Jones's search and rescue work had benefitted mere "Indians and Mexicans," it had gone unheralded by the press. Even Jones had neglected to record the names of the beneficiaries. Back in Ottawa Deputy Minister Gourdeau was skeptical. Why had he seen nothing in the press about these rescues? He wrote Gaudin in August, asking for details of Jones' lifesaving exploits which were always rich grist for the department's public relations mill. Gaudin was able to furnish only two names while affirming the "rescue of . . . two Mexicans was a well-known fact of the time." Local journalists were as frustrated as Gourdeau. According to the *Province*, Jones never mentioned any of these incidents, though it was "well known that a couple of the rescues were made at no small risk to himself, and only accomplished after a severe struggle in the icy waters."[4]

In July 1906 came the inevitable collision in the Narrows. There could be no hedging afterward about Jones' alleged heroism; he had scores of witnesses this time. They were all milling around the Brockton Point Lookout at 2:00 p.m., Saturday 21 July to watch the *Princess Victoria*, celebrated "white flier" of the Canadian Pacific fleet, pass by outbound. A lowly Union Steamship tug, the *Chehalis*, chugged ahead of her, under charter by local businessmen interested in buying up northern oyster beds.

As her two hundred or more passengers lined the rails, waving over to the envious onlookers at Brockton Point, the graceful steamer gathered speed, gaining steadily on the tug. Aboard the *Chehalis*, Captain Howse altered course toward the north shore to detour the flood tide. "I thought we were making good time and did not trouble to look behind," he confessed before collapsing in shock and grief in the aftermath. It was a fatal blunder. "I had just altered course a little more to starboard when suddenly I heard a whistle and as I looked out astern, I saw the *Victoria* on top of me."

In a final, desperate lunge Howse hauled the wheel hard over as more than a couple thousand tons of steel, sharpened to cleave through water at twenty knots, sliced into the *Chehalis*, "throwing its occupants high into the air." The steamer kept right on going, huge propeller blades churning through the wreckage. A small motor boat picked up one survivor, a woman aboard the steamer flung a life ring to another, and an alert passenger threw out an orange crate to a third.

Over on the viewpoint the spectators' mood changed abruptly from exaltation to shock. Captain Jones hurried over to his skiff, shoved his boat down the ways, and rowed out. Dean, the *Chehalis'* engineer, had gone down inside the tug as she plummeted stern first. He clawed his way out of the crushed hull and swam toward daylight as the *Victoria's* propellers, two terrifying tunnels of foam, passed by overhead. When Dean broke the surface, gasping for air, Jones seized him and hauled him into the skiff. The engineer was one of eight of the *Chehalis'* fifteen passengers and crew to testify before a long, drawn-out enquiry. The rest are still trapped in the *Chehalis* somewhere among the huge boulders under ten murky fathoms a few hundred yards off Brockton Point.[5]

In March 1907 Jones mailed Gaudin a *Daily Province* clipping "calling attention of the public to the services which he rendered in the cause of humanity by saving some sixteen persons from drowning in Burrard Inlet." This was the stuff which cast the government in the best possible light, and the department arranged for Templeman, the acting minister, along with R.G. McPherson, MP, to present a gold medal "in recognition of his humane services."[6]

Brockton Point 1914 showing old fog bell with new tower under construction.

Brockton Point 1901. Light was mounted in bay window off keeper's bedroom.

Jones probably contributed more to the stereotype of the lightkeeper in western Canada than any other. Even before his ceremonial elevation to public hero in 1907 he had become a colourful and well-known figure, the most accessible of all the lightkeepers on the coast to a curious public. When tourists went home to Moose Jaw or Red Deer, when farmers migrated back for seeding in the spring, they would hold court at crossroads stores with their accounts of visiting a lighthouse and meeting its keeper. That light was invariably Brockton Point and its keeper Captain William D. Jones.

The spring of 1909 brought the semaphore station with its promise of more work for less pay. Like Grove at Prospect Point, Jones trudged around downtown for days trying to discover the lowest wages a reliable man would want to assist him. And, like Grove, he concluded, "It will be impossible to find reliable assistance for 365 night and day watch a year for less than $600 per annum." For his part, Jones pledged, "I am prepared to do my duty to the best of my ability . . . for that amount in addition to my salary." Gaudin sympathized with his keepers and the difficulties they had "to contend with in obtaining assistance for the work," when the cost of labour was "so high and men so independent." He recommended they be given an extra $500.

"*It is a cruel injustice,*" Jones declared in August 1911 after Captain Robertson received complaints about the signals at Brockton Point and threatened to replace him. Since he was spared the long climb up the bluff that John Grove faced at Prospect Point, Jones tried to man the signals with a lone assistant. It was too much. Even worse, the Parks Board was complaining that the grounds at the light were being neglected. Jones defended himself:

> Now, Sir, I will ask you how am I to keep this place in order and a credit to the Department if I am to spend every moment of my life attending to these Semaphores? For that is what it amounts to. And another thing the assistant is getting more money than the Principal in this case, that is rather an unusual state of affairs, is it not? And worse still I am at least $5.00 per month out of pocket with it. I will attend to these Signals under *Protest*.[7]

As far as the grounds were concerned, he had expended "hundreds of Dollars and years of hard labour in turning a howling wilderness into the loveliest spot in Vancouver." He had even constructed a huge floral sundial measuring twelve feet in diameter with "the hours marked in vari-colored flowers." Jones neatly scotched the slur by securing an appointment as Parks Board Commissioner. In April 1913, when there were more complaints about the signals, Jones demanded to know "who the persons are that sends these malicious reports," and extolled his night assistant, an old fisherman who lived nearby, as "absolutely dependable."

In 1914 Colonel Anderson transformed Brockton Point. Opportunities to display his architectural flair were all too rare since most lights were so isolated. At Brockton Point he outdid himself, pouring a curved concrete seawall and mounting the tower above arches so tourists strolling along the seawall could pass on the palisade beneath. Jones' spacious, gabled dwelling stood behind, surrounded by a lush flower garden. He was the first horticulturist to begin cultivating ornate flowerbeds in the park, raising sprays of flowers for the Military Hospitals Commission during the war. In December 1916 the commission's secretary-treasurer wrote Ottawa, relating how Jones had cleared Brockton Point himself. His house was "one of the beauty spots to see in the park on account of the climbing roses." Jones hit upon the idea of selling flowers to raise $100 for the Returned Soldiers Club in 1915. He contributed $150 the next year, and in 1917 announced "he was going to make $1,000 from the sale of flowers during the year." Enlisting the Women's Canadian Club as a retail outlet, "he accomplished the almost incredible feat through his own initiative of donating. . . $1000" to the club, as well as $35 to the Prisoner of War Fund, and another $200 for presents of tobacco for the club's Christmas program. Jones was literally growing more money on trees than he was paid.[8] In May 1918 he received the welcome news that he could turn his whole attention to the station and grounds—the semaphore station was taken out of service.

The Canadian government sailed into dire financial straits in the 1920s. There were huge interest charges on war bonds. Bankrupt railways, like the ill-conceived Grand Trunk Pacific, demanded to be nationalized so their directors and share-holders could be compensated by the public for their foolhardy venture. Income tax, initiated in the war, was here to stay but could never keep pace with government expenditure. The nation's debt skyrocketed from $462 million in 1911, to well over $3 billion by 1925.[9] Under mounting pressure to generate revenue the Ministry of Finance drew up a novel scheme to swell its coffers with involuntary contributions from public servants—a scheme so sly and nefarious that it almost commanded respect.

The 1924 Superannuation Act legislated compulsory check-offs amounting to 5 percent of each employee's wages. The contributors would have no say whatever in how their money was put to use; rather, the Treasury was given a free hand with the windfall, and civil servants would see only a portion of it in the form of a pension.

Prior to this time all lightkeepers were appointed by Order in Council; the new act would bring them into the public service. Those who wanted no truck with the plan could resign immediately and take whatever was coming to them under the previous scheme, the Calder Act, which granted two months' gratuity on retirement and a monthly pension equalling half their average salary during their service. Those who stayed on would make retroactive payments *for every year* they had worked before 1924. And they had to make up their minds fast; after 1924 there would be no provision to pay back what they "owed," nor would they receive benefits for previous service. In one fell swoop the Treasury reached back thirty years or further to plunder the life savings of public servants who might otherwise invest them. Lightkeepers, always the lowest paid of all government workers, would now shoulder an even heavier burden.[10]

When the disastrous superannuation scheme came into force, Jones wisely elected to resign at once rather than make retroactive contributions for each of his thirty-five years' service. Under the Calder Act, his average wage of $607.50 entitled him to $344 per annum, $29 a month. Not much, but far better than handing over more than $1000 in a lump sum to the government under the new scheme.

Captain Jones turned eighty-one that year. He agreed, as a favour, to stay on at the station until, he said, "[I] receive further instructions to vacate my position or as long as I am able to do so which should be at least for another *20 years*." W.C. Shelley, chairman of the Parks Board, welcomed the news that his fellow commissioner would stay on a while yet "with great satisfaction." At its next session the board drafted a letter to Ottawa congratulating the department. For all the years he had been at Brockton Point, Jones had fired the nine o'clock gun—a muzzle loading cannon brought over from Esquimalt and installed on nearby Hallelujah Point in 1884—while Vancouverites set their watches. "Now, when the 9 o'clock gun sounds," the *Province* exalted, "all Vancouver will continue to realize that the gallant captain is still in harness."

But by late January 1925 Jones charged, "The Department is benefitting at my expense and I am to be the victim of Departmental economy." Some shrewd clerk had decided that since Jones was officially retired, he should only be paid the difference between his pension and his previous wage. As early as October, when

Showpiece tower at Brockton Point designed by Colonel William Anderson, 1914.

his pay stubs brought this chicanery to light, he telephoned Wilby to explain that, if he had retired when he originally planned, the department "would have been in a position of having to pay not only [his] superannuation under the Act but also the full salary of a permanent official." Moreover, he had evicted his tenants from his house downtown in October, expecting to retire then, and had lost $105 in rent. In the past year he had also paid $97 to electrify the dwelling and fog bell. Even so, he was still prepared to stay on in his unfurnished dwelling if he was given full pay. The present arrangement, he declared, "I cannot entertain for one moment."[11]

He didn't. He left the next day and never lived to see the Parks Board eradicate every last vestige of his presence in that one-time "howling wilderness," knocking down his house and paving over his beloved flowerbeds and sundial for a parking lot along Stanley Park Drive. All that remains today is Anderson's concrete.

Colonel Anderson's Brock-
ton Point complex from the
sea.

Capilano

The *Vancouver Province* heralded the construction of a fourth harbour light in August 1908. The Vancouver Shipmasters' Association had long wanted a light somewhere on the north shore across from Prospect Point to bracket the Narrows at night. "Vancouver pilots especially have fought hard for it," the *Province* reported, though tugboat owners were "not very interested" since the course was so familiar. The "big steamers," which traded to the port "very often," decided the issue.

Like the Fraser over at Sand Heads, the Capilano River shipped tons of rock and sand into the Narrows as fast as dredges could heave and haul it up to waiting barges. Wide variations in the shallows from one year to the next, together with sixteen-foot tides, drove mariners over as close as possible to Prospect Point, increasing the odds for collisions. And with only Grove's bell to go by in the fog, many ran aground. Even when the light was built over the Capilano shoals, its second (and last) keeper recorded forty-two groundings in twenty years.

An unwatched beacon standing on a black cylindrical tank was installed, and James Gaudin hired M. Rood to row over to maintain the light and wind the fog bell. In 1915 a dwelling and tower were built on piles three hundred feet north of the original site. Later that year more piles were driven next to the tower to support a fog alarm. The local Conservative Association nominated George Harris for the post of lightkeeper and fog alarm engineer. Harris, with his wife as assistant, took over the station that March. After nine years' service he declined a promotion and transfer to Entrance Island. "I would not hesitate a moment in taking the position if I was a younger man," he explained, but he was "not enjoying the best of health.... Although this has been a strenuous place... and has put a few years on my life," he added, "I still feel it is home and keep hoping for conditions to change for the better round the buildings." Harris also hoped to "be able to fulfill the duties required here... for a few more years."

Three years later, in March 1925, Harris died on the station. "I am at the lighthouse & you may rest assured I shall see every duty is attended to," his widow promised Wilby.[1] The marine agent instructed Gordon Halkett, his superintendent of lights, to offer the post to Alfred Dickenson at Kains Island when he landed there in the course of his annual tour of inspection.

Alfred and Annie Dickenson had long yearned for the Capilano light during their stint at Kains Island light in Quatsino Sound, well up the west coast of Vancouver Island. The transfer, when it finally came in September 1925, entailed a revolutionary transformation in their lives. They moved from a station where one motionless month succeeded another without social contact, to a light from which they could row to the centre of a city or visit other lightkeepers like the Groves across the Narrows, or Tom Grafton out at Point Atkinson.

In the beginning, trips to town were set down as special events, like the day Alfred took "5 hours for the purpose of visiting the Strand Theatre and buying a pair of trousers." Annie, who had been wistfully unsettled in their last years at Kains, staring out to sea with her binoculars for hours, hoping to see a boat—any boat—to break her monotonous existence, now had an endless, polyglot parade of shipping at her doorstep and soon made up for her five lost years by visiting old friends and making new ones.

The move to Capilano was a deliverance and the Dickensons, through their diligence, repaid the department tenfold. On 8 August 1928 "a 14-foot rowboat containing Mr. and Mrs. Roberts was swamped near this station," Alfred reported. "I got them ashore and dried them out and they left at 1 p.m." Three weeks later Eric Hope, aged seven, and his eight-year-old mate "went through narrows in a 12 foot skiff out of control (strong tide)." Dickenson "went after them, overtook them at Lumbermen's Arch and put them ashore at Mr. Newman's farm, absent 1 to 4 p.m."

Dickenson's log for 17 August 1930 records the first casualty:

> I rescued from the water about 100 feet SW of this station George C. Leighton and John McCormick, they being in a rowboat which was swamped by swell from SS *Prince David* throwing boat and occupants on shoal and the back-wash drawing them in about 8 feet of water. Mr. McCormick was semi-conscious when I drew him in my boat, he weighing about 200 lbs. it took me about 5 minutes to get him in, in the meantime Leighton had disappeared. I cruised around and found him about 2 foot below the surface, I was assisted then by 3 men in a dinghy in getting him into my boat. He groaned when dropped on bottom of boat.[2]

Dickenson tossed his painter to the men in the dinghy and laboured over Leighton while they towed him ashore. An hour later a doctor pronounced "life extinct." After a hot bath, McCormick left for home, "a very sick man."

The next week Alfred saved another couple in a swamped rowboat. The woman was "in such a nervous condition that she could not proceed." The Dickensons took three hours to persuade her into the station boat, and he rowed her over to Ambleside Wharf.

In December 1934 the steamboat SS *Cruiser* went aground in a dense fog near the Capilano's west arm. Hearing her distress signals between the blasts of his own horn, Dickenson hiked over the estuary of polished gravel, helped the crew and seven passengers ashore, and brought them home "to be warmed up," then led them to the railway tracks which they followed to the ferry dock. The following June he rescued another man who had collapsed in his rowboat "under the influence of drugs or . . . a Epileptic fit." Then, in a reversal of fortune, Dickenson was rescued himself when he was making his way back from Vancouver in a skiff with a friend. Their boat was swamped and Alfred clung to it while his friend swam ashore and summoned help. After drying out and resting up at a house nearby, he set off alone again at two in the morning.

Of course there were drawbacks to their home on piles. At Kains they had been well beyond reach of the sea; Capilano often "got a real dusting," with the swells at high tide washing clear up to and over the landing and veranda. "Very rough seas today," Dickenson observed on 12 November 1929. "Rails on south bulkhead broken and sea washing through basement." The water came over their porch again in July 1931, and on 11 January 1932 the platform on the south bulkhead broke up. "About half flooring in the basement was washed away along with coal and salvaged lumber." The weather vane, chimney, and yards of shingles blew off the roof in a gale of March 1942. "8 years since we have seen a sea like this morning," Dickenson recalled, "shall be very glad to pull out of this wreck." The light repeatedly suffered "a very severe pounding" from runaway logs and snags

Capilano Lightstation at low tide c. 1935.

borne in the current. As Alfred and Annie lay in bed the whole station would reel and rock under them.

The most terrifying phenomena were earthquakes; the first lasted a full minute, which must have seemed like an hour. "The station certainly did rock," Dickenson reported. "I ran on bulkhead to see if some vessel had struck." Five times over the next two decades the china rattled and the dog whimpered when the earth began to shiver and shrug under them. At high tide there was no escape and they counted the seconds, praying the shuddering pilings would hold and the dwelling wouldn't fall into the sea. One shock followed hard on the heels of another on 30 January 1942, "each lasting about half a minute separated by a quarter minute. Shaking sensation, rattling pictures, etc." Three months later Dickenson "distinctly felt this station rock with short trembling movements which lasted about 2 minutes." The worst happened at 7:20 p.m., 16 February 1946, "very severe while it lasted."

They also had a front row seat to witness human events of a gargantuan scale, as engineers poured concrete and stretched cables across First Narrows above them, and the grandiose suspension bridge reached inexorably for the north shore. "Lions Gate bridge open to pedestrian traffic today," Dickenson recorded on 12 November 1938, an event which added another grim chore to his workload: rowing around under the bridge, looking for suicides.

The Dickensons brought with them their reverence for natural things which had sustained them in the absence of human companionship throughout their exile at Kains Island. Pods of "blackfish" (killer whales) entering and leaving the

Capilano Light with tide in, 1944.

inner harbour were set down in the logbook with as much detail as shipping; seasons were ushered in by the "advance guard" of swallows and the departure of the last stragglers. In spite of the earthquakes and high water, the Dickensons were as content as a couple could be as they sat outside holding hands on the evening of 24 September 1944, their day's work and the dishes done, and watched "the most prettiest sunset" they had ever seen. They could judge sunsets, for they had seen every one over the past twenty years. Alfred and Annie had been together all that time, *really* together, with no distractions to come between them, under conditions few would tolerate for more than a month, and they had reaped this "in station" as their reward. Two months later, "this being my birthday I thank God for all his blessings bestowed upon me," Dickenson confided to his log, adding, "Hope we are out of this moth-eaten outfit before another birthday. This is Annie's fervent wish also."[3]

These were strong sentiments indeed, especially for a pair who had weathered five years at Kains (notorious even in the public's mind after the "Sadler affair" when a keeper and his wife went insane, and their children nearly starved, with scarcely a complaint). The cause of Dickenson's bitterness was "Lizzie," a fog alarm engine which continued to behave like a cranky invalid despite all his rehabilitation efforts, and the hours he spent tarting up her brass work.

Though it seemed laughably perverse to outsiders, the relationship between lightkeepers and their machines was as intimate as any that could be forged between lonesome men and an inanimate mass of gleaming metal. After decades of disemboweling and reassembling them, each piston, crank, and valve was as familiar a part of their existence as the contours of their wives' bodies. Visitors at Capilano were greeted with the command, "Shoes off in the engine room, you!" and many flinched under Dickenson's tirades if they so much as touched a block, a belt, a flywheel, leaving a fingerprint to mar the engine's outward appearance.

But inside, Lizzie was a mess. The first harbinger of twenty years' despair came in July 1925 when she broke a timing rod and Dickenson rowed over to town for another. In October both Lizzie and her sister quit for three-quarters of an hour in heavy fog, and Dickenson had to drag the handhorn out of storage. He diagnosed dirty fuel oil and revived the engines by mixing the oil with gasoline. In December Lizzie "choked herself, dirty fuel," at 1:00 a.m. while Dickenson was out rescuing a man adrift on a raft. Three days later his diaphones quit altogether when their pistons jammed. "Can only get a wheezing noise out of it," he wrote. "Have tried three pistons." Next night he worked on them for three hours, gave up, then squatted next to the handhorn all night. "Started horn at 8:30 gave few blasts then went dead," he wrote 8 January, "tried 3 more pistons no sound from any. Made a rubber gasket and fastened down and horn going irregularly at 9:45. Fairly good at 11:30 a.m. cleared at noon. Started again at 8:45 p.m. very irregular until 10 p.m. when went dead and could get no sound from any of 4 pistons. Worked on it until 1 a.m. and my wife used hand horn. Am beat. Very foggy during night."

From that point on the engines and horns ran in sporadic bursts between lengthier periods when Dickenson had their entrails spread over the floor and his tool bench, searching for an explanation in that clutter of steel. Annie pumped away at the handhorn outside, night after night, week after week. Fed up, Dickenson stripped Lizzie clear down to her block in mid-January 1928. The fog rolled in around 6:30; Lizzie took fifteen minutes to start, "no kick at all." Number two engine started, but the piston jammed in the diaphone again. Dickenson dismantled it, cleaned it with gasoline, oiled the cylinder walls, and had a horn until 3:20 a.m. when Lizzie blew her head gasket, spewing oil all over the floor and walls.

"Unable to start No. 2," Dickenson wrote in disgust as the sound of horns hooting derisively all over the harbour broke the stillness in his slippery engine room. "Changed igniter and fresh gas in priming can and away at 4 a.m. Stopped 4:15, started 4:25, stopped 5:00. Put in new gasket, ground valves, cleaned manifold on No. 1 and had misfortune to break cylinder head stud had no die to thread new one so had to use smaller stud with packing but it does not act, water entering head." He gave up at 4:00 p.m. as it was "too dark to do anything more."

Month after month Dickenson's log catalogues his frustration as gaskets blow, rings crack, timing rods and belts snap, diaphones cleave to their cylinder walls, water pours out gaskets, and filthy black oil spits all over the floor and walls. Mechanics dispatched from Victoria had a go at the engines with no more success than their custodian. "I changed over to 'Lizzie' at 11 a.m. to examine oil level in No. 2 engine," he wrote on 12 November 1935, "she lasted 35 minutes, then died, cannot find anything wrong with it, cause is 'Bad Construction' am discouraged with said engine, have been 8 years trying to remedy it."

By now Dickenson had a bleeding ulcer and had contracted pneumonia as a result of his frequent spells at the handhorn. In October 1935 a doctor was summoned. Dickenson "was so weak" he was "ordered. . . to North Van General hospital," where the keeper confounded nurses and his fellow patients by scraping leftovers off his plate out the window for the seagulls. A year later he confessed he was "utterly discouraged with this outfit." He celebrated Christmas Day 1937 by putting in three hours' work on Lizzie. "Was working on same old pile of junk on Christmas 1924," he recalled with black nostalgia.

On New Year's day a doctor came to take "Capt. Dickenson to West Van nursing home on account of nerves." He returned three weeks later and was hospitalized again in January 1942. "In the meantime Mrs. Dickenson kept light and fog alarm in operation alone—and with a straight 65 hours of continuous fog! That was a real feat! Congrats."[4]

Lizzie's sibling, who never rated christening beyond "No. 2," was a poor substitute at best. In December 1943 Dickenson replaced Lizzie's exhaust valve and began to strip down No. 2, slipping new rings over her pistons, but was "unable to get piston back at present (6 p.m.)." "Oh What a life," he despaired. "Looks like a night of fog. At 6 p.m. dense fog Lizzie in operation again, knock in cylinder but thank God she is percolating, Annie and I got pistons in No. 2 8 p.m., on tightening head broke a stud, too tired to do any more repair work, quit at 8:30. Lizzie pounding away sounds like music to my ears, fog very dense, pup is asleep and Annie going to bed. What a life for me, Christmas is a mockery at this joint." This, he hoped, would be his last Capilano Christmas. On 2 January No. 2, freshly overhauled, wouldn't start and Dickenson burst out, "Am just fed up with junk, in fact it is telling on my health. . . what a life, always patching up."

At times it seemed as if the two engines conspired to torment Dickenson, one quitting even as he mulled over the innards of the other. All through the week of 14 December 1945 he was virtually a prisoner in their cage. Annie brought meals to his work bench as Alfred fought off sleep with a wrench in his hand. Dickenson's log:

Dec. 14—At 9:30 p.m. timer belt broke at fastener and became entangled in shaft, repaired same, 15 minutes silence. Have been nursing Lizzie all day, water entering cylinder (after replacing gaskets twice in the last month). At 2:40 a.m. Lizzie finally died. Placed #1 light plant to operate horn, oh what an outfit, will have a look at Lizzie in daylight.

Dec. 15—New gasket on Lizzie, soaked it in linseed oil as have no gasket cement, cleaned rings and timer. Belt on compressor broke at 11:30 a.m. needs new one. Don't know what to do for Lizzie, certainly is a moth eaten outfit, 72 hours continuous fog to 6:30 p.m. We have no fresh water and too risky to go to ferry wharf to fetch a pail full. Pump belt broke again at midnight, "rotted" #1 light engine operated horn all night.

Dec. 16—I had to shut down #1 light engine, all lubricating oil shot up exhaust pipe, and leaky gasket, placed Lizzie in operation again at 8:45 a.m. silence about five minutes, commenced to nurse Lizzie at about 10:40 unreliable outfit. At 10:55 piston stuck in horn, silence 5 minutes, inserted a new one, terrible noise, I have ceased to worry anyhow with the best able bodied assistant [Annie] I have had in my life. A Merry Christmas, just a mockery at this scrap heap. At 1:35 p.m. Lizzie died, no ignition, placed the light engine in operation, silence 5 minutes. Fog cleared 3 p.m. 92½ hours continuous fog. At 8 p.m. dense fog. At 8:35 Lizzie died, #1 in operation, silence 5 minutes, installed new points on coil for Lizzie going strong again at 9:10 p.m. passed out again at 11 p.m. silence, 5 minutes, #1 in operation again and ran all night but it won't last much longer. What a life.[5]

By the end of that fog-bound December Dickenson had restored Lizzie to some semblance of working order. Much to his astonishment she pounded away for four hours before he went back to the engine room. When he opened the door, he found that she was "throwing all the oil out," and he spent the day cursing, soaking up the viscous swamp with coconut mats, and washing down the walls again.

Lizzie went out in March for a thorough overhaul at the Victoria Marine yards. By September water was into her cylinder head again, and in December Dickenson spent five hours overhauling her carburetor. "The outfit is as reliable as a snowball in hell," Dickenson sneered, reflecting upon "20 years running this wreck." They were "both discouraged," he confessed, "but will not worry, but hate to be beat." Two weeks later, in a crescendo of frustration, he declared, "This is the last gasket I will make. . . I don't mean maybe."

His prediction came true. In the spring of 1946 the department entered into an agreement with the National Harbours Board to electrify the Capilano light and run it from the signal tower up on the Lions Gate Bridge. It meant the end, at last, of Alfred's star-crossed relationship with Lizzie. He received a letter raising the possibility of superannuation, but Dickenson was reluctant to leave the lights if he could take a transfer instead. Confirmation came that May of his appointment to Sheringham Point, up the Juan de Fuca Strait past Sooke. "Certainly delighted to leave this wreck," he exalted, "such change to be made about 2nd week in June." While electricians wired the station to the bridge, Dickenson hammered his crates together on the landing. He tore down the veranda 1 June. A week later he was "nearly finished packing, just few odds and ends left." The *Berens* dropped anchor in the Narrows on the morning of 13 June. While deckhands loaded their belongings, Dickenson boarded up the windows, then climbed down into the workboat. Capilano light's last keepers steamed away twenty-four years after they had arrived.

They hadn't been aboard a ship in all that time, and whatever high spirits they shared quitting Capilano were soon dampened. The *Berens* anchored in the harbour that night. Next day the crew stopped briefly at Capilano and "dismangled" the old derrick. A heavy southeast gale was blowing with heavy rain. Annie and Alfred watched despondently from the wheelhouse as their belongings soaked up the torrent on deck. "On our way at noon," he glumly wrote in his diary, "moderate sea running in Gulf, Annie very seasick." The *Berens* docked in Victoria and deckhands transferred their crates to a truck for the last leg to Sheringham. "Most of the stuff is soaked," Alfred raged, "damned disgrace how things are handled, several things broken." They crowded into the cab with Tom Morrison, the marine agent (who was Pattie Cox's son), and drove up the coast.

No one in the real world can fathom the mixed feelings a keeper experiences when he changes stations. Leaving behind years in a place he will doubtless never see again, he has no inkling of what awaits him. If the Dickensons expected an improvement over their hard life at Capilano, their hopes were dashed upon arrival at Sheringham. "In all my life I have never seen such a disgraceful condition for a government lightstation," Dickenson wailed. "I do not blame the temporary keeper, this dump was never looked after, hell of a mess. . . Engines just a bunch of junk, Mr. Morrison and self tried to start them, also 2 of the *Berens* crew, no success, proceeded to tower, my, what a mess there. Had place to myself at 8:30 p.m. Light stopped 12:30 p.m. and again at 1:10 a.m. What an outfit, fine thing... no bed, everything soaked." He almost longed for Lizzie again.[6]

They had inherited the aftermath of patronage. A loyal Tory named Arden had been granted the station over much more experienced men in 1912. Whatever Arden's virtues, lightkeeping certainly couldn't be counted among them. Dickenson was sixty-one, and after twenty-seven years on the lights he was starting all over again.

The light he left behind continued operating until February 1969 when a concrete beacon was poured nearby. Much to the dismay of the residents of the North Shore, the original lighthouse was put to the torch on the afternoon of 26 February. Dying embers were its last beacon until they sank hissing into the swirling current of the Capilano after sixty-one years' service.

Lighthouse tender *Berens*.

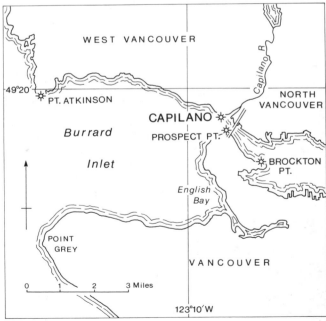

Capilano Lightstation 1938.
Dwelling in centre, tower
and engine room on right.

Entrance Island

Robert Dunsmuir founded a coal mine at Nanaimo in 1869. The "black gold" gave birth to the town with its humble cluster of company shacks. Men and boys tramped to the pits at dawn and homeward at dusk, streaked with grime and sweat, owing their souls to the company stores of Wellington Mines. In 1871 Wellington's reorganized as Dunsmuir, Diggle and Company, and began shipping coal to Departure Bay for export to cook stoves, blast furnaces, and boilers all round the Pacific Rim. By 1874 the town was incorporated as a city of fifteen hundred.

Carrying coal out of Departure Bay was as risky a venture as mining it. The *Prince Alfred* was lost in a dense fog with all hands on 15 June 1874. Four years later, in January 1878, the 1042-ton *Grace Darling* suffered the same fate somewhere off Cape Flattery. In November 1879 the American vessel *Marmion* left Departure Bay bound for San Francisco, and sailed into a howling gale out in the Strait of Juan de Fuca. Her seams opened up and she foundered. Fortunately the crew was snatched up by the *Tam O'Shanter*. In 1886 the *Barnard Castle*, under charter to Dunsmuir, left for her final destination on the shoals at Race Rocks.

Early in 1873 D.W. Gordon, MP for Nanaimo, wrote the minister of Marine and Fisheries to boast that 500,000 tons had cleared Departure Bay the previous year. Surely it was time that "such important interests" received "immediate attention," and that Nanaimo be granted the necessary harbour lights which Victoria and Esquimalt had "enjoyed for 13 to 25 years." This local political pressure meshed neatly with Langevin's priorities and the department called for tenders to build a light on Entrance Island, outside the harbour, on 30 December 1874.

On 25 March 1875 Nanaimo contractor Arthur Finney told the *Nanaimo Free Press* that the station was nearly complete. Three months later the *Free Press* announced the lighting of the beacon at nightfall on 8 June, noting "one strange feature" about the event: no notice had been issued to mariners. The editor trusted that, "for the sake of humanity," no casualty would result "from the cheese-paring policy of the Dominion Government."[1]

Unfortunately, a fire in the department's Victoria headquarters on 5 August 1900 consumed Entrance's early records, along with those of many other lights. The *British Columbia Coast Pilot*, the well-thumbed Bible of the wheelhouse, provides one of the earliest comprehensive descriptions of the island and the characteristics of the light. Lying half a mile north-north-east of Orlebar Point, the station sat on a bare sandstone rock thirty feet above high water. All traffic bound northward up the strait was advised to round Entrance. "There is a passage between it and Orlebar Point named Forwood Channel," said the *Pilot*, "but as there is a rock nearly in the middle, this channel should not be attempted by a stranger." The *Pilot* also warned ships away from "reefs and broken ground" lying two cables off the south and west side.

In December 1891 Stone-Chance of Birmingham shipped a fifth-order dioptric light apparatus for the square white tower that rose sixty-five feet above high water. The beacon exhibited a red sector over the Gabriola reefs and was visible fourteen miles away on a clear night. In May 1905 the apparatus was replaced by a larger fourth-order lens with a twin capillary burner, replaced in turn by the standard revolving lens floating upon a mercury bath in 1921.

The new Vancouver firm of Baynes and Horie built an engine room, in 1894, to house a steam horn which bellowed for eight seconds at forty-five second intervals. In 1915 the horn was converted to diaphones with gasoline engines driving their air compressors.

John Kenney, an Englishman from Newcastle, took charge of Entrance in June 1876, succeeded soon after by Robert Gray. Gray's annual salary totalled $600. Kenney, Gray, and those who came later kept precise and detailed logs which survive as a catalogue of the ever-increasing traffic in and out of Nanaimo. They also documented annual supplies and daily work, as well as some bewilderment at bureaucratic routine. "Received a note and form from William Smith Esq., Deputy Minister of Marine and Fisheries Department," Gray noted with exasperation, "accusing me of not returning. . . forms previously sent to me which I never received so I could not return which I did not get."

In July 1902 M.G. Clark saw a canoe carrying two Indians capsize off the station. He and his assistants launched the station boat, rowed out, and saved them by towing their canoe ashore. They were each rewarded with a pair of binoculars, presented in Nanaimo by Ralph Smith, MP, in "recognition of [their] humane service in rescuing the two Indians. . . from a watery grave."

Clark was keeping Entrance when the steamer SS *Portland* ran aground in the early morning of 16 February 1907. Mason, her captain, complained that the horn could barely be heard. Clark protested to Ralph Smith and demanded an official investigation to clear him of any charges of negligence. Since the *Portland* had struck just below the fog alarm building it seemed inconceivable that Mason would blame the horn. Clark's log confirmed it had been blowing at the time. This evidence was enough to convince James Gaudin, who tactfully wrote Smith suggesting he in turn contact Clark to tell him that no blame had been attached. Gaudin added, "If [Mason] is wise, he will let the matter drop."

In light of subsequent events, Clark may have had compelling reasons to prove his competence. He and his wife were investing most of their time and money on a ranch near Orlebar Point across on Gabriola Island. Mrs. Clark stubbornly refused to live on Entrance, so Clark depended upon assistants to run the station and, as it turned out, his ranch as well. Hugh Brestin was sent out to Entrance by Captain Gaudin in February 1909. He wrote the agent in May claiming that Clark had cheated his predecessor out of a fortnight's pay. "When I got there, I was made to feed the chickens, dig his garden, clean his house down for his *angel* wife," he complained. When he gave notice in April, Clark told him to leave immediately "as he had got another man." He still owed Brestin nine days' pay.

Brestin's successor was also conscripted as a ranch hand. At sundown on 20 November 1910 he set out to row home after another long hard day's work on Entrance Island.

Gabriola. He never arrived. Clark waited until the next morning before sending a telegraph: "ASSISTANT DROWNED LAST NIGHT, BOAT CAPSIZING." Captain Barnes was at Mary Anne Point in Active Pass with the *Newington*, installing a gas beacon, when he received the message. He immediately steered for Entrance and went looking for the boat and body. Neither was ever found. Why, one wonders, did Clark make reference to the boat capsizing, yet wait hours to inform the department?

Whatever the reason, he certainly wanted off Entrance a month later. Claiming that his health was in such a state that he couldn't work, that his failing eyesight was so bad he could no longer even clean the lamp, Clark declared, "I have not got a five-cent piece that I can call my own," and asked if he could have a pension if he retired after fourteen years' service. At least he had some political capital. "I have always been a supporter of the Liberal party (and my whole family before me). . . there ought to be something done," he wrote Ralph Smith.

The superintendent of lights rowed over to Entrance in February and confided to Gaudin on his return that, for a man who could barely see to clean the lamp, Clark was quite adept at reading small print. Halkett had asked Clark to climb up with him to inspect the lantern and noted, "He followed me up the stairs very quickly." The pension was refused.

Disturbed by the assistant's death, Alexander Johnston, the deputy minister, ordered Gaudin to investigate and determine whether Clark's "private interests on Gabriola Island interfered with his duties." Halkett looked into the matter. Clark assured him that he and his wife had separated; she ran the farm with hired help, he was "with his assistant stationary at the lighthouse." Suspicions lingered on in Victoria, fueled by a report that the light was out at 5:00 a.m., 26 February 1911. Clark lamely attributed it to a faulty ventilator; an excuse which Halkett

Entrance Island Light, showing original tower.

pronounced "very poor." The agent threatened to write Ottawa if he received another complaint.

In June 1911 Allan Pope walked into a Vancouver employment agent's office and stood scanning one of the boards until his eye fell on Clark's advertisement:

MAN & WIFE WANTED FOR LIGHTHOUSE
Must be able to manage a boat

The agent explained he would be expected to "keep things clean and smart about the lighthouse," and care for a flock of chickens. Mrs. Pope would be expected to do the housework—all for $50 a month plus board.

When they arrived, the Popes abruptly discovered they were expected to work at the ranch in the daytime and tend the light at night. Incensed that he should be doing another man's work for a fraction of his wages, Pope wrote Gaudin a letter in July. It should have sealed Clark's fate. "I have been here since the 13th of June," Pope reported, "and Mr. Clark has only passed one night at the lighthouse. Now Mr. Clark expects me & my wife to go across to his ranch & work all day there & then attend to the light nights." Clark had instructed him to check on the light every two hours. "Cannot see how I am to get any sleep," the assistant claimed. Moreover, Pope's wife had to bring the Clarks' laundry back and wash it, as well as clean the lighthouse "top to bottom." Pope closed by accusing the keeper of using station lumber and nails over on Gabriola, and asked the agent "to request Mr. Clark to deal a little more fairly" with them, as they were "not the first people that Mr. Clark [had] treated unfair." Clark finally sacked Pope because he was tardy getting across to Gabriola in the mornings.

Captain Robertson, Gaudin's successor, proceeded to Entrance 10 July to inspect the station and look into Pope's claim. The island was deserted. Next day a letter arrived from Clark, apologizing for his absence. As for Pope's charges, Clark admitted that he had only spent one night on the island but denied stealing lumber. Contrite, he implored, "Give me another chance and let the matter drop." If given a reprieve, the keeper pledged to repair his reputation and give up farming for good. The farm belonged to his wife, he explained, "and as she will not stop at the lighthouse and try to do what is right, she can stay where she is." But Clark's reputation, launched upon an act of heroism eight years before, was foundering. Halkett climbed ashore on 9 August. No one home again. Robertson wrote the deputy minister in Ottawa recommending Clark's dismissal.

Clark's dereliction of duty was exceptional: no other keeper throughout the history of the West Coast lights ever proved as shiftless or irresponsible. But many, many more would continue the trend he established of mistreating and exploiting assistants.

W.E. Morrisey, who took over Entrance from Clark, hired Edwin and Bertha Perdue to assist him in October 1914. Shortly after they arrived, Bertha wrote Victoria to ask if there were a set of rules and regulations for lighthouse keepers. If so, were assistants allowed to read them? She wanted to know, too, if there were set watches or if assistants were generally required to stand watch twenty-two hours a day in addition to feeding pigs and chickens, and cleaning their pens.

She complained of living "cooped up in two rooms"—one on the first floor of the tower and the other over Morrisey's diningroom. Could they use the wash-house? she asked. "Things have come to such a pass that although we have only been here a short while, we are forced for the public's safety as well as our own to inquire into these matters," she concluded. Robertson replied that the lightkeeper was the only employee of the department at Entrance Island and that assistants were "wholly under the orders of the lightkeeper," although the department expected him to "behave in a fair manner to all his help." [2]

The Perdues had answered Morrisey's advertisement in the *Vancouver Daily World*. It sounded too good to be true:

> The wages are 25.00 a month and board. If you should come you would have free rent and a chance to catch lots of fish. I would rather help a married couple than a single man.

A few days later, Morrisey wrote them offering the job if they wanted to start 30 September. He promised to pay the expense of their move from Vancouver.

When Perdue went to ask for his wages a month later, Morrisey told him he would pay them $100 after three months. They should pay their own expenses. He wrote his grocer in Nanaimo guaranteeing $50 credit for three months.

Attractive new tower on Entrance Island, 1982. Jim Ryan photo.

"Consequently from Nov. 23rd until Dec. 7th we had scarcely anything to eat but salt pork and potatoes," Perdue reported. The first time they went to town, on 1 December, the Perdues took Morrisey's letter to a lawyer who then wrote to Morrisey about breach of contract. As soon as he opened the lawyer's letter, the keeper ran over, livid, and shouted, "Get to hell out of here, there will be no work for you here."

So the Perdues found themselves sitting on their trunks on the quay at Nanaimo. There were fewer trunks now, since they had had to sell off some furniture to pay for the move and get a meal. Morrisey had garnisheed their wages to pay the grocer, the hardware, the butcher, and his lawyer. "He claimed there is only two and a half dollars ($2.50) coming to us after Dec. 31st, 1914," Perdue explained.[3]

In the summer of 1924, Entrance was taken over by Michael O'Brien and his wife. The O'Briens had certainly paid their dues. Michael had served on the Sand Heads lightship, then up at Triangle Island, the nastiest light of them all, where ferocious winds blew away chimneys and chickens, and rocked houses on their foundations. He transferred to Chrome for three years, then moved over to Entrance.

There they were within easy rowing distance of Nanaimo with its shops and schools. It was a fitting reward, a dividend long overdue for all their suffering and isolation, compensation of a sort for Michael's arthritis. They had only four good years. "MY WIFE DROWNED LAST NIGHT," he radioed Victoria in mid-October. "RUSH A RELIEF IMMEDIATELY."

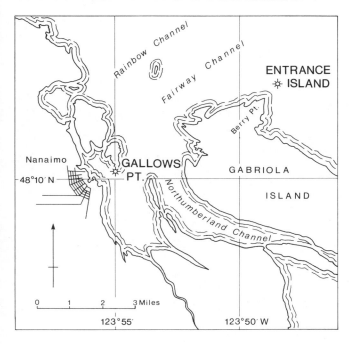

Gallows Point

In 1905 Gaudin built a light on Protection Island in Nanaimo's inner harbour. It stood at the site of a gallows where two Indians were hanged in January 1853 for the murder of a shepherd—a grisly parallel to the Execution Rocks light in New York harbour. A fixed red anchor light was first moored off Gallows Point in 1900 at the behest of the Western Fuel Company, to assist "pilots bringing large steamers" to Western's Protection Island wharf to take on coal.

In May 1901 the pilots complained that the light's radius reached less than a mile into the night and would be better shown from the south side of the channel to define their position relative to nearby tidal flats. The agent ordered that a more powerful beacon be installed upon a platform supported by copper-sheathed piles.

Mechanical fog bell established on Gallows Point, Nanaimo, 1906.

In April 1906 the company requested a mechanical fog bell. Gaudin obliged in return for a promise to have miners wind the bell in thick weather for a payment of $10 a month.

The Western Fuel Company abandoned their nearby pits in the autumn of 1918. In October the department hired Jack Hutching, a transplanted Newfoundlander living aboard his gas launch in the harbour, to tend the beacon and bell for $20 a month.

In October 1922 the *Princess Patricia's* captain ordered FULL STOP and sent his steward around to the first class cabins to fetch A.W. Niell up to the wheelhouse. When the MP entered the bridge, the captain explained they were a few cable lengths off Gallows Point and invited him out on the catwalk to listen for the bell. He heard no sound whatever. Next day he wrote Colonel Wilby asking to have an "adequate fog signal" installed.

In December 1923 Nanaimo's Board of Trade complained that, "during the recent foggy weather period," steamers had been forced to lie at anchor outside the harbour, "unable to be brought in owing to inadequate facilities in the way of light and fog signals." But Nanaimo's businessmen ranted at the ships' lost time for sixteen more years. Then in 1936 the CPR's *Princess Elaine* stranded on Gallows Point and diaphones were installed soon after.

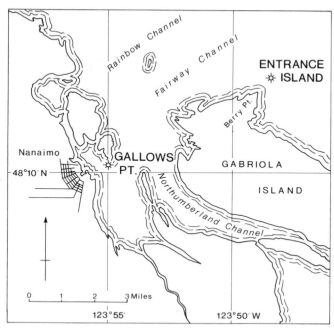

Berens Island

In the early 1860s the colony gave top priority to the British naval base at Esquimalt, the fleet's leading Pacific station. But even then Victoria's inner harbour was evolving into a hub of commerce; a transition completed when the postcard port became seat of the provincial government in 1871. It was a waste of time hauling all that freight out to Esquimalt when stevedores could sling it aboard a few blocks away. The city desperately needed a light in its own right, and there seemed no better place for it than Berens Island, off the mouth of the harbour.

Work gangs completed the new light in the winter of 1874, and "fit and lit" a fixed blue light on top of its forty-foot tower in March 1875. The accommodations were cramped and spartan, with a lower floor measuring nine by twelve feet. "The passage way upstairs to the lantern can scarcely be called a bedroom," the agency's chief engineer remarked. A. McKinnon took over the new light which was equipped with a fog bell timed to ring every five seconds in reply to signals from approaching ships. In 1895 the department installed a revolving lens to set Berens Island apart from its backdrop of Victoria's street lights.

McKinnon had apparently been in ill health for some time. From the outset his wife shouldered most of the burden at Berens. In May 1886 William Smith, deputy minister of marine, learned that McKinnon was sick again, and that the trouble was "clearly traceable to habits of intemperance." He ordered the agent to send "some well known Doctor" out to Berens Island to examine the lightkeeper and "set forth plainly the precise nature of the disease."

But McKinnon was reprieved by a curious twist of fate. One fogbound night in August 1887, the SS *Abyssinia*'s captain paced angrily in her wheelhouse. He had been blasting his horn for hours to summon the Victoria pilot to come steer his ship through the fog to Vancouver. Finally a rowboat appeared out of the mist. The crew dropped a rope ladder and McKinnon hauled himself aboard, demanding to know what all the commotion was about. The Captain explained his dilemma and "evinced great anxiety to proceed," so McKinnon took the helm, ordered up steam, and sailed off to Vancouver! Needless to say, the Victoria pilots were incensed by a lowly lightkeeper's usurping their authority, and they complained bitterly to the minister in Ottawa.

James Gaudin explained, "This is the first time he has been absent from his station for ten years"; moreover, McKinnon had left a competent assistant (his wife) in charge. William Smith replied that, under the circumstances, McKinnon's explanation was satisfactory and Gaudin could "inform the complainants accordingly." In future, however, the minister would rather McKinnon abort his

The first Victoria Harbour light, built on Berens Island in 1874.

career as a pilot unless, Smith added, "such vessel is in distress and he considers it necessary to render assistance for the purpose of saving life and property."

In December 1890 McKinnon suffered a paralytic stroke. Smith endorsed the agent's proposal to retain his wife in his place. For the next five years she safeguarded shipping on its way in and out of Victoria harbour while she spoonfed, bathed, and turned her husband, numb from the neck down, in that closet of a bedroom. When he died in May 1895, Gaudin left the station in her charge for two more years until a replacement could be found. McKinnon's widow, he pointed out, "has operated the light satisfactorily for many years." But now a new steam fog alarm was on the drawing boards for Berens Island. Gaudin was soon swamped with applications for the post, and in spite of patronage priorities, the agent hoped, "Some person who is able to operate it will receive the appointment." William Henry Harrison replaced Mrs. McKinnon in July 1897.

In the summer of 1899, when Harrison was in hospital, Elizabeth Sea relieved him. While on watch on Sunday afternoon 4 July, she saw a sailboat capsize offshore. She ran down, launched the station boat, rowed out, and rescued two weekend sailors.

In June 1905 Victoria pilots petitioned the department to move the light to Nicholl's Folly to give them better guidance for vessels making for Royal Roads. The *Colonist* reported, "Masters and owners of ferry steamers which come and go. . . daily are said to be opposed to such a change." The ferry masters carried the day. In 1925 Berens Island light was converted to an automatic unwatched beacon and survives as a fifteen-foot day marker on a concrete base.

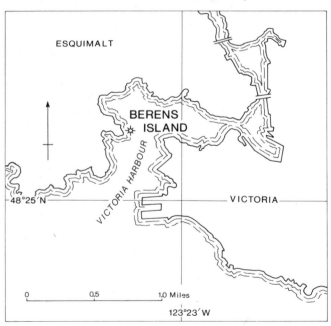

Trial Island

After a refit, British ships of the Pacific station would sail out of the shelter of Esquimalt Harbour, past Fisgard, to an island off Oak Bay and back again, while shipwrights checked the caulks and seamen cinched up the standing rigging. Inevitably the island came to be known as Trial Island. Only three hundred feet of water—Enterprise Channel—sets it apart from Oak Bay; today a golfer can easily slice a drive over to the lighthouse. But as in any narrow channel, tons of seawater sluice through at six knots or more when the tide runs, making Trial's proximity more deceptive and tantalizing than that of any other station. "Vessels should give it a good berth in thick weather on account of the strong tide races," the *BC Coast Pilot* cautioned in 1905.

The island is a barren, treeless hump rising some eighty feet above high water, carpeted with brush and grass. Long before the light was built the place was a refuge for John Kergan, a hermit, and a haven for a bootlegger named "Liverpool Jack." Kergan was finally hounded off the island by increasing numbers of visitors at the turn of the century. His body was later found in the surf off Sombrio Head.

The crew of the *Velos* and the hulk of the *Pilot* she had under tow on the night of 22 March 1895 underwent the worst trial of all in that boiling channel. A former Columbia River tug, the *Pilot* had suffered the humiliation of having her masts amputated and was hauling stone blocks from up-coast quarries for the facade of the new legislative buildings in Victoria. That morning, by eerie coincidence, Frederick Adams, her owner, decided to sit down and make out his will.

Aside from Adams and Captain Anderson, five crewmen were aboard the *Velos* and twenty-four more were astern on the *Pilot*, hunkering down against the wind and spray as the tow rope drew tight and the tug laboured out of Victoria Harbour at 6:30 p.m. After a bitter hour's pounding against a southeast gale, the hump of Trial Island loomed up ahead. Anderson had no time to turn and elected to make for shelter in Cadboro Bay via Enterprise Channel. Once into the narrows, the rip tide and the battering wind had him at their mercy. Anderson tried to escape by turning his tug about, but the larger and heavier tow was already caught in the current's powerful grip. The *Velos* was now the *Pilot*'s prisoner, their roles reversed. The cable fell slack, then snapped taut with every gust, and the violated tug charged them. Well into her turn, the *Velos* stood broadside to the violent current. A wave slammed into her hull and sent the tug careening into the rocks.

For a few desperate minutes it seemed as if the *Pilot* was sure to crush her. First Mate Andrew Christenson watched petrified as the maimed hulk came out of the squall "like a steam engine." He "knew that if she struck she would go clear through!" But they were reprieved when their tow struck another rock. The towline snapped tight again, clearing the water. Christenson clawed his way hand over hand back to the *Pilot*, shouting for the others to follow. Time and again he went under when the line slackened but finally reached the tow and was hauled aboard. Frank Duncan followed suit, but was carried away by a wave. The *Velos* was nearly submerged now. Trapped below in the galley, Frederick Adams drowned, the ink barely dry on his last testament shut up in a desk in Victoria. The cook and the engineer leapt over the side into the racing current, clung to a rock for a while, then were swept away. Captain Anderson and Law, his engineer, clung desperately to the wheelhouse as the *Velos* broke up. Finally Anderson struck out for a nearby reef.

The twenty-five men stranded on the *Pilot* held on as the waters carried her back and forth in the channel, smashing and splintering her hull. The *Velos* was their anchor until the hawser ripped the capstan clear off the deck. The punished hulk finally grounded on Trial Island. The men clambered ashore and listened through the night to the wails of their shipmates from the *Velos*. One fell silent, then another, and they took turns shouting encouragement to Law and their captain out there somewhere in the dark.

They listened as Law passed through the worst nightmare a seaman can imagine. Men have been known to tread water and chew off their thumbs at the root when snared by the wrist, but Law had a line cinched around his ankle. He could only pray the tide was ebbing. It wasn't. "Won't someone *please* help me," he wailed as he tread water and swam hysterically in turn toward his mates on Trial, then back over toward the darkened dwellings on the Oak Bay shore. Hearing Law's shouts above the storm, Christenson tried to launch a lifeboat from the *Pilot* but the waves smashed it against her hull. The swirling water rose inexorably. As the slack went out of his leash, Law's frenzy mounted. The sea lapped up to his neck, his chin, then went into his nostrils, drowning out his last scream. Captain Anderson and the others survived to carry that hideous memory away with them from Trial Island.

With the *Velos*'s fate Trial Island went down in log books as a place to be shunned, especially in thick weather. No one needed reminding to stay out of Enterprise Channel.

In late September 1898 Captain Smythe of the survey ship *Egeria* recommended that a light and fog alarm be installed on Trial as they "would doubtless be of great assistance to navigators in foggy weather." Smythe appreciated the need better than most; he ran his *Egeria* aground there in the fog on his way back to Esquimalt. Seven years later the department put up tenders to build the light and fog alarm building. Specifications called for concrete foundations for the combined tower and dwelling. "From this a chimney with three flues" was to be built, and "under the kitchen a cistern. . . with a capacity of 800 cubic feet." Up above, the architect envisaged "a neat two-storey building about thirty by thirty and shingled with cedar shingles on the sides with a tower on top."

In October 1906 James Gaudin informed Deputy Minister Gourdeau in Ottawa that the building at Trial was practically finished. Gaudin had also ordered the new keeper to sound his handhorn on request, since the *Twickenham*, "a large and new steamer" with a cargo of five thousand tons of sugar, had "stranded itself in the vicinity" a few days before the diaphones were installed. The fog alarm, twenty feet above high water near the west shoreline, had been operating since August. A temporary fixed light was installed until the Fresnel lens arrived from Birmingham.

Trial Island 1982 with Enterprise Channel in background. Jim Ryan photo.

The first lightkeeper was Harrold Shorrock O'Kell—according to Gaudin, "The son of one of our most respected citizens who has had several years' experience at sea and holds a Mate's Certificate for Coasting Canadian waters." O'Kell's promising career at sea had been cut short when a cable snapped, whooped through the air, and shattered his shin bone. He came ashore at Trial that August with a "cork leg." Here was a rare combination which reconciled patronage and competence. Three years later Gaudin praised him as "one of our most reliable lightkeepers," who kept the light and signal at Trial "in a highly efficient condition."

North Americans are only just beginning to appreciate the pricelessness of fresh water, but for O'Kell and his fellow keepers at those arid stations in the rain shadow, conservation of water always ranked highest in their priorities. (Even today keepers sound their cisterns weekly as a matter of routine.) If the O'Kell's check of their water supply indicated that the level was steadily dropping, it meant that water went from the bath to the laundry to the gardens in turn. Seawater had to be hauled in pails for the toilets. There was also the problem of fresh milk for their baby. O'Kell purchased a cow in Oak Bay, built a raft on the beach, looped a rope around her horns, and rowed her home.

Harrold O'Kell set out to transform Trial Island. Every summer for twenty-five years he rowed to Oak Bay, packed tons of topsoil into pails and sacks, and ferried them home in his rowboat. Then he ground inches off his peg-leg as he roved the island with a wheelbarrow, levelling potholes in the rocks and filling stone planters. On weekends the O'Kells rowed to town for a bath to conserve water for their parched and precious flowers.

Unlike most of their contemporaries they had a telephone link to the marine agency in Victoria, which doubtless accounts for the sparsity of correspondence to give some insights into their life at the light. O'Kell could pick up the phone instead of a pen. When his father died suddenly in Victoria in 1910, the department sent A.E. Roberts and a boat party out to Trial one Friday morning to bring him word. "There was such a storm raging that it was only with great difficulty we were able to reach the Island to tell him the sad news," Roberts reported. It took them a day and a half! "Had there been a wreck off the island Friday night," he pointed out, "the men on the island could not possibly have launched a boat and would have looked on in utter helplessness while their fellows drowned before their eyes." If they had a telephone, Trial's keepers could notify Victoria and rescuers might be dispatched. The storm had raged all that week and "it was impossible to launch the lighthouse boat owing to the heavy waves beating against the slip." "Something should be done immediately," Roberts recommended.

The telephone link to Trial bound it tightly into the emerging search and rescue network in Victoria. Forty years later the Department of National Defense wanted to remove the submarine phone cable to the light, claiming they needed it somewhere else for search and rescue purposes. Appalled by this warped logic, Tom Morrison wrote Ottawa, pointing out that Trial Island was "a very important link in [the] chain of search and rescue reporting stations." How, he wondered, could the military require the whole cable for emergency search and rescue purposes when they were "not even using the pair of wires...available"? The agent reviewed Trial's history dating from the *Velos*, carefully constructing his argument to retain the service. In 1944, for example, the keeper saved five people off a smashed yacht and brought them home. The navy was unable to land a boat. One of the passengers was seriously injured and the keeper was given medical advice over the telephone to treat him. The cable stayed.

Aside from such exploits which went far beyond their normal duties, Trial Island's keepers telephoned local weather reports mornings and evenings to be broadcast twice daily from the Gordon Head radio station. They stood ready "at any hour of the day or night" to assist pilots or other navigators. "Due to its location and natural phenomena such as winds and tides," Morrison wrote, "local weather and sea conditions are of the greatest importance and frequently the governing factor to all but the largest type of seaborne traffic in and out of Victoria."

In 1970 the department poured a new concrete tower at Trial, a few feet away from the original tower and dwelling. The old lens and lantern room were carefully dismantled, trucked to their final destination in Victoria's Bastion Square, and reassembled. Trial Island's light still flashes through the night, guiding a very different sort of traffic through another enterprise channel between Government and Wharf Streets.

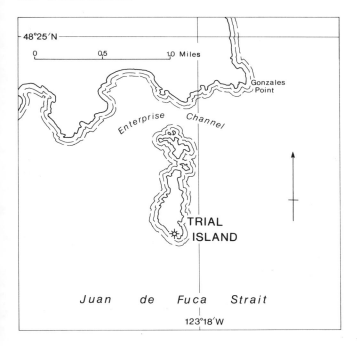

Fiddle Reef

James Gaudin had the luckless Captain Anderson into his office within a week of the wreck of the *Velos*. Law's shrieks carried a long way. That such a shocking tragedy could unfold within a stone's throw of Oak Bay had created a stir even in Ottawa, and the department anxiously awaited a report. For his part, Captain Anderson confessed that he had misjudged the distance to Trial Island in the dark and rain. Gaudin advised that a light on Fiddle Reef, between the harbour and Trial, "would have been of assistance in judging the distance from Trial Island."

Lighthouse Board chairman William Anderson gave his agent the go-ahead, and construction of the Fiddle Reef light commenced in August 1898. Barges brought out the quarry stone and within a month, "what with the steps and cellar floor," stonemasons had completed a hundred square yards of masonry. By mid-September Gaudin had exceeded his $500 budget, "but it is a good solid job," he boasted.

He also had a man in mind for the place: John Davies was "an old sailor. . . who would be glad to undertake the job for about $20.00 per month." If, on the other hand, the minister appointed someone with a family, Gaudin predicted, "There will be no end of wants." At high tide there was barely standing room left on the reef and the carpenters joked that its name was a misnomer—there was hardly enough elbow room inside to play a fiddle. The single room on the ground floor measured ten feet square.

"I have had two comfortable rooms fitted in the tower (which is a small one) which would accommodate one person comfortably," Gaudin wrote in October. There was also "a large and commodious boat house." He had originally proposed that the keeper should "reside on shore and row out to the light night and morning" for $25 a month; now he had changed his mind "because no landing could be effected in rough weather." He once again advanced Davies as a suitable candidate. Not only was he "sober and reliable," but "this pittance with his small savings would enable him to live in comfort."[1]

John Davies won the appointment. For once, patronage was no problem. Any Liberal interested in the post need only ride out to Oak Bay to see the light and its claustrophobic setting to be moved to consider a career in the post office or customs shed instead. Davies was marooned on the reef during his first winter, after the boat house and skiff were "totally wrecked during a heavy S.E. gale." The agent immediately dispatched a crew to erect another as it was "urgent that the lightkeeper should have the means of leaving the reef in case of accident." This time he would build to last, trusting the new boat house would "not meet with the same fate."

When Gaudin came to work on Wharf Street on the morning of 2 May 1902, John Davies was lying in wait for him. The agent ushered the old salt into his spacious office and learned he no longer considered his "small pittance" enough compensation for claustrophobia. "I very much fear we cannot find any person to relieve him, on account of the scant dwelling accommodation," Gaudin confessed to Anderson. He proposed instead that the light be converted to an unwatched beacon, linked by submarine cable to Oak Bay. He cajoled Davies to remain in charge until Anderson's planned trip west that summer so the chairman of the Lighthouse Board could see the place for himself. Davies quit in March 1903 "on account of failing eyesight and general breaking up."

Colonel Anderson rejected Gaudin's automation scheme. M.G. Douglas took over from Davies in the spring of 1903. He was near the end of a rather checkered career, having meandered from one odd job to the next. He had found some security behind the bar on the CPR steamers, "but owing to his advancing age, was discharged from that service." In April he wrote Gaudin asking for a raise. Back in Ottawa Anderson reckoned any man at Fiddle Reef should surely be able to take on outside work as well, as the place was so close to town. Gaudin tried to correct the delusion. There was no problem in fair weather, "but should the weather become at all stormy, landing would be impossible at the station, without serious risk," he explained. "It may be possible to find a person to take charge of this light who could supplement his salary by working at his regular business on the premises," the agent conceded, "but I must admit such people will be hard to find." For what it was worth, he would inform Douglas that he was at "liberty to supplement his salary by . . . work onshore." Douglas quit that May after two months' service.

His replacement, C.M. Black, wrote Gaudin a year later, in April 1904, for the same reason. This time the agent argued, "According to the market price of necessities . . . in this province, $25.00 per month is scarcely sufficient to sustain a person with any degree of respectability and comfort," especially if he lived "on an isolated rock," in a dwelling that was "very cramped, consisting of one room about ten feet square which he has to use for all purposes." Black also suffered from "the disadvantage of being shut up on the rock for several days at a time in stormy weather. . . . According to the rate of wages in this province," Gaudin concluded, "I should say that the salary paid to the keeper is inadequate." At the

Fiddle Reef Lighthouse, built in 1898. Keepers lived in tiny room in tower.

very least, he recommended a raise of $100 per annum. Black received the increase in July 1904.

Like any other port, Victoria was accustomed to seeing sailors well into their cups weaving up and down her streets without rudder or compass. As long as they confined their antics to Wharf Street, Government Street, and Trounce Alley, they were tolerated. Like most other upright members of Victoria's Establishment, James Gaudin turned a blind eye. But one Saturday afternoon in February 1905 he saw a man who looked remarkably like Black, carousing with a motley crew. "I met Mr. Black in the street in a state of intoxication," he wrote Anderson the following Monday. "I used every effort to get him to go back to the lighthouse but I am sorry to say without avail." Doubtless the beery keeper gave the agent precise instructions where to deposit his paltry $33 per month. Gaudin faced a real dilemma now: getting someone else out to the Reef by nightfall. Fortunately he came across an "elderly seaman named Owen Thomas" on the street and persuaded him to take over until a permanent replacement could be appointed. First, he had to promise him $50 a month.

Word of Gaudin's encounter with Black made the rounds of the public houses with much guffawing and slapping of thighs. Donald McNeill, a member of "one of the pioneer families of" Victoria, heard the story and called upon Gaudin Monday morning to seek the appointment. McNeill's grandfather, Captain William Henry McNeill, had steered his brig *Llama* into Victoria harbour on 1 May 1831, the first ship ever to anchor there. The McNeills were also the first white settlers at McNeill (Shoal) Bay, and the family had rescued crewmen from the *Velos*, *Emma*, and *Islander*. His father and brother had joined Don McNeill in agitating for the Trial Island light. "He claims to have rendered some services to the Government by which he lost two fingers of one hand," Gaudin reported.

A week later Deputy Minister Gourdeau sent a wire questioning McNeill's appointment:

DONALD McNEILL FOR KEEPERSHIP FIDDLE REEF OVER AGE LIMIT DOES THAT MATTER? ANSWER

to which Gaudin replied:

AGE DOES NOT INCAPACITATE McNEILL TAKE CHARGE FIDDLE REEF STATION

"All the lightkeepers who have hitherto been in charge of this station have been old men," Gaudin elaborated. "It would scarcely be practicable to obtain a young man to take charge of Fiddle Reef for the salary allowed to a lightkeeper of this station."[2]

Though Gaudin was mixing geriatrics with economics, the agent was never more astute than when he pronounced Donald McNeill fit for the keepership of Fiddle Reef. For the next twenty years he would amass a compelling record saving ships and lives—a record that makes a mockery of mandatory retirement at sixty-five.

There was no horn during McNeill's stint at Fiddle Reef. A lesser man might have contented himself with tending the light and lens. Not Donald McNeill. He would launch his skiff into the blackness any time a vessel seemed to veer too close. Around 9:00 p.m., on 9 February 1907 he watched a Seattle freighter, the *Montara*, blunder into foul ground lying off nearby Chain Islands. He rowed out, screaming "Back Water!" at the top of his lungs, then shouted to drop anchor. He climbed aboard to point out their perilous position on the charts. At daybreak McNeill came out again. Taking the wheel, the keeper piloted *Montara* well out into the Straits, then rowed back to his post as her captain, much relieved, charted his course to Skagway.

Gaudin forwarded McNeill's report to Ottawa. Gourdeau took it in to Brodeur, the minister. In an unprecedented gesture, the deputy wrote McNeill in person to express his gratitude and the minister's. The minister, said Gourdeau, "read [the report] with much satisfaction and...highly commends your conduct. By his direction I hereby convey to you the thanks of the Department for the efficient service rendered by you to the officers and crew of the above-mentioned steamer, and assure you that your action is much appreciated at headquarters."

This was heady tribute indeed, but McNeill treasured even more those letters of thanks from people who faced much greater peril than an upcoming election. "Dear Sir," M. Buckley wrote, "I have to convey to you the united thanks of myself and sister for your much valued service rendered off Trial Island, when we were swept out in the Straits by a strong flood tide and westerly wind. We were unable to get back in our small skiff and you were the only person who rowed out and showed yourself able to get us back. I consider your conduct in this case deserves consideration from the Marine Department of Lighthouses," Buckley concluded, "and I think you should be promoted to a better lighthouse." F.C. Pauline wrote in a similar fashion to thank McNeill for coming after him when he "was fishing off Trial Island one Labour Day, and being caught in a strong flood-tide was swept out in the Straits, exhausted and seasick and unable to row back to shore. I was very pleased when your boat hove in sight," Pauline understated, "and pulled me ashore, as the sea got so rough afterwards."

But McNeill, if always eager to put his own life at risk, resented doing the work of Harrold O'Kell over at Trial Island too. He sent the letters to the office, an in-camera enquiry was convened, and the agent concluded that O'Kell, "notwithstanding his misfortune in having a cork leg. . . is one of the most reliable lightkeepers." McNeill was cautioned to cease "making an attack upon his neighbour." He called O'Kell's competence into question again in March 1919 after he went out after someone in distress off Trial Island. The assistant deputy minister instructed his agent "to severely censure [McNeill] and to inform him that such reprehensible conduct will oblige the Department to consider the advisability of disposing with his services as lightkeeper."

When McNeill set out on his missions of mercy, he never knew if he would get back ashore. The landing at Fiddle Reef was notoriously difficult and he doubtless approached it with foreboding, heaving up and down in the heavy chop, arms aching from towing someone, and with only two fingers clenched around one oar.

In April 1908 the keeper left for Victoria in fair weather for supplies. By mid-afternoon the sea turned nasty as he headed home. After swamping his loaded skiff, McNeill "just managed to reach one of the rocks where he found temporary shelter." The telephone jolted Gaudin awake in the middle of the night and he padded downstairs in his pyjamas to learn that Fiddle Reef light was out. He hurriedly dressed and made his way out to Oak Bay. By then the sea was so rough that no boat would dare put out. The agent paced back and forth wringing his hands, squinting out at the reef, knowing full well that nothing short of injury or death would keep a man of McNeill's mettle from his work. It was not until midnight that McNeill felt confident to dive in and swim home. Gaudin, much relieved, saw the light flash on.

Sobered by his experience that wild night, McNeill wrote asking for "much required improvements at his station," especially for a breakwater and concrete boat slip which could easily be poured during summer's low tides. "There is no protection," he stated, "and it is dangerous and a risk of life to land. . . in rough or windy weather—the boat sometimes being filled with water and swamped—the provisions lost and the boat itself only saved with considerable difficulty." McNeill also asked for an addition on the northwest side of the tower, for better accommodation and more structural strength. "The fierce wind lately and during last winter made the old tower crack and tremble considerably," he reported. A breakwater on that side "would shear off the heavy sea and the logs that strike against the foundation of the lighthouse, and damage it in stormy weather." He might also store firewood in the annex "since the Department stopped the coal supply." He also asked for "a good marine telescope."

Gordon Halkett rowed out to the Reef to assess McNeill's plans for improving his station. He reported that Fiddle Reef had been "maintained satisfactorily under present conditions for a good many years," so he didn't see "the necessity of the requests." McNeill's reliability, it seems, was a liability as well.

When the sledgehammer Superannuation Bill descended in 1924, McNeill jumped aside. Under the new scheme he would have had to scrape together *a years' pay* and turn it over to his employers. McNeill wrote Colonel Wilby, pointing out that failure to do so would deprive him of any pension. "I have served over 19 years at Fiddle Reef Lighthouse," he reminded the agent, "having commenced on March 5, 1905, and worked *continuously* ever since, serving the Government faithfully both day and night. *No holidays at any time*." Now he was seventy "and still thoroughly fit for the work at Fiddle Reef Lighthouse," but he could no longer afford the position. "I am still able to continue the work," he claimed, "but I am very anxious not to lose the chance of the Superannuation Pension."[3] McNeill agreed to stay on for as long as it took the agent to find a replacement.

Walter Ward replaced him on 26 January 1925. Ward was sixty-eight. In late February he resigned "owing to. . . poor physical condition and nervous temperament." Reginald Graham took over at Fiddle Reef a week later. The department issued him a new boat and he purchased an outboard motor which was, he said, "a great help to me against wind & tides Except when I am making a landing and then it is rather in the way." Early in January 1926 he made three tries to land and "the motor got drowned. . . each time." A fishboat en route to Discovery Island detoured to give him a tow and stood by to see if he could make it. "After some hard manoeuvring I managed to make a landing & save myself & boat," he reported.

In November the next year Graham set out to fetch his provisions and a sack of coal. By 1:30 p.m. "it came to blow from the South East"; by the time he reached the reef "their was very heavy seas running." He continued, "I got the boat upset making a landing & was thrown into the sea but got ashore but could not save the boat from being broke up."

The gale which careened up the Straits Christmas week 1932 was one of the worst in memory. Marooned on Fiddle Reef, Graham watched as the waves washed over his porch, uprooted the winch and sixty feet of boardwalk, then pried the boathouse off its foundation. The storehouse mounted on his water cistern was swept away. All his stores were lost and the tank flooded with sea water. The stone foundation cracked. Water sluiced through, flooding the basement.

Wilby brooded over Graham's damage report, then wrote the deputy minister, recommending once again that Fiddle Reef be automated. Aside from removing a man from his perilous perch on the reef, automation would allow the department to forgo making any repairs since there would be no need for fresh water or a boathouse if an unwatched Aga light were installed. At the same time he dutifully informed C.D. Neroutsos, manager of CPR's steamship service, of his plan. The CPR insisted that a fog horn be retained and urged the department, "having in view a desire for economy," to establish a fog alarm "without the maintenance of residence." George McGregor, managing director of Victoria Tug Ltd., also insisted upon retaining a fog alarm. Without it he must route his towboats around Discovery Island, "adding hours to the passage." H.R. Ellworthy of Island Tug & Barge also informed Wilby that the channel between Fiddle Reef and Oak Bay was "used practically exclusively" by his tugs "and it would be a great hindrance if the horn was discontinued."

By 1936, after ten years at Fiddle Reef, Reg Graham had ample reason to want off. Each time he went for supplies he never knew if he would come back alive to those four walls with so little space between them. Even if he did, the experience of the gale four years before suggested he may not be secure inside. He had a wife and two children ashore, and the demands of keeping Fiddle Reef ruled out the possibility of holding another job. It was the pay, finally, which drove him to resign.

Yet when Wilby informed Ottawa of Graham's decision, the deputy minister welcomed an opportunity to cut wages at Fiddle Reef. Wilby objected. The salary might appear high because of the station's proximity to Oak Bay but, he explained, "it is necessary that the keeper's services be available especially during the winter and foggy season, thus precluding any possibility of his performing work outside of his lightkeeper's duties and so I do not think that any reduction in the present

Fiddle Reef from seaward.

salary is feasible." Wilby recommended the department reconsider removing the horn and pulling the keeper off Fiddle Reef, but shipping interests still wanted the horn.

Nevertheless, as C.D. Stuart discovered when he replaced Graham in July, the pay was cut. Stuart was a Boer War veteran, with a pension to supplement the pittance paid at Fiddle Reef, but he was appalled by his working conditions and by the intransigence of the marine agency in Victoria. Stuart wrote the minister in December to say so:

> My pay is small and I have to furnish all my food and coal here. Last month I had lots of fog, and the hand horn was used in one 4 nights straight. I became sick and had to see a doctor on 30th Nov. I was ordered home to bed, and I took a doctors certificate to Col. Wilby. I was then told my relief would be paid by the Dept. I was later informed by Col. Wilby that the pay for my relief would be deducted from my salary. I am alone and on duty 24 hrs. a day. Since 27 July I have had just 10 days leave. I am getting less pay than my predecessor and cannot get any information on this from the Office. I received fog horn allowance for Aug. by separate cheque. Since that month, I have had none. I have asked Col. Wilby for information concerning this for 2 months without effect.[4]

As if the minister would object, Stuart confided, "I am of the opinion that some Politics are being injected into the work of the Victoria office."

On Christmas Eve he called at Wilby's office to see about a loan until his pay came through. Much to Stuart's astonishment, he found the office deserted that afternoon. He stomped around looking for someone, even a clerk or secretary. Finally he picked up a telephone, leafed through the directory, and dialed Wilby at home. Incensed, Wilby arrived at the office and the two went at it hammer and tongs: Stuart demanding his pay and Wilby demanding to know why he smelled of liquor. The dispute stopped just short of blows. Wilby sacked Stuart on the spot and the two charged downstairs and went their separate ways, elbowing last-minute shoppers aside. Stuart headed home, anticipating Christmas bleak and broke. Wilby, hardly infused with the Christmas spirit himself, made for the telegraph office and sent a cable off to Ottawa:

HAVE FOUND NECESSARY TO SUSPEND C.D. STUART KEEPER FIDDLE REEF FOR DRUNKENNESS AND INSOLENCE. . . .

Whatever peace Wilby found Christmas Day was interrupted by a knock at his front door that afternoon—Stuart. Hat in hand the keeper sheepishly explained he was no drinking man but had had a few nips, "Christmas apparently being looked upon as a special occasion." Fiddle Reef may have its drawbacks but it was still better than nothing, especially in 1936. All contrite now, Stuart asked Wilby to forgive and forget his harangue, to let him go back to work. It was Christmas after all, and the agent was in a forgiving mood. Stuart could go back to Fiddle Reef all right—after two weeks suspension without pay. Next day the keeper sat down and typed out his letter to the minister. He went back out to the Reef 27 January and resigned in December.

For the next two decades keepers came to Fiddle Reef and left as soon as a better station was offered. Oscar and Pearl Edwards lived there with two children. Pen and Elizabeth Brown began their career on the lights with a honeymoon at the Reef, and ended it with a narrow escape when a tidal wave swept over Pine Island ten years later. The main floor doubled as kitchen and living room. Pen brought his coal up through a trap door in the floor. Upstairs "there was just enough room for a mattress and spring." Roosting seagulls had contaminated their water supply so the Browns brought fresh water in five-gallon cans from the Oak Bay Marina. They bathed outdoors, on the seaward side of the Reef, using a dipper and washtub. Neither had been near the sea before and a *Times* reporter told how they "felt as if they were on the bridge of an ocean vessel when gale-force winds hammered the walls of their home."

Taking on a shipment of fuel, Fiddle Reef c. 1930.

James Heanski was the last man at Fiddle Reef. The department had already decided early in 1959 to automate the beacon, and Heanski's experience confirmed their wisdom. On Easter Sunday, 29 March, Heanski cleaned his lamps and windows, topped up his fuel, then clicked on his radio to hear the weather forecast. He wanted to attend Easter services with his wife in town. The wind came up while he was ashore and Heanski spent all night over at Oak Bay waiting for a break. "This is the first time in a year and a half that I've been caught off base," he apologized to the agent. "I won't trust the radio so much in the future."

In November he set off from Oak Bay with supplies. The wind "started to freshen." By the time he approached the station it was very fresh indeed, howling at "50 & 60 miles a hour." Heanski steered past his landing, then turned about to approach upwind. He scrambled ashore, tied the painter, then lowered the hook from the winch. The boat was impossible to board by now and Heanski was leaning out, trying to slip the hook under its cable with a boat-hook, when the cleat ripped clean off the bow. "I watched it till it neared the Chatham Islands but it got quite dark and I lost track of it," he explained. "Boat, motor, groceries, oars, and life preservers were gone."

Heanski's harrowing experience coincided with CP Steamship's decision to discontinue its ferry service through the channel. Only two requests had been made for the aging handhorn the previous year, so in September 1959 Fiddle Reef was finally automated. Heanski, having narrowly escaped drowning there, perished in a fire at Portlock Point light four years later.

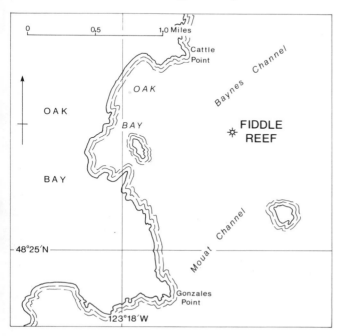

Bare Point

Bare Point juts out at the mouth of Chemainus Bay, an important exit for Vancouver Island's timber for over a century. In January 1896 the directors of the Victoria Lumber Manufacturing Company, "one of the largest and best equipped Mills in the Province," wrote James Gaudin and asked for a lighthouse on the point for the convenience of sailing vessels coming and going in the night, decks laden with fir and cedar planks. The agent forwarded their petition to Ottawa, adding that there were also plans "to ship coal at this point from the new mines being opened."

The fixed white light shone eleven miles out to sea from a tower thirty-six feet above the keeper's dwelling. James Crozier, an Irishman, assumed his duties immediately upon completion. Crozier doubled as a lumber inspector at the Chemainus sawmill with the agent's approval, since his keeper's salary of $10 a month was not enough to support him. The light on Bare Point stood a mile by boat from the dock, two miles away on foot. Every evening Crozier would row or hike over to the tower to light up, go home for the night, then make the same journey again at sunrise. The passage by water could be precarious. "I am afraid that during the November gales which blow with great violence in winter," Gaudin informed Anderson, "some difficulty may be experienced in reaching or landing by boat." The station boat, once used by Gaudin to get around Victoria harbour, had been condemned before it came to Bare Point.

Crozier always slept over at the light in stormy or thick weather. Storms hurled volleys of deadheads and mill scraps at the station. When the tide rose, the debris threatened to tear the boat house and landing from their pilings so much of Crozier's labour consisted of bucking the logs with a Swede saw, and shoving them away with peavey and pike-pole. It was hard going for an older man, and Crozier implored his MP to press for a raise in pay. Gaudin recommended an increase of $5 a month, especially since "the price of labour" was on the increase "owing to the gold excitement." In October 1909 Crozier was up at low tide four nights running, clearing the flotsam and repairing the boat house. All his labour was in vain. A March gale in 1911 tore the entire landing away. In August of that year the keeper advised Robertson he had been "incapacitated twice from illness from lighting and attending to [his] duties."

Crozier resigned shortly after and handed his keys over to Philip Stevenson. In April 1912 Stevenson was felled by "some kind of a stroke" and asked to be relieved. "I think from what Dr. Ewing says that grave consequences are threatened," he confided. Stevenson continued keeping the light on borrowed time, never knowing if he would return from a trip to Bare Point. Later that summer, on 4 August, he was delayed. His wife was last seen alive that evening, pacing anxiously back and forth at the end of the dock, alone in the rain. A few days later Captain Robertson found a letter from Stevenson on his desk: "My wife having been found drowned this morning, I have asked Mr. James Chalmers to take care of the lighthouse for me until after we have put her away." Grief-stricken, Stevenson never went back.

James Chalmers relieved Stevenson in August 1912 and maintained the light until 1926. Mariners were perplexed when the light was out for a few nights that September and they complained to the port authorities. A party from Chemainus entered the building and found Chalmers lying dead on the engine room floor. When the news reached Ottawa, Hawken, the deputy minister, noted that Chalmers had been earning $330 a year. He proposed the pay be cut to somewhere between $180 and $240, and asked Wilby to advise if a keeper could be hired for even less. Wilby settled upon an even cheaper scheme and converted Bare Point to an unwatched light tended by government steamer.

This "Aga" apparatus soon proved unsuitable due to vandalism and frequent break-ins. By 1940 the wooden tower was so dilapidated that it was put to the torch and replaced by a white steel skeleton tower with a red lantern.

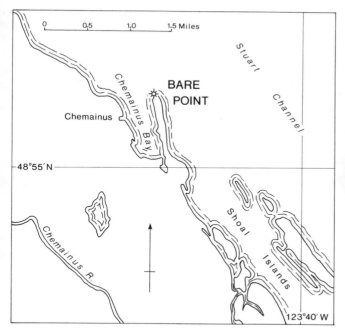

Bare Point Lighthouse, built 1896 to guide lumber ships into Chemainus Bay.

Albert Head

Many place names in and about Victoria bear the indelible stamp of the city's colonial mentality. The sheltered cove at Esquimalt, appropriated by the Royal Navy for the Pacific fleet, was christened Royal Bay, later Royal Roads. Captain Kellett followed suit in 1846 by naming the adjoining headland "Albert Head" for the Queen's consort.

On the morning of 13 October 1929 the 627-foot Canadian Pacific liner *Empress of Canada* drew near the end of her passage to Vancouver via Panama. Ninety-six impatient immigrants from Southampton crowded her decks and cabins. At a time when smallpox, tuberculosis, and cholera commonly booked passage from foreign parts, immigration laws stipulated that all prospective immigrants be examined and cleared through quarantine stations. The captain, E. Griffiths, RNR, steamed through the fog toward the station at William Head. Unfamiliar with local conditions, and apparently unwilling to heed the advice of his subordinates, Griffiths ran the steamship hard aground on the rocks at Albert Head at 11:30.

Water poured into three of the liner's holds. Extra pumps were lifted from the *Salvage King* alongside. Griffiths immediately wired Victoria for a relief ship and ordered lunch served to the shaken passengers in the diningroom. The SS *Otter*, under Captain J.A. Harrison's command, came out to take off the passengers and their baggage. As they departed, the passengers "cheered the Captain and crew to the echo."

The tugs *Salvage Queen*, *Burrard Chief*, and *Hopkins* fastened cables and tried in vain to free the crippled *Empress*. "Clouds of smoke and steam poured from the funnels of the staunch crafts," the *Colonist* reported, "hawsers strained almost to the breaking point but the ship moved not an inch from her rocky berth." In the end the liner was finally dragged free, pumped out, and towed to drydock in Victoria for repairs.

Many of her passengers never forgot their first terrifying contact with Canada—on hands and knees in a bedlam of flying trunks and baggage. Always quick to respond to petitions from the CPR, the department laid immediate plans to construct a manned light on the spot. Before the year was out, contractors erected a square steel skeleton tower supporting a white wooden watchroom and tower. Edwin Parkin transferred briefly from Kains Island to break in the station. Harrold Shorrock O'Kell moved over from Trial Island three weeks later on 23 September 1930. In May 1939, after thirty-three years' service on the lights, O'Kell advised Colonel Wilby that he was nearing sixty-five and eligible for superannuation. "As you know, my wife passed away at the station recently after a very trying illness,"

he wrote, "and naturally after so many years together in the service I feel the loss very keenly." He thanked the agent for "the considerations and associations" which he and his wife had "enjoyed in the Light House Service." O'Kell resigned and was awarded the Imperial Service Medal. Peter Georgeson, a second generation lightkeeper, moved over from Active Pass to replace him.

The *Empress* was the first and last vessel to come to grief on Albert Head. Ever since that morning all shipping has steered clear of the five-second flash and diaphone horns blasting through the fog.

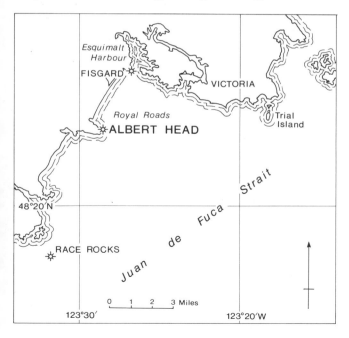

Above: Albert Head Light-station 1978.

3 The Pacific Graveyard

After lighting up the main harbours in the 1870s, the Department of Marine and Fisheries waited twenty years before working its way up Vancouver Island's West Coast. The department's bureaucrats had built Cape Beale light at the mouth of Barkley Sound when that was envisioned as a major port, but they left the rest of the coast in darkness until the mounting toll of shipwrecks and drownings forced them to act.

The public dismay and private anguish aroused by modern-day aviation disasters provide a familiar standard with which to compare the impact of news about shipwrecks—news that arrived in Victoria weeks, sometimes months after a wreck occurred. Any vessels forsaking the sanctuary of Victoria for points north faced foggy days and fearful blind nights when their crews frantically cast lead lines while suspense mounted over the depth of water beneath their keels.

So desolate, so storm-tossed was their course that whole ships and crews were swallowed up by the Pacific's insatiable appetite. In December 1860 the schooner *Ino* sailed into Victoria with a splintered headboard on her foredeck bearing the name *John Marshall*. After combing the silent shoreline for miles, her crew saw no bodies but much wreckage, rigging, and shattered masts. As if this were not enough to disquiet the *Ino*'s hands, they retrieved the headboard of the *Dancer* and some of her rigging as well. Only after the trio of West Coast lights— Carmanah, Pachena, and Cape Beale—were manned, jutting up like white headstones along the graveyard of the Pacific, could the count of casualties begin. The tally of earlier victims will never be fully known. Fractured ribs and crushed hulls of ships were often found a decade or more after they were due in Victoria or Anchorage. Some West Coast tribes fed and clothed themselves almost exclusively from the cargoes washing ashore.

The most macabre imagination can barely conceive the dreadful fate awaiting seamen who heard the sudden roar of breakers coming through the night and fog. Once locked in their embrace, the stoutest vessels were borne by the relentless five-knot swells toward their doom on the shoals.

Few were as fortunate as Captain Frederick Mosher whose forty-year-old bark, the *Atlanta* foundered off Cape Flattery on 8 December 1890. Mosher's account was the one so many dead men could never tell. The tug *Tyee* towed her out of Port Gamble, then cut her loose. As soon as her crew put sail on, *Atlanta* started to take on water. Since his cargo was lumber, Mosher decided she was buoyant enough to plow on through the spume of the windward swells. They blundered on to the mouth of the Columbia where the wind changed abruptly and snow squalls set upon them. Captain Mosher:

> The sails all blew away on the night of Dec. 13 and soon after the heavy deck load of 80-foot timbers broke adrift. On the morning of the 14th, the fore and main masts went by the board, the foremast smashing the long-boat, destroying our means of leaving the ship. The seas were washing over us, fore and aft at that time. As we had been many hours without food, I went to what was left

of our cabin and found one can of tomatoes and one of peaches. From these, each man was given a mouthful to relieve his thirst. About noon on the 14th, the vessel commenced to break up, and at about 3 p.m. she parted just abaft the main hatch, leaving 14 of us on the after house, with nothing to eat or drink the two cans being lost in the excitement.

Night began to set in, and a night in December off Vancouver Island is a long one, even when one is comfortably situated. The mizzen mast went shortly after daybreak, and took nearly one half of our limited raft. Through all that day, and the next night, the sea was making a clean breach over us, but on the morning of the 16th we sighted land, which was a relief even though it was far away. The steward, John W. Wilburn, became temporarily insane at noon, on the 16th. The first officer's leg was broken, and all hands were inclined to be despondent. We had fully made up our minds that we would either be dead or ashore by morning, as we were all badly chilled. When morning came, few of the men could speak on account of thirst and cold.

The rudder had been jammed with a lot of the deckload, forming quite a raft, and as our house was breaking up piece by piece, John Anderson, second mate, and four men went to it, so as to make room for us on the house. They had hardly crawled on to the timber, before it parted from the rest of the wreckage and we drifted away from each other at 8 a.m.

By some "singular coincidence" the two rafts drifted together again at 5 o'clock that afternoon and landed safely, two hundred yards apart, in Clayoquot Sound. Mosher and his men had been swept a hundred and seventy miles north over four days and nights. Clayoquot Indians took them in and cared for them until the schooner *Katherine* took Mosher and his men away to Victoria.[1]

Usually any seaman lucky enough to stagger ashore had little time left to give thanks as he watched his ship's remains carried away in the swirling water, and took stock of his situation. Soaking wet, dazed and mesmerized by shock and hypothermia, he faced slow but certain death without food, water, and warmth unless someone out there on the unbroken line of gloom saw a fire or heard his wail of hurt and distress above the pounding surf. *Janet Cowan*'s crew, wrecked off Pachena Bay on New Year's Eve 1895, languished for two weeks on shore, knee-deep in snow, frostbitten and starving, never knowing where they were. Their captain perished on the fifth day; two seamen and the cook followed him the next. A makeshift tarpaulin tent, their only shelter, caught fire and nearly incinerated the sick and injured cowering inside.

The most able-bodied among them elected to split up and strike out for help. One party headed south, the other northward. By sheer chance, a lookout aboard the *Tyee* spied the *Janet Cowan* on the rocks shortly after the tug cut its tow free in the Strait. They veered in as close as was safe and sent two boats ashore. These came back with fourteen survivors who were too weak to show the rescuers where the bodies of their shipmates were stowed. On 14 January the *Princess*

Louise anchored off Carmanah lighthouse to take away nine more survivors who had been found by Phil Daykin, the lightkeeper.[2]

As early as 1887 the British Columbia Legislature, citing increases in traffic stemming from coal and lumber, and the anticipated boom in trans-Pacific commerce following completion of the Canadian Pacific Railroad, had petitioned Ottawa to recognize "the great and urgent importance of having a life-saving station established on the West Coast of Vancouver Island." The lieutenant governor cited the recent wreck of the *Belvedere*, whose crew was saved only by the "timely and accidental arrival of a tug from Victoria." The crew of the bark *R.J. Foster* would certainly have perished too had they not stumbled upon a Catholic mission. The Japanese current, he explained, conspired to bear all ships to the West Coast, an area which afforded "little or no natural protection" and was "entirely destitute of life-saving appliances."[3]

The province's petition was duly referred to Colonel W.P. Anderson in his capacity as chairman of the Dominion Lighthouse Board. A life-saving station would doubtless entail a "very serious outlay" in terms of wages, Anderson calculated. "[It is] inexpedient to establish a lifeboat at least until the danger becomes more urgent or the white population denser," he concluded. Instead he advocated that Indians, "wonderfully expert" at handling canoes in surf and swells which would swamp an ordinary boat, be drafted as search and rescue teams. In short, Anderson was upholding the status quo, though he suggested that the tribesmen might be paid whenever they "turned out," and awarded a bounty for every life saved. He argued that the lighthouse he was proposing for Bonilla Point would "decrease the dangers on that rugged coast" as soon as a telegraph line connected Victoria to Bamfield in Barkley Sound.[4]

The issue lay dormant until October 1893 when the Port Townsend Chamber of Commerce wrote the Victoria Board of Trade, boasting that the United States government intended to put up a first-class life-saving station near Flattery at a cost of $80,000. They called upon Victoria businessmen to lobby their government for a similar installation at Bonilla Point in order to bracket the worst stretch of coastline. "We do not deem it necessary to go into detail regarding the names of vessels wrecked on the Vancouver [Island] coast," they wrote, "as all the facts are only too well known in Victoria."

The Board of Trade sent the letter on to Sir Charles Tupper, minister of finance. From there the issue bounced back to Anderson. He drew his minister's attention to his earlier report, reiterating his staunch faith in the cooperation of Indians as an economy measure. The chief engineer explained that the new Carmanah lighthouse, built near Bonilla Point in 1891, had a twenty-foot whaleboat but admitted it "would not be large enough for lifesaving purposes even if the keeper had a crew on hand to handle it." If the department undertook the expense of hiring, training, and housing a nine-man crew, they ought to station them at Carmanah. Though poor at best, the landing there was still superior to anywhere else between Cape Beale and Port San Juan. Otherwise, Anderson suggested, the

Quadra should be placed on standby since the telegraph now stretched from Victoria through Carmanah and Cape Beale to Bamfield. "Her speed and stability might enable her to reach a vessel in distress more quickly and more effectively than any lifeboat," Anderson claimed.

Sobered by Anderson's estimates, the British Columbia Board of Trade conceded the drawbacks of a life-boat station in February 1893 and recommended instead the construction of a series of less sophisticated (and less costly) lifesaving stations, to be manned only during winter, supplied with "the usual appliances, rocket apparatus, etc." Anderson calculated a cost of $1500 to man the stations for four winter months. Even this was too high; he recommended that action be deferred "at least a year or two." Meanwhile the whole correspondence should be forwarded to the marine agent in Victoria for comment.

The man on the scene, Captain James Gaudin, submitted his report in April 1894. He advocated placing the proposed stations between Port San Juan and Cape Beale. Compiling a list of wrecks to illustrate that most vessels came to grief along that stretch, he argued that loss of life was greatest from Bonilla Point to Pachena Bay. North of Cape Beale, the agent noted, in clear weather, a vessel could be steered safely where the sea was not breaking. Lighthouses with fog alarms remained the key to safe navigation. When fog cleared, he reported, the Coxes at Cape Beale light often saw sailing vessels drifting perilously close to shore near the entrance to Barkley Sound. Many lost their anchors to the foul ground there. He advocated that more lights and fog alarms be constructed north of Cape Beale.

Gaudin also advanced a novel solution to the plight of sailors marooned ashore: shelter shacks scattered every five miles along the coast, well stocked with blankets and provisions, "in which would be found printed instructions in different languages stating the direction and distance of the telegraph wire and how to communicate through it to the nearest station." Since coastal Indians already made adequate wages fishing and sealing, he doubted they would ever idle the winters away in their villages waiting for rescue work.

Anderson took Gaudin's report in to Sir Louis Davies. The minister endorsed the proposal to build shelter shacks and concluded, "Under the circumstances . . . establishing life-boats may be postponed without leaving the Department open to the charge of cruelty."[5] Ottawa was giving the West Coast short shrift; by 1893 there were *seventeen* lifesaving stations on the Great Lakes and along the East Coast.[6]

Nine months later all the flags in Victoria were at half mast, and throngs of hatless spectators lined the streets to watch four hearses, flanked by two detachments of blue jackets from HMS *Royal Arthur*, in a grim procession to Ross Bay Cemetery with the *Janet Cowan*'s dead.

Carmanah

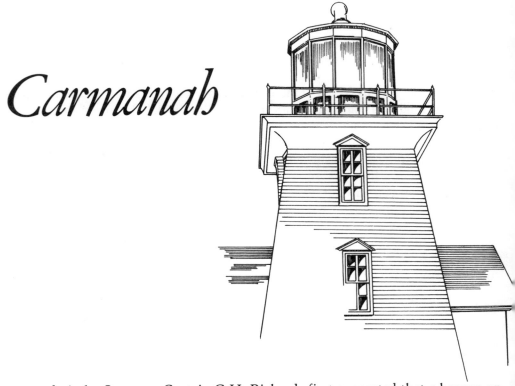

Admiralty Surveyor Captain G.H. Richards first suggested that a beacon on Vancouver Island's south shore could work in concert with Cape Flattery to bracket the entrance of Juan de Fuca at night. Mariners had long clamoured for a light and fog signal on Bonilla Point. In 1887, however, forty years and hundreds of casualties after Richards' time, the CPR had only to lean lightly on Ottawa to bring it about. W.C. Van Horne wrote George Foster, minister of Marine and Fisheries, in August to complain that SS *Port Augusta*, twelve days out of Yokohama, had wasted two more days waiting outside the Strait in fog.

Threats to the railroad's profits precipitated action in Ottawa in a way compassion never could. Foster demanded an immediate report from his agent in Victoria. Gaudin explained, as he had done so often before, that the only fog signal was eleven miles south at Flattery. Since vessels bound in from China usually made landfall somewhere between Cape Beale and Bonilla Point, the latter was clearly "the most suitable place for a fog alarm."

Ironically, the plan was thwarted by the heavy weather it intended to overcome. A shore party off-loaded supplies under a thick carpet of fog, and manhandled them up the steep cliffs. When the clouds finally scattered, the dismayed crew found themselves on Carmanah Point looking out over at Bonilla. Rather than drag everything back down to the shore to load and unload it again, they elected to build the station where they stood.

On the chart, Carmanah Point lay a mere sixty-five miles by calipers up the Juan de Fuca Strait from Victoria, yet the intervening stretch of coastline and the lack of road access left it as isolated as if it were in Stanley's Congo. When completed the new beacon appeared much the same as its sisters constructed in the period: a wooden tower forty-six feet high, with an attached dwelling, exhibiting a light from an elevation of 173 feet that was visible for nineteen miles on a clear night. And what a welcome sight it was, the "next one up" from Flattery, a cone of light to break that long, horrific stretch of disaster leading to Cape Beale.

Carmanah was also the pioneer ship traffic control centre. A steam whistle, separate from the fog horns, allowed ship-to-shore communication through the night and on fogbound days, "using the Morse or Continental telegraphic codes." The lightkeeper was charged with monitoring the progress of west coast vessels and reporting their movements by telegraph to Victoria, to be passed on to Lloyds of London.

The *B.C. Coast Pilot* broadcast regulations for communicating with Carmanah. All vessels "exhibiting their distinctive numbers" would have their names and registry transmitted to Victoria by the lightkeeper for publication free of charge. Messages "by flags of the international code" were forwarded at tariff rates. All traffic was informed that a stock of "provisions and other necessaries for shipwrecked persons" was maintained at the lighthouse.

W.P. Daykin came ashore with his wife, five boys, and invalid mother at Carmanah on 17 April 1891. He began to keep a daily journal which survives, in nine tattered volumes, as the most compelling first-person account of early life on the lights.[1] Half his logs are a dismal record of weather along that rainswept, sodden coast: a relentless cycle of gales blowing between monotonous lulls of drizzle and fog, with all-too-brief respites when a fugitive sun burned its way through the gray mantle.

Whatever the weather, Daykin toiled. There was coal, tons of it, to be packed up from the beach in sacks, tipped into bins, and, whenever the fog crawled in or a ship signalled, shoveled into the ravenous maw of his steam boilers' fireboxes.

Carmanah Point Lightstation c. 1912.

Parlour of long-suffering Carmanah lightkeeper W.P. Daykin.

Every four hours every night Carmanah's keeper had to rouse himself, climb the tower, and crank up the counterweights to keep the lens turning. In those days before radio Daykin flew signals in the day, blew them on the horn at night, and set down the name of each ship and "whither bound," then transmitted the news along the fitful telegraph line. When ships and men went to wreck, there were miles of shore in both directions to patrol seeking their shattered remains — fragments which might provide some clue to the vessel's identity — and there was five dollars apiece for the recovery of any body or "portion thereof."

The journals continue for twenty-one years; two tormented decades were ushered in by the confident, artful script of a dedicated civil servant and were brought to a close with a sickening scrawl as Daykin's last ounce of patience and sanity bled out the nib of his pen. For Carmanah, insatiable, took away almost everything the keeper prized: his wife, two of his sons, his health, in the end even reaching out for his mind.

It is hard nowadays to imagine the verdant bounty of the sea off the West Coast before man depleted the stock of whales, herring, and salmon. As Daykin scanned the horizon for shipping he was astonished, in late summer and fall, by the awesome spectacle of "water alive with salmon," a leaping, boiling turmoil of sleek silver bodies herded along by killer whales or sea lions. "Great many salmon around taking hook," he wrote excitedly. One June day he pulled two hundred from his trap in the Nitinat River.

Walkway to beach, Carmanah Point lightstation.

At least the salmon kept to their schedule. Supplies ordered by telegraph from Victoria came ashore with much less regularity. In January 1902 the keeper wrote Captain Gaudin, complaining he had only received $200 of the salary owed him. He sent the letter off to a passing ship by an Indian courier but "the idiot brought it back in the mail bag." On the morning of 2 February Daykin's boys rowed out to fetch provisions from the *Queen City* only to be told: no cash—no goods. He was frustrated again six weeks later:

> 10 A.M. Quadra in sight, hired an Indian to take the letter off to Capt. Gaudin. . . and although the canoe was within 200 yds of the Quadra, they would not stop. Fired 3 shots but they took no notice, but they turned back a mile at Clo-oose to pick up. . . two American prospectors.

Daykin was still writing futile pleas about his salary to Gaudin in Victoria six years later. On 1 August he telegraphed Port San Juan to enquire if the *Quadra* had his provisions below in her hold. The tender finally dropped anchor off the station on 5 August and, Daykin reported, "[It] sent boat ashore with provisions and *fresh* meat which Capt. Hackett denied having on board when I telegraphed to San Juan.... The meat was *alive*... sent it back on board. It had been on board about a week."[2]

Next week, when the *Quadra* was back in port, Daykin tapped out another meat order to his supplier, only to learn that Carmanah was not scheduled for supplies. "The weather is too good and smooth," he snorted, dripping sarcasm. "She would most likely be able to land things without getting them wet." In a single month the Daykins lost sixty pounds of meat and were forced to bear the cost. They resorted to their own devices to obtain fresh food. A flock of chickens yielded a ready supply of meat and eggs. Daykin's sons took full advantage of the bountiful salmon runs up the Nitinat and brought down deer coming to drink. Mail service was as sporadic as the food deliveries, just another "one of the inconveniences you must lamely submit to," James Gaudin explained.[3]

Landing at Carmanah, or even getting the station boat out to the tender, taxed all a man's strength and seamanship, and made a mockery of Colonel Anderson's claim that it would make a suitable lifeboat station. Every gale at high tide delivered tons of logs, stumps, and roots to the foot of the landing. At low tide the boat had to be manhandled over the slippery log-jam for a hundred yards or more. When the task seemed beyond him, Daykin dipped into his dwindling reserve of cash and paid local Indians $1.50 a trip to go out in their canoes.

Returning from the U.S. lighthouse tender *Manzanita* in February 1901, Daykin nearly smashed his boat against a jumble of logs five feet high. "Reported this to Capt. Gaudin," he wrote in disgust, "and asked for help to remove them but he has not answered the letter." The logs stayed, rearranged by successive tides and storms, and much that was wrestled over, under, and around them, including a piano, arrived damaged and soggy.

As if lack of supplies and mail were not enough to drive Daykin to despair, the equipment on the station bedevilled him constantly. At 2:30 one December morning in 1898 the "lamp commenced working badly... stopping every few minutes," so he stayed up the tower all night long, oiled all the revolving works and gears, and ran it with the clockwork uncoupled. "Can find no hitch in it," he wrote. Two nights later he was up again after the light stopped at 2:00 a.m. He overhauled the works, crouching by the dim flickering light of a kerosene lamp, and noted, "The worm gear is badly worn."

Two years later a broken bolt in the pulley shaft kept him up in the tower again two nights running. In late February 1902, the "lamp working very badly," he had no choice but to climb up and crank it by hand until sunrise. The apparatus pilfered his sleep for years. In March 1908 he hoisted the lamp to replace a worn shaft bearing only to find the new part "worse than before." By December Daykin

Getting supplies ashore at Carmanah was backbreaking work.

had done "everything possible but could not make her work properly." Every six months he strained the mercury through a chamois and topped it up.

Then there was the "fearful coal." In late September 1900 the *Quadra* steamed up from Port San Juan and sent her workboat over with eighteen tons of coal and eighty-four cases of oil. For days the Daykins packed sacks and rolled drums up to the engine room only to find, a month later, that they might just as well have left them down on the beach. Daykin wrote in his log: "4 PM started signal—had to stop few minutes at 5 to clean grate—*very poor coal*." Two days later he shut the plant down again to clean tubes and boiler grates of "a great many clinkers." The "*very bad coal*" tormented him all that winter and spring. The next shipment was as bad, if not worse, and Daykin, cursing, sweating, and coughing under a plume of ash, shut down his boilers time and again, dumped out the grates, and scraped the tubes with a wire brush. "Have great trouble with the coal," he wailed, "never saw worse." One day he noted it "took one hour to raise steam from hot water (*coal*)!"

Moreover, the lamp oil was as useless as the detested coal. "Wound lamp and trimmed wicks every night, will soon have to trim wicks twice a night," Daykin wrote, exasperated. "The wicks char for ½ an inch in 6 hours." The light had to be stopped ten minutes each time he trimmed. When they charred, he had to wipe soot off all the prisms and windows.

The telegraph was also a problem. Telegraph wires linked Carmanah with Cape Beale and Victoria, with relay points south at Port San Juan, Jordan River, and Sooke. Although linemen were nominally assigned to patrol each section weekly— checking for fallen wires, short circuits, or other interruptions—they often gave their patrols short shrift, viewing them as something to attend to after checking their cattle and traps. Even when windfalls were discovered, the sheer labour involved in cutting through virgin coastal timber, up to ten feet thick, with an ax and Swede saw kept the line mute for days, often weeks. One morning after a gale the wires were smothered under eighty fallen trees along a ten mile stretch. As Bruce Scott, the resident historian of the West Coast, concluded, the lifesaving network brought no fiscal return so its budget "was skimped until such time as a public outcry demanded improvements."

As a result, Carmanah was cut off for days, weeks, months at a time. As a backlog of skewered messages piled high on his spike file, the flinty keeper fumed about the line and reported linemen for "neglect of duty." On 3 March 1899 HMS *Pheasant* "ran in to signal. . . 'Please telegraph'." Daykin replied: "telegraph communication interrupted," and hoisted more signals requesting her captain to report the situation to his admiral. The line to Victoria had been down twenty-five days, with no connection to Port San Juan for five days, "and the lineman at Clo-oose [was] attending to private business." A week later he sent in his weather reports and attempted to get a message off to the agent, but gave up in disgust after ten minutes. On 29 March Gaudin cabled Carmanah to inform Daykin that the government was about to take over the line. "Glory Hallelujah!" he exclaimed. The line would also be extended beyond Cape Beale, strung tree to tree all the way along the Canal to Alberni. But succeeding entries confirmed that Daykin's enthusiasm was unfounded as he poured scorn on those responsible for communications:

> May 29, 1901. Line working from Victoria to Alberni, which is something unusual. Must be someone in authority in Victoria.
>
> August 14, 1901. Victoria talking with Vancouver on this wire via Cape Beale. *First Time*!
>
> January 28, 1902. Steamship *Maru* signalled. Line down as usual. Over two months east and 85 days since I had Alberni.
>
> March 21, 1902. 5:30 PM., got Alberni for the first time in over *four months*! Reported the *Athenia* inbound to Lloyds.

As all the frustrations with the telegraph, rotten coal, filthy oil, and faulty equipment mounted, lack of sleep and fresh food began to exact their toil. Daykin complained of days and weeks of "all hands sick," reduced by "La Grippe" to a helpless state, "unable to make out returns" or even to venture out after the provisions they held so dear. The increasingly spidery quality of his writing bespeaks more trouble than even he knew: mercury poisoning. Yet he would still lurch feverishly from a sweat-drenched bed, haul himself up the tower to do battle with the lamp, and shovel the cursed coal to raise steam for signals. "A Merry Xmas & Happy New Year," he glumly wished the outside world on 30 December 1900. "All laid up with Grippe. A dry Xmas and New Year. Supplies did not come."

Ottawa spent seven years charting a course between cruelty and cost while ships and men went down all round, leaving the wreckage of hulls and humans behind. All through the gale season, howling in in November and tapering off to a whimper in March, Daykin and his boys trudged for miles in both directions from the light station, and came home with grim tidings of smashed hulls, scattered cargo, rudders, rigging, and corpses—even one of their own kind, the battered and bloated remains of Cape Flattery's lightkeeper. His assistant's headless corpse washed up at Cape Beale a week later. More often than not the trail of evidence littering the beaches yielded no clues beyond "several pieces of painted boards, blue white, a lot of salmon tins washed up. . .piece of ship's tumbler rack and keel of small boat painted green." The schooner *Dare* disappeared off Bonilla Point 23 December 1890, the bark *Sarah* sank with the loss of two hands at Pachena Bay 23 November 1891, and *Lillie* went down somewhere in Barkley Sound. *Laura Pike*, an American schooner, went to wreck at Klanawa in 1891; on 19 November 1892 the *Erikson* was lost off Barkley Sound. The SS *Michigan* lurched aground on 2 January 1893 at Pachena Point, with two lives lost. In September 1894 *Ivanhoe* foundered somewhere along that awful stretch and disappeared with all hands.[4]

At sunrise on 13 November 1896 Daykin's son Tom saw a four-masted schooner skewered on the rocks at Bonilla Point. He hiked over and found the *Puritan*'s crew crammed into the hut of a local Indian, Frank Nighton. Nighton had been out all night, trying to take a line off the vessel. After swamping his dugout and being washed off the jagged reef countless times, he finally snagged a fish-line and hook cast out by the crew. He pulled over a line, cinched it to a rock, and the crew made good their escape. Daykin loaded them all into the lighthouse whaleboat, then rowed and sailed sixty miles to Victoria.

A year later he was headed east down the coast again with the captain, mate, and six fearful seamen of the *Vesta*, the morning after a monstrous wave had hoisted the puny 286-ton schooner clear over a reef and dashed it into the forest. This time it was a rough trip, right into the teeth of a gale. There was no hope of steering up Juan de Fuca, not with swells pouring over the stern where Tom wrestled with the tiller, in water up to his knees, while his frantic passengers bailed for their lives. Instead, he ran along the troughs for Neah Bay on the American side. When reporters buttonholed him in Victoria next day, Tom gave graphic testimony to the gargantuan size and power of the swell. The *Vesta*, he related, lay in drydock back among the trees. "She is standing high and dry and you could plant potatoes in her," he said. For years to come, *Vesta* served as a lineman's cabin on the trail.

The night of Boxing Day 1901 was wild, with "fearful squalls shaking house badly blew in two windows. All fences down." Like a giant crowbar, the shrieking wind wrenched the flag pole's guy spikes out of their stumps. Daylight revealed "hundreds of trees down in all directions" behind a "fearful sea." Young Roby Daykin pulled on his sou'wester and gumboots and struck out to take stock of the

Bamfield surfboat coming alongside tender *Estevan* for supplies, 1924.

night's flotsam. Midway to Clo-oose he heard the distant lament of a steamer's distress whistle and siren, punctuated by the muffled gunfire of popping rockets. On his return trek Roby picked his way across beaches carpeted with new wreckage—"several large butter casks. . . lower half of a schooner rudder (copper painted). Ship's taffrail of hardwood painted white. . . great many broken oars and a raft in two parts two miles apart. Nothing to identify by."

Through rain and hail squalls a week later Daykin spied another vessel drifting "bottom up" off Bonilla Point. He sent Roby to investigate. "Seemed to be a sloop or small schooner," he wrote, "with part of a mast sticking out of water—still attached to hull." By October 1910 the *Colonist*'s scorekeepers reckoned that "700 lives and millions of dollars had been lost in that vicinity through wrecks due to fog."

The cold, wet gale season brought not only wrecks but also arthritis. This affliction was to lightkeepers what Black Lung was to coal miners. In his very first letter from Carmanah, Daykin begged Gaudin for a fireplace to drive out the perpetual damp. Pointing out that Carmanah enjoyed, at best, four rain-free months a year, he insisted it was necessary that there be a fire in every room. His request was turned down.

Whatever the genetic underpinnings of the disease, the clammy conditions allied with them and assaulted Daykin with a vengeance. He first thought of escape. Seldom a year went by without Gaudin fending off his desperate appeals for transfer. The keeper would reach for a pen at the slightest rumour of a vacancy or a new station in the works. Each time Gaudin dutifully forwarded his entreaties to Ralph Smith, M.P. for Nanaimo, noting "that the damp climate at Carmanah cripples him." The declining health of his wife and his mother made isolation at Carmanah all the more desperate. In January 1903 Mrs. Daykin went away to Victoria for a mastectomy. Yearning to be near her, Daykin applied for the keepership of Discovery Island, five miles south of Victoria. He was turned down and she died in hospital alone.

By December 1903 Gaudin was peeved by the rising torrent of Daykin's applications. "I'll give you a piece of friendly advice," he offered. "Stay where you are, or face a cut in pay." It was government policy to retrench (which might explain the quality of the coal) and Gaudin warned, "The lopping off does not commence at the top of the tree, the lowest branches are handiest, and that applies to you as well as myself."[5] Gaudin's caution tempered Daykin for awhile. By 1906, however, his mother was failing fast and demanded constant attention. No nurse could be enticed to Carmanah. While sympathizing with his problem, Gaudin decided her removal was "almost out of the question."

The marine agent came up that April and was shocked by the shell of a man who greeted him on the beach and made his way, like a rusted robot, up to the house. So horribly had the rheumatism bent and warped his frame that Gaudin pronounced Daykin "beyond the attention to the operation of the light and fog alarm." A week later his mother died. The *Quadra* turned back and took her corpse away to Victoria. In June Daykin appealed for yet another move—this time to Trial Island or maybe even the new light at Estevan Point further up the West Coast. Gaudin wrote Colonel Anderson on his behalf. Politics again: "I would very much like to feel that your application will be granted," Gaudin apologized, "but I am afraid other arrangements have already been made by Mr. Sloane, MP."

For two more years the pain came and went in waves, lapping up to ever higher water marks, then engulfed Daykin, leaving him a stiff and crippled marionette, his elbows and knees kinked, hands contorted into gnarled claws. In July 1907 he pounced on a rumour that Cape Beale might become vacant. At least there was no foghorn there! He bent over his typewriter and pecked out another appeal: "I have today put in the last boiler tubes (4) that I am able, I can not stand the jar of cutting out and beading the tubes, my wrists are too weak from rheumatism, and it cripples me for weeks." There would be none of this work at Cape Beale, and no need to handle a boat.

He cited another reason for a move, even more compelling. After his first wife died, Daykin had written proposing marriage to her sister in England. She accepted. Now he watched in horror as the arthritis flared red in Anna's joints too, making them partners in pain. He implored Robertson, Gaudin's successor, for a transfer to Cape Beale, where they might have easier access to medicine and assistance.

The proposal had possibilities. Though the stations lay in separate constituencies, both were "under control of the Liberal Govt," and Daykin calculated he could pull the exchange off since he would be creating a vacancy at Carmanah. Brewster, another MP, wrote Daykin that he had "strongly recommended" his transfer. As a matter of form, though, he would ask the secretary of the Alberni Liberal Association to make a nomination. "This he did—his brother-in-law," Daykin caustically informed Captain Robertson. A one-time beneficiary of patronage, who had nudged Albert Argyle off Race Rocks, Daykin was now a victim himself. His response was identical. "I don't pretend to any right for an exchange," he admitted, "but after 25 years service, it is hardly fair to give a station with the same pay as this—with half the work. . . to a new man."[6]

There were even worse trials than pain and patronage. One day he cranked up the gas-driven donkey engine which ran the sky-line, installed in 1900 to carry freight up the cliffs from the beach. One of his sons climbed into the bosun's chair to make the descent. Midway down the cable began to unravel, then parted. The boy plummeted down and hit the rocks with a sickening smack. It was as if the father had killed him by his own hand. Something in Daykin's spirit snapped that day, like the frayed cable, and left his mind dangling at the end of its tether.

A second son set off up the Nitinat hunting with a friend and never came home. Searchers later found their canoe floating on the placid lake, fully loaded with their gear. Both were capable swimmers and their disappearance remains one of the West Coast's unsolved mysteries.

As all the torments of Job thickened and swarmed around him, Daykin was reputed to have poured a bottle of Scotch whiskey down his throat every day with no apparent effect. After telephone replaced the telegraph, eavesdroppers on the party line would flinch at the lightkeeper's explosive temper when the tender steamed by without landing his case of "pain-killer." "You didn't know if he was in a bad humour or not," one recalled. "He used to yell and shout as if he was goin' away or somethin'."

But Daykin was "goin'" nowhere. Applications for transfer went unheeded year after year as he sat alone through the nights, staring endlessly out through the rain-splattered window panes at the same expanse of water, hearing again the voices of his sons, his golden years turned to lead by the perverse alchemy of isolation. Late in 1911, twenty years after he came ashore at Carmanah, Daykin's mind had become as disordered as his handwriting: a cramped, spidery scrawl tinged with torment as the mind guiding it wandered in ever-widening circles from the centre of sanity. References to a cryptic "Keno" began to appear as he plunged into hallucination. "And all's well, Keno," he scribbled New Year's Eve 1911. "Goodnight, Keno—where ever you are," reads another.

Finally it ended. On 29 March 1912 Daykin began packing his belongings. Two weeks later he received word that he would be transferred, in two more weeks, to MacLaughlin Point, a beacon in Victoria Harbour. Meanwhile, with the self-forgetful devotion of a mother with a spoiled tyrannical child, he went about his routine as conscientiously as ever, painting the engine room floor

Carmanah Point Lightstation 1978.

(again) and making repairs to the engine, a project he had to abandon since all his files were worn toothless. Three more months dragged by as he waited for his replacement. On 19 July 1912, after twenty-one years and two months, W.P. Daykin was taken away to MacLaughlin Point.

Gordon Halkett, the superintendent of lights, came to inspect Daykin's new station late in November 1912. The keeper was absent, given to shuffling along Victoria's back streets, prodded on by the sharp memory of his vanished way of life. Halkett drove back to the marine office and reported he was "not at all satisfied with the conditions existing there." The engine room was locked. Anna Daykin confessed she knew nothing about operating the fog alarm. Their surroundings were in a "very poor state of tidiness, . . . very different to what it was when you took charge," he wrote. A platform Daykin had laid down two months before appeared "very cumbersome," not yet having "received any paint." A clapboard porch he had built without authorization looked in poor condition. "You will have to see that these conditions are altered as soon as possible," Halkett warned. They never let up.

Daykin died 20 November 1916. His wife was granted leave to stay on until the end of January while she made arrangements to go back to her family in England. "I have quite decided not to apply for a light," she explained. "I am not strong enough to undertake such a thing."

Helicopters transformed life at remote stations like Carmanah.

George Woodley took over Carmanah in the fall of 1912 and soon wondered why Daykin had stuck it out for so long. One foggy night in September he cranked up number one fog engine. Two hours later he and his assistant were in the engine room when the crank-pit blew out, hurling pieces of machinery like shrapnel all over the room. Luckily neither was hurt. Try as he might, Woodley could never regulate the lantern to turn at the correct rate. "So I have completely had my fill. . . get someone to take my place as soon as possible," he demanded.

Price, Halkett's assistant, went up to reason with him. A week later he telegraphed Victoria that Woodley was "practically finished with this station," and refused even to order food or cook it. Captain Robertson cabled back that the keeper would be relieved as soon as possible. Until then, if an accident occurred through negligence, he threatened, "It will be a serious matter for you." For Woodley, though, escape was a much more serious concern. He replied that, if he were not relieved before the *Tees* called next, he would "come in and take the consequences." He lasted six weeks. James Davies (son of the ill-starred George who perished at Race Rocks) came to Carmanah after Woodley. He was horribly burned and disfigured when the spirit can exploded in his hand as he was lighting up, spraying his face, trunk, and arms with flaming methyl hydrate.

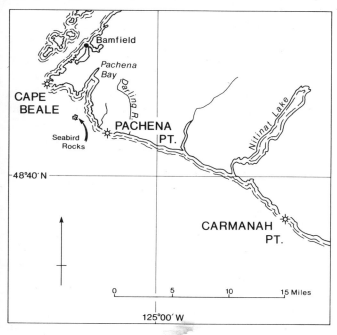

Lennard Island

I nbound navigators of the new century had only to keep between Cape Flattery and Carmanah Point to find the elusive mouth of Juan de Fuca. If their approach was from the south, they could feel their way into Juan de Fuca with the sounding lead. While the continental shelf off the Washington coast would read a steady fifty to sixty fathoms on the leadline, the bottom dropped off sharply as soon as Flattery was cleared. When the weights bounced down 150 fathoms or more, the quartermaster brought the bow around 130 degrees, and the bo'sun barked out his commands to send sailors scrambling up the ratlines. Hanging from the booms, bare calloused feet stretching the stirrups, they set more sheets to the wind. Lookouts squinted ahead for the Dungeness light on the American shore, then for Race Rocks. The helmsman steered wide around Race's awesome rip-tide, then hauled the wheel over hard toward Fisgard and Esquimalt, or aimed the bow for Berens Island.

If they were bound further north, ships' masters cleaved to a northwest course, seeking Cape Beale light after Carmanah went by, always keeping a respectable distance out from the foul ground and harrowing breakers of Barkley Sound—the harbour that never was. From Beale on up, all was a void of endless undulating swells for two hundred miles to Cape Scott at the northern tip of the island. Worse trials lay ahead: the frenzied expanse of Queen Charlotte Sound; then the Hecate Straits dividing the Queen Charlottes from the mainland, a natural funnel for wind and weather which earned it the nickname "Hectic Straits" everywhere outside the chartroom.

Past Cape Beale in the night they were hissing along like Columbus four hundred years before, headed off the earth's edge into oblivion. And fog made the void complete. It is simple, today, to recreate the awful burden of command for captains northbound in 1900: simply switch off the headlights and wipers of a crowded car on a moonless, overcast night in a pelting rain, then steer for 150 miles according to instructions from a passenger with a compass and map in his lap.

In January 1901 James Gaudin reported there were fifty sealing vessels out each season. "With the settling up of agricultural districts and the development of the fishing and mineral resources of the West Coast of Vancouver Island, the trade is rapidly increasing," he observed, and boasted, "We now have a tri-monthly Mail Service to all points on the coast." The Canadian Pacific and rival steamship companies had ten steamers assigned to coastal trade throughout an area that was "rock bound with dangerous reefs extending a long distance off shore, and without aid and few remarkable points to guide the Mariner or give him any assistance in verifying his position."

Gaudin enthusiastically endorsed the application of Ralph Smith, MP, for a light at Lennard Island near Tofino, fifty miles north of Cape Beale. A light at this location would have the advantage of marking a landfall for the steady stream of tramp steamers bound in from the Orient, and would benefit any sailing ships driven off course by the "adverse winds and stormy weather" of the autumn and winter every year. The Victoria Ship Masters Association and Captain Troup, superintendent of the CPR fleet, also lobbied hard for the Lennard Island light. Troup had recently been appointed to the Lighthouse Board, assuring the CPR that its demands would be met.

Gaudin dispatched Captain Walbran with the *Quadra* to Clayoquot Sound that spring. Walbran came back with a chart tracing, indicating a suitable site for a new light. In September Colonel Anderson sent plans and specifications to Gaudin, telling him, "You may make arrangements for having the buildings erected by days work whenever you think it can be done to advantage."

An iron lantern room and lens were on order in Birmingham and would be shipped in a few weeks. Anderson instructed his agent to leave the lantern base open or unfinished on one side. Befitting its importance, Lennard Island would be topped off with the largest light on the coast, an eight-foot high, first order classical lens, cast by Chance Brothers. The only other of its kind had recently been installed at St. Catherines light on the Isle of Wight. "The sections of this apparatus are very large," Anderson advised, so George Frost, the construction foreman, had to be sure he left a large enough hole in the floor "to pass in any section of the apparatus," including the mercury tub—three feet in diameter with a capacity for eight hundred pounds of the deadly quicksilver.

Gaudin advised Colonel Anderson that, owing to the importance of Lennard Island, the station would "require a person of good average intelligence to operate it." Such a man "should be worth six to seven hundred dollars per annum." Anderson agreed and approved a $600 salary. And not to worry about finding the keeper: Ralph Smith had already wrung a promise from the minister that "his man," Frank C. Garrard, would have the appointment. Meantime, Gaudin must take pains to write Garrard at Alberni and offer him work "during the construction of the buildings."

Frank Garrard had certainly "knocked around" before the day he opened that letter from Victoria and learned about his next destination. He was born in 1863 at Broxbourne, Hertfordshire, and shipped before the mast fifteen years later. Over the next decade he made sixteen voyages, six times around the world and seven more around the Horn. He tried his hand ashore, at prospecting and homesteading near Nanaimo, then went back to England to fetch Annie, his bride. He worked as a labourer, widening inland navigational channels for prospectors, then signed on with a crew slashing the telegraph line overland from Alberni to Clayoquot. When that link was forged they strung another wire back over the same track to join Clayoquot and Alberni to the world's longest submarine cable, between Bamfield and Australia.

Garrard had previously worked with George Frost, foreman of the Lennard Island job, in Nanaimo. When he arrived at Clayoquot he found the construction crew at the landing, waiting in the rain to off-load supplies from the *Queen City*. Garrard rowed out to the site with forty coal-oil cans full of fresh water. When he landed at Lennard he found the concrete had already been poured for the foundations of the tower and dwelling. The crew lived in tents. Frost's wife and daughter fed them all. On weekends the workers rowed over to Clayoquot to take on local settlers in baseball games.

On his forty-first birthday Frost handed Garrard a telegram from Victoria, confirming his appointment to Lennard. He set off for Alberni to pack his belongings and bring his family to Clayoquot. They steamed down the Alberni Canal on the *Queen City* and made the trip out to Lennard aboard a scow, hemmed in by two sea-chests, a chest of drawers, sewing machine, cow, calf, and dog. Annie and their four children took up temporary residence in the cramped oil shed while Frank helped the crew finish the house.

A few days later the *Quadra* anchored off Lennard and sent over a workboat with the celebrated lantern equipment aboard. The crew rigged two tree trunks as sheerlegs and began winching the works up by block and tackle—first the cast-iron mercury tub and turn table, then the catwalks and railings, and finally the framework and copper sheeting for the roof, every piece stamped with its identifying number. The framework was bolted together first. They had installed half the roof before someone noticed the holes for bolting it to the framework were out of line and they had to drill additional ones—a slipshod innovation which made life miserable for Lennard's keepers afterwards. "The consequences of this was that after I was left in charge of the lighthouse and when we had some heavy rain, the roof leaked badly, so much so that I found it advisable to wear oilskins while up in the lantern attending the light and clock attachment which controlled it," Garrard complained. Finally the crew uncrated the lens, lifted the semi-circular refracting crystals like eggs out of their straw nests, carried them lovingly one at a time up the tower, and puttied them into place in their brass mounting. The last of the workers quit Lennard on 26 October "as they did not wish to be marooned during the autumn months."

Garrard lit up for the first time on the night of 1 November 1904, wound up the weights, gave the gleaming five-ton lens a shove, and Lennard Island light,

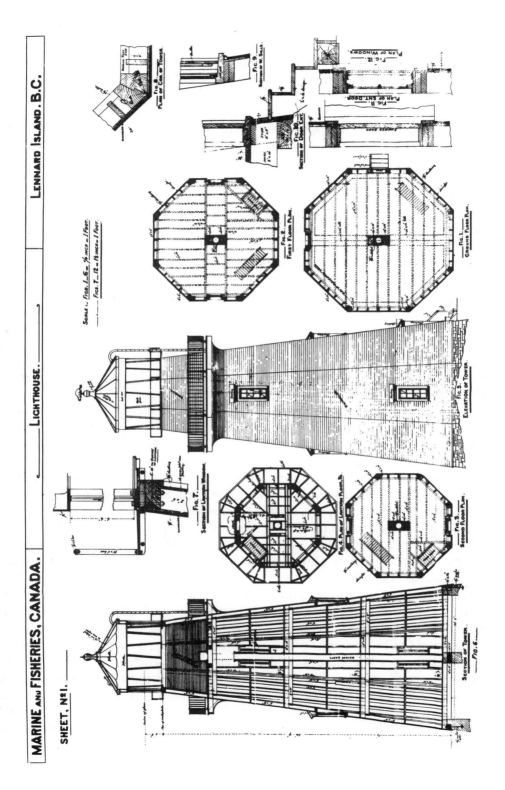

"the most up-to-date on this continent," went down on the lengthening List of Lights with its flash every 11¼ seconds from an elevation of 108 feet, visible sixteen miles "except where obscured by trees on island."

Before they were marooned themselves, Frank rowed over to Clayoquot to post his supply requisition to Victoria and leave an order with the grocer. He also implored Mrs. Carter, the postmaster's wife, to come out and visit Annie from time to time. Then the first series of long gales cut them off. Food ran short; by the time the roaring seas abated they were cutting flour with bran. Frank set out for town again with his two oldest children, Lilly and Burdett. They loaded pipes and elbows and a barrel of salt pork into their sixteen-foot boat at the pier, then set off for home in a hurry, hoping to take full advantage of the ebbing tide before the waters between Lennard and the Sound erupted again. They were nearly too late.

Where the tide collided with the groundswell, they slipped into a surging rip, "and [I] naturally headed the boat up into every breaker as it came, so as to take it head on, but the trouble with that method was that the tide was taking us out as we headed out to the ocean we were rapidly getting into the breakers across the entrance of that channel." The pork barrel made them perilously top heavy. Wrestling with the tiller to head the bucking bow directly into the swells, Frank ordered his children to open the barrel and haul out the pork, slopping it piece by piece into the rising water in the boat. Then he seized the barrel, tipped it over the stern, and laid a plank across the thwarts. "I unshipped the rudder," Garrard recorded, "and sitting on the plank pushed & steered at the same time, Burdett rowing; I kept the boat's head to the breaking seas, in the tide rip & by alternately rowing ahead and astern, facing the seas all the time, we let the boat drift in the current to Lennard Island."

Getting there was the simple part. They heard Lennard long before they saw it. The heaving combers reared up ten feet or more, thundering over the barnacled rocks in huge welters of spray. It was the ultimate test of a man's seamanship to land a rowboat under such conditions. Garrard waited, grimly issuing instructions to his crew, then rose up on the crest of a swell, rode it well up onto the rocks, jumped out, and seized the painter as the wave retreated, the boat crashing down.

It would be their last trip till spring. The following April the *Quadra* called. James Gaudin came ashore, shaken by his rough landing on the rocks. "He complimented me on my ability as a boatman," Garrard wryly noted in his diary. "I told him that I had to be to manage the trips between the Island and Clayoquot." On his return to Victoria the agent sent a crew back to blast out a boat landing since the place was "dangerous and destructive to boats." He also brought Garrard confirmation of his permanent appointment at the annual salary of $600. "Although it was not a very excessive remuneration," Garrard hoped it was at least a steady income which might allow them to clear their escalating debt at the store. He had already borrowed money from A.W. Niell, an MLA, for supplies.

The *Quadra* took Annie and Lilly back to Victoria. Lilly had been hired as an au pair girl in Victoria, which gave her a chance to attend school. She came home during the summer. "During this time at the lighthouse I managed to give the children some schooling, making a schedule by which they attended their lessons and the regular routine of the lighthouse was carried on," Garrard recalled.

> I spent the night up in the tower, winding up the clock every 2½ hours, this did not necessitate my keeping awake all the time, as there was an attachment on the clock, which when it ran down or began to slow rang an electric bell. . . .
>
> I really did not need this as if I was dozing I would immediately hear the stopping of the clock, and the lens platform would continue revolving for a little while. . . .
>
> I was able in this way to do the other work connected with the light, cleaning the lenses and brass-work in the tower, painting, as for instance the roof of the tower. . . and later on painting over the whole tower & dwelling.[1]

In June 1905 Frank received a welcome letter from Victoria advising him that he would soon receive an increase of $400 a year since the machinery must be wound at such short intervals, and that a steam fog alarm was slated for Lennard. He hired Annie as his assistant. That summer the construction crew came back to build the fog plant.

Garrard left a detailed description of the new building and its machinery. A cistern under the floor held water fed from gutters on the roof. Brick walls enclosed two huge steam engines which drove air compressors with their fan belts. The boilers stood in a separate room "which was entered from the tramway leading past the tower and on which the coal was hauled up." Coal bunkers occupied half the boiler room, and each boiler had gauges "built on the principal that as soon as the water was low in them they shewed it. . . giving ample time to start the injector pump."

The crew finished in mid-December, hoping to catch a boat out on the

The original tower on Lennard Island.

seventeenth. This time they were too late. A hurricane-force gale engulfed the West Coast on 23 December; two days later the *Pass of Melfort* went down with all hands off Amphitrite Point. On Christmas Day the Garrards and their unbidden guests sat on the rocks, marvelling at the sheer force and fury of the sea around them as it swallowed up fifty-foot reefs; "the next moment the reefs would again appear, but a cataract of water would be foaming down over them."

It was a pleasant change from the dreary salt-pork Christmas of a year before. While spray lashed the windows, the crew doted on Garrard's children and enjoyed "an evening's entertainment of games, using the old fashioned ones, Earth, air, fire & water etc." When the labourers shipped out a few days later, they left R. Pollock behind as a qualified assistant and steam engineer.

Lilly went back to school in Victoria. Frank and Annie agonized for some time about their three younger children and finally decided to board them out in Tofino. Ethel, Noel, and Olive would raise the enrollment and enable the new school to qualify for a provincial grant. Frank gave them a canoe with a sail, which he ordered them never to rig. Every Monday at sunrise they rowed over to Tofino, stayed with friends through the week, then rowed home Friday afternoon. Frank would meet them halfway to Lennard in the station boat. One Friday he took Burdett, Annie, Lilly (who was home on a visit), and Mrs. Davidson, a Clayoquot friend, with him. They could see the canoe off in the distance, "about half a mile" away. The oarlocks had broken and the children were standing up, trying to rig the sail. As the family watched, the canoe capsized. Frank and

Calm weather was essential for landing supplies at Lennard Island.

Burdett pulled frantically on their oars, racing against time and temperature. Facing the bow, the women saw only a "dot about the middle of the canoe," and "a splashing in the water." Frank remembered:

> When we arrived, we found Noel had managed to get on the upturned canoe, Ethel was holding herself up by having one arm across the bottom of the canoe, which having no keel made it a very precarious hold, between them they were holding Olive so that her head was well out of the water, they had at first when the Canoe upset lost track of her & she could not at that time swim, Ethel and Noel could a little, and had managed to get a hold of her & as I said were holding them up between them when we reached the upset canoe, we ran alongside on the opposite side. . . and pulled them into the boat over the bottom of the canoe.

Frank righted the canoe and bailed it out. Burdett climbed in and paddled home behind them. They wrapped little Olive in a coat and wedged her between Lilly and Mrs. Davidson. Noel, shivering, took one of the oars. As soon as they landed, Frank sawed the canoe in half to make feed troughs for the cow. "For some days," he confessed, "I had the vision before my eyes of the upturned canoe & the splashing in the water."

He nearly lost Ethel on his next trip out for mail. It was a calm day, a welcome breathing spell between storms, and they were nearly home, coasting over a heavy swell. They passed Village Island and were watching across the unwrinkled water for a large breaker opposite the landing channel. Ethel, holding the tiller, screamed, "Here's one now!" Burdett and his father hauled hard on their oars. The boat spun around and the oarlocks popped out. "We got the boat shouldered on to the wave," wrote Frank, "& as it broke about eight feet above the bow of the boat which for the second was almost perpendicular, I thought she would capsize end over end, the sea thundered down into the stern where poor Ethel was. . . the full weight of it. . . must have beaten her down into the boat, instead of washing her overboard." Luck was with them again and Frank was even more grateful that Annie wasn't. She "expected another addition to the family," and had gone to Tofino.

Then came another chain of gales. Frank had only Ethel and Pollock with him; the other children stayed in Tofino with their expectant mother. The two men spelled each other off in the fog alarm building, and kept a sharp eye on the water. The morning of 8 December 1906 Garrard climbed up to extinguish the lamp and saw, "drifting through the broken channel, just inside the reefs, a vessel with her top masts gone and a torn signal on the lower masts."

Pollock helped him launch the boat. Frank and Ethel set out after the wreck. When they were halfway out the shattered hulk drifted around the far side of nearby Wickaninnish Island; they heard the awful splintering of timbers and watched her masts collapse behind the wind-sculpted pines. Father and daughter would suffer the same fate in the pounding surf if they approached from seaward, so Garrard steered through the undulating kelp tentacles and landed on the island's lee side. They dragged the boat up and ran across the neck of land. "It certainly was a spectacle that greeted us when we arrived there," said Frank, "the vessel having been loaded with lumber and all the fore part having broken up, the whole shore was covered with lumber, pieces sticking up and then being washed out again thrown end over end on to the shore and the wreck or part of it was grinding on the rocks."

Frank held his daughter's hand, watching helplessly as the surf casually engulfed and dismantled its prize, sweeping away her boiler and donkey engine. The mizzen mast jutted up like a splintered arm; next to it a skiff, with its hull stove in, was still lashed to the poop. No sign of life aboard. Only the gulls shrieked back as their shouts echoed over the water. Frank Garrard could just make out the name on her broken bow: *Coloma*. Though he had no way of knowing, her crew was safe in Bamfield, thanking God and Minnie Patterson for their lives.

The two rowed and sailed over to Tofino but the lightkeeper was unable to report the wreck because the line was down. A man named Rhodes gave them a tow back behind his launch. They found the derelict stranded high and dry at low tide. Frank climbed up the rigging and crawled into the cabin from which Captain Allison had stepped only forty-eight hours before, pistol in hand. He took away some provisions and fittings, including "a hanging lamp and a looking glass that had been cracked & to hide the crack, a wreath of flowers painted over it." Rhodes salvaged some blocks, tackle, and rope. Frank noticed a strange ball, nearly a foot in diameter, lying on deck covered with sand and wood chips. He took it home and, "by melting & skimming off the chips of wood," discovered he "had got a supply of butter." He also retrieved some hams. Later that day *Tees* sent her longboat over to Lennard, and Garrard learned the lucky fate of the derelict *Coloma*'s crew. During the next week he went out and salvaged some cargo which he later used to frame a house on the mainland.

Annie came home with the baby boy soon after, just in time for Christmas. The sea was flat calm that year so in the afternoon they took the infant Edward out for his first time, rowing out past the reefs over to Wickaninnish. All that remained of the *Coloma* now was the spine of her keel and a few ribs arcing out of the sand.

The Garrards turned Lennard Island into a virtual menagerie, adding a herd of goats, seventeen cats, and flocks of ducks and chickens to their tiny herd of cattle. The ducks cultivated a taste for Annie's poppies, waddling up to feed in the flowerbeds every morning, then lying around in a daze, barely able to quack, all afternoon. They never grew "and later died off one by one. . . a horrible example of indulging in opium or its derivatives." The goats took a special dislike to Pollock, butting him whenever they could catch him off guard. They once held him captive in the blacksmith shop; on another occasion Garrard found his assistant up a stump surrounded by goats pawing the ground.

Frank and Annie decided to send the children off to Tofino again when the new school opened that spring. They rented a cottage there, where the children stayed during the week. Frank purchased a new-fangled gasoline engine for his skiff and towed the children across to Tofino in an extra skiff on Mondays. Friday afternoons they caught a tow back by launch. Sometimes the children made the crossing to school by themselves, and their parents never knew "if. . . they arrived there until. . . the end of the week when they returned to the lighthouse." The baby stayed at home, though, and like any child born in his parents' middle age, Edward was the brightest light in their lives. He grew up "full of life & vigour and never seemed to be ill in any way."

Outboard engines revolutionized the lives of all the lightkeepers who could afford them, easing the awful tension of mail crossings or going out to fish. But the pioneer models could be dangerous in their own right, as Frank Garrard soon discovered. As he steered through the shallows off Vikings Beach one day, with Annie holding the baby in the stern, Frank cut inside some rocks to cross a sandbar at low tide. Annie leaned over the side to check their clearance and "the hub of the flywheel, which had a projection for use with the crank handle, caught her skirt & in a second pulled her down onto the gunwale of the launch." Annie clung to baby Edward, screaming as the motor stripped off her dress. The fabric coiled around the shaft and seized up the engine. Frank wrapped his stunned and naked wife in his coat "so as to go up to the house."

That fall Annie became very depressed. She already had serious misgivings about the endless boat trips, and her melancholy deepened when she learned of her father's death in England. Frank scraped his savings together and came back one day with a phonograph and a collection of wax discs. "We got a certain satisfaction from these as can be imagined," he related, "some of them being very good & I was duly impressed when I first heard one of Harry Lauders 'I love a Lassie'." Thomas Edison gave them "a very happy Christmas," as everyone took turns at the crank after dinner and sat back to marvel at the cascade of sound coming out the horn. But then Annie lifted the spindle, packed the wax discs away, sent the children off to bed to succumb to their delightful fatigue, and Frank went out to climb the tower; it was the last time they would know true happiness together at Lennard.

Shortly after Christmas they learned the *Quadra* was steaming north with supplies. Gordon Halkett was aboard. The fastidious Halkett had caught them completely off guard last year. In spite of "the natural state of the place and the difficulties to be encountered," he was appalled when he climbed the tower and saw rags littering the floor to soak up the water leaking through the honeycombed roof. The superintendent of lights sent Garrard a blistering reprimand. Aside from the littered floor, "the lamps were in a filthy condition and had not been polished for a long time," he wrote, "in fact looked as if they had not been properly cleaned since the lighthouse was established."[2]

One blemish on his record was enough. Frank set to work in the tower while Annie supervised an early spring cleaning in the house, thankful they had some notice this time of Halkett's impending arrival. They scrubbed walls and floors with lye, rubbed down and blackened the stove, beat carpets, washed drapes, wiped salt spray off the windows. During a lull in their labours, Burdett sat at the kitchen table cuddling Edward. The toddler's sharp eye fell upon some white flakes lying on the table. His arm shot out, he snatched up the "sugar," and swallowed it. Suddenly he began shrieking and fighting in Burdett's lap. At first Annie suspected it was just a tantrum brought on by fatigue and neglect; "only after he had been crying for some time & Annie noticed his little fingers were burnt. . .did they understand what had happened." Lye.

Noel ran out to the tower and screamed up the zigzag staircase to his father polishing the lantern. Frank administered some "sweet oil" and Edward vomited

Lennard Island 1982. Jim Ryan photo.

up blood and stomach lining. The weather was "very rough," but they launched the boat anyway and ran into Tofino, with the sharp auger-bit of fear turning in their stomachs. Dr. Raynor (who should have known better) forced the baby to swallow white of egg and he vomited again—the third time the alkali made its searing passage along the tiny esophagus. Afterward Edward "seemed easier & he even slept & was able to take nourishment for a day." They brought him home again but his esophagus was perforated and he died a few days later.

The next trip to town, with the tiny coffin lying at their feet and Annie's sobs rising above the grinding outboard, was one of their last. Though Pollock had taken Frank aside and counselled him not to bring her back, Annie returned to the stillness of the house. It would never be the same, not with sullen meals taken at that same table, even though all the wooden toys, diapers, overalls, socks, and tiny rubber boots were packed away out of sight. Frank tried hard to mend their scarred hearts—bringing friends out in relays from Tofino, cranking up Harry Lauders in the evenings, reading aloud to Annie—but he could never again dispel "the element of danger" pervading their lives. He mailed off his resignation and they began crating their belongings for Tofino. In July 1908 Garrard opened his last letter from James Gaudin, acknowledging his resignation. "I . . . sympathize with you regarding the cause which has led up to it," the agent wrote. "I may state that since you have been in charge of the station our relations have been of the most cordial nature, and trust that those with your successor will be equally fortunate."

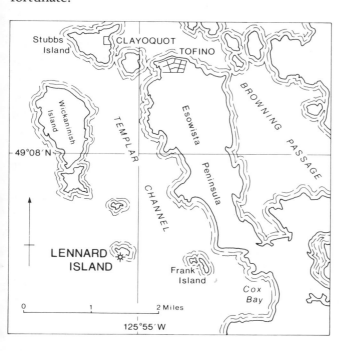

Valencia

O ttawa's sly hope of avoiding "the charge of cruelty" over its policy of shortchanging the west coast on lifesaving facilities finally backfired in the government's face in the winter of 1905-6.

On 19 January, the *Queen City* tied up at the docks in Victoria. Her crew carried down the gangway a coffin and seventeen cadaverous crewmen from the steel bark *King David*, given up for lost after 116 days at sea. Davidson, *King David*'s captain, related a tale which, in spite of its drama, had become monotonous.

His charts were out of date and Captain Davidson had misread a makeshift private light at the entrance of Nootka Sound for Cape Beale. At 9:00 p.m. on the night of 10 December his lookout screamed "Breakers ahead!" and Davidson ordered both anchors down. The chains rumbled out for a few seconds, then found bottom—in only eight fathoms. *King David* held out against the assault of the swells for three terrifying days and nights. "On the 13th, the wind increased to the point where the strain was so great that the windlass broke and she was swept up on the rocks. Soon after she started to break up. A large portion of the bow broke off and was carried by enormous waves high on the rocks," the despairing Davidson related. "There was little we could do but hold out until the sea subsided, and pray that the ship didn't fall to pieces under our feet."[7]

Finally the crew escaped ashore in their lifeboats, and later rowed back to the wreck to salvage provisions. They stumbled upon an abandoned fish camp, then kindled and stoked a huge bonfire. Weeks later, as their food supply ran out, Davidson's first officer, with seven volunteers, set out for help in a lifeboat. Day after day the others kept an anxious lookout. The *Queen City*'s lookout spotted their signal fire and sent a boat ashore on 14 January—only a few hours too late for a sailmaker who went insane and died raving on the ground. All that time they were only nine miles from the village of Nootka. The party in the boat was never found.

The *King David* set the mood for that winter of disaster, but she was swept from the headlines three days later by the international scandal Colonel Anderson and his restraint-minded colleagues in Ottawa had gambled would never happen.

The wreck of the San Francisco passenger ship *Valencia* near Pachena Point on 22 January 1906 surpassed any other shipwreck before the *Titanic* in terms of sheer horror. Yet there was a certain grim dignity in the latter's fate. None of that for *Valencia*, whose crew and passengers were virtually tortured to death in a manner which sent a shock wave of revulsion around the world.

The passenger steamer *Valencia*.

Valencia's last run from San Francisco to Victoria on 20 January 1906 began as innocently as all her others. Deckhands uncoiled hawsers, and stokers below decks kindled the firebox, while the captain's wife stood at the parlour window in their apartment overlooking Meiggs Wharf, watching and savouring each minute before her husband steamed away again. The canvas-sided gangplank was retracted, *Valencia*'s whistle boomed out over the harbour, and 160 passengers stood waving at the rails. Captain O.M. Johnson emerged from the wheelhouse for a secret parting ritual: one last look up at the bay window where his wife sat waving, with their little daughter bouncing excitedly on her lap. Then, with a final wave of his own, the twelve-year veteran of the Pacific Coast Line turned all his attention to the task of piloting his 1598-ton ship and its human cargo safely up coast.

Fog engulfed the steamer soon after she left the harbour. Blindfolded, *Valencia* groped her way northward. Johnson fell back upon his reams of charts, the patent log spinning in his wake, and "dead reckoning." By keeping careful track of the time and *Valencia*'s speed, Johnson guessed their position. By Monday evening, after fifty-four hours at sea, his tables told him the entrance to Juan de Fuca lay at hand. At six o'clock seamen began throwing lead over the side, calling the mark as they threaded the lines back through chilled fingers. The wind rose steadily with the seas to a full howling gale and passengers kept to their cabins and the saloon, puking into spittoons and muttering about the lousy weather.

Four hours later the leadsman shouted out sixty fathoms. Assuming he was still a few miles south of Flattery, with the Umatilla Reef ahead, Johnson put his calipers to the chart and ordered a change in course to north by a half east. But there was still no sign of the Umatilla lightship behind the shroud of fog. Half an hour later Johnson, confident in his navigation, altered course eastward again. Much to everyone's relief the fog began to flutter in ragged patches before the wind, offering tantalizing glimpses, like a fan dancer, of the rugged shore off to starboard.

Sixty fathoms still lay under *Valencia*'s belly at 10:30. Perplexed, her captain rang the telegraph for HALF SPEED, then around to DEAD SLOW. The steamer lumbered awkwardly at four knots through the fog as the leadsmen's shouts rose over the rushing wind and the pulsating throb of her engines every quarter hour. 10:45, "eighty fathoms"; 11:00 p.m., "sixty"—much too shallow for the mouth of the Straits, where a sounding would disclose a depth of 150 fathoms or more.

Peterson, the second officer, stood on the bridge with Johnson, the quarter-master's knuckles white on the wheel between them. "We must be somewhere around the Umatilla Lightship," Johnson speculated, "but I don't believe the lightship is out." Soundings kept coming in, increasingly ominous: 11:15, "fifty-six"; 11:30, "thirty-three." The mountainous seabed was rearing up at them. Then Peterson dimly saw a black object ahead. He pointed it out to Johnson. "By God!" the captain exclaimed in shock. "Where are we?" He ordered a course hard to starboard. Peterson pushed the helmsman aside, seized the wheel, and wrenched it around just as the mate yelled up "Twenty-four!" Johnson lunged for the telegraph arm to ring FULL STOP when he was thrown off his feet by the impact of steel against stone. "In the name of God," he roared, "where are we!"[2]

Johnson had somehow failed to take the Japan Current into account. He was ten miles west and north of Carmanah light, three hundred yards from where the *Janet Cowan* struck ten years before. The *Valencia* grazed the rocks and passed over. Down below the engineer coaxed full power out of his engines while Johnson, breathing a sigh of relief, held the wheel hard over and swung the bow seaward. Halfway round his turn the steel prow crashed into a neighbouring rock. Now, with dreadful certainty, Johnson knew he was nowhere near Juan de Fuca.

Once again he cranked the telegraph through to FULL ASTERN. The engine roared, whipping seawater white and foaming at the stern for endless, agonizing seconds. Finally, with a wild ripping shriek like ten thousand fingernails scraping down a blackboard, the *Valencia* shuddered free.

At first it seemed like a second reprieve, but no sooner had Johnson hollered down the copper voice tube for a damage report than oilers came grappling up on deck, flushed like rats out of their engine room by a rising torrent of sea water. Only one chance remained now—the most agonizing a captain can choose. Johnson took it. "I will not sink in deep water," he declared. Downing, Johnson's chief engineer, still stood at his post down in the belly of the ship, up to his waist in the oily swirling flood. He answered his captain's bellowed command for FULL SPEED AHEAD to run her up on the rocks.

The sprawling fog, having done its best to delude Johnson, began to clear at last. It might have given more comfort had it hung around. They beheld their position: held fast on a pinnacle a mere thirty yards from the shore which heaved up 100 feet above their funnel. "It was so handy," an officer would later testify in tears, "you could almost take an orange and throw it on the cobbles on the shore...."

Swells rushed headlong at them all the way from Japan, and the *Valencia* lay helpless before their onslaught. On and on the combers came with savage monotony, smashing her hull, leaping the rails, sweeping the decks. Frank Lehm, a freight clerk, came out on deck and beheld a spectacle he would always want to forget.

> Screams of men, women and children mingled in awful chorus with the shriek of the wind, the dash of the rain, and the roar of the breakers. As the passengers rushed on deck, they were carried away in bunches by the huge waves that seemed as high as the ship's mastheads. The ship began to break up almost at once and the women and children were lashed to the rigging above the reach of the sea. It was a pitiful sight to see frail women, wearing only night dresses, with bare feet on the frozen ratlines, trying to shield children in their arms from the icy wind and rain.[3]

In spite of their hapless situation, Captain Johnson rallied his panic-stricken passengers and shepherded them to the upper decks to abandon ship with some semblance of order. *Valencia* carried a full complement of lifeboats and two rafts, as well as a Lyle gun designed to fire harpoon lines ashore. He first ordered the port amidships boat swung out. No sooner had it cleared the deck than the sea swept it away with part of its crew. Next the portquarter boat was lowered, only to be crushed under the heel of another swell lunging over onto the deck. Then the crew ran over to the starboard quarter and let down another boat to the saloon deck, the call "women and children first!" was given, and they clambered in under the muzzles of officers' pistols. The seamen swung her out and lowered away.

Part way down the stern fall parted. The bow plummeted down, cutting a seaman in half against the hull. Women and children spilled over the seats into the boiling surf. It was all over in a matter of seconds. All were sucked down and swept away under the eyes of fathers, brothers, and sons. Johnson, his voice cracking with grief and rage, ordered the amidships boat out. Frank Lehm again:

> The boat was filled with more women and children and safely launched. Oarsmen's faces were contorted as they strove to pull away from the ship's side in the boil of the surf and the undertow from the cliffs. At last they started to forge ahead. A great cheer for those who were to be saved went up from the hundred left on board. Even the faces of the terrified women in the little boat looked more hopeful as they began to clear the wreck.
>
> We all thought them saved when suddenly a great breaker, larger than any I had ever seen, aided by a terrible gust of wind, struck the boat, slewing her around in spite of all that the man at the steering oar and the sailors could do. The next moment she was overturned.
>
> What a sight! The searchlight showed every detail of the terrible tragedy — the men and women struggling in the water, their faces ghastly in the glare; eyes that stared at us unseeingly, already glazed with the touch of death; the bodies of children swept toward the terrible rocks, in a wild chaos of boiling surf. Suddenly all of this vanished, the searchlight revealing only a tossing, rolling, terrifying rush of water.[4]

Four boats gone and all hands dead, save for nine men who managed to make shore and cowered, shivering, in a sea cave at the foot of the awesome cliffs. Johnson elected to save his last two boats for daylight. Throughout the rest of that dark night *Valencia*'s anguished master fired distress rockets. One exploded, blasting away two of his fingers. Tying a rag, with one hand and his clenched teeth, around his bloody fist, Johnson ordered the steward to pass out blankets and food to the sodden passengers. Water rose steadily in the engine room, then snuffed out the lights.

That darkness was a blessing of sorts was confirmed when the sun rose grey-dull behind a heavy overcast like ground glass, the colour of no hope. Bodies hung suspended from the rigging like flies in a web. Once rigor mortis had run its course they loosened their hold and tumbled into the water or onto the deck with a flaccid thud. More corpses drifted between ship and shore, scoured of flesh and features as if by a giant cheese grater. The swells carried them up on the barnacled rocks and the pink, frothing undertow gargled and spat them out again. There was some small excitement when voices were heard ashore: three survivors from the ill-fated lifeboats. The rising tide drove them up the sheer face of the cliff but, as numb fingers and toes clawed in vain for purchase, each lost his footing in turn and fell shrieking into the surf.

Captain Johnson and his remaining crew readied the last two boats. Hysterical, the women balked and the seamen gave up trying to pry their fingers off lines and rails, and drag them along the decks. Two hand-picked crews set out instead. One boat with five men would try to land ashore to fasten a line shot over from the Lyle gun; the second, with a crew of nine, would row northward for help. This time, free of the weight of passengers, the boats made good their escape.

One landed at the base of a cliff. The other disappeared for seven months. The men waded ashore, scaled the rocks, and soon stumbled across the telegraph trail. They followed the wire to a lineman's cabin on the banks of the Darling River. From there they rang through to Cape Beale; Minnie Patterson sent first word of the disaster over the wire to Victoria via Bamfield and Port Alberni.

Meanwhile, a handful of bruised and bleeding survivors, ashore from the night before, began to trek overland. "The underbrush—you could not make 100 yards in a hundred years!" one of the party recalled. Carrying a sail, some sodden hardtack biscuits, and an ax, they limped westward along the beach until they blundered into quicksand, then headed back into the woods. Finally they spotted telegraph wires nailed to the trees and followed them to a rude hut. A white signpost outside proclaimed "3 MILES TO CAPE BEALE." "That was the first we knew where we were; that was the last place I thought of being," one survivor explained.

Tom and Minnie Patterson already had word of the wreck. When their watchdog began barking furiously, Minnie, eight-and-a-half months pregnant, ran out with her children to the bedraggled trekkers, mistaking them for the party who had telegraphed earlier. "You are the shipwrecked crew, I was so sorry we could not connect with you," she exclaimed. All Minnie had been able to make out was the word "telegraph." Upon learning this was a different group, she ran back inside to her headset. She instructed the men in the shack down the coast to check connections and tighten the wiring on their set.

After making a clear connection, Minnie learned there were seven passengers and two firemen at the other end, crowded into the shack with only a few biscuits between them, "and they didn't think they could last much longer." She wired W.P. Daykin at Carmanah, gave him their position, and he promised to dispatch a party with clothing, provisions, and ropes. "She started to tell us about this lighthouse keeper, what a good man he was," one man remembered, "if there is any possible chance of any body getting there; he will die on the trail, he will never give up." All through the night Minnie and Tom monitored the line. The survivors shucked their boots and wet clothing, slept in snatches, let their imaginations wander back down the trail to the *Valencia*.

Back on board Johnson bawled out orders and tried valiantly to keep spirits up. Perhaps he really believed the ship would hold together for days under them, even as he could feel the rivets popping and the steel plates buckling below. Now a line ashore was their only hope. He ordered deckhands up the mainmast to cinch a heavy rope to the mast. They dragged the heavy coils over to the Lyle gun, then broke out the shells and cartons of line. The Lyle harpoon was designed to carry a quarter-inch line ashore. A shore party could then haul the rope over, and everyone would roll across, one by one, on a breeches-buoy. Johnson was confident someone was over there, somewhere high above them. He had seen some climb the cliff that morning, and surely the fugitives from the lifeboats would soon arrive with help.

Johnson slid the first shell into the breech and fired. The line frayed on a corner of its box as it snaked out, and the barb flew over, trailing a few pathetic feet of tarred marlin. He cursed, loaded, fired again. This time the missile and its cord vaulted high over the brow of the cliff. They waited. An hour. Two hours. Nothing. Then they watched in horror as their slender hope slid over the cliff and fell into the water, chafed through by the ship's constant teetering on the rocks. The men who might have saved them were even then warming themselves in the Pattersons' parlour, or shivering inside the Darling River cabin, as the life line lay limp in the flotsam.

The only means of getting a line ashore now was round a man's waist. John Segalis, a Greek fireman, volunteered. After a half hour's flailing through the surf he surrendered and was hauled back on board. Lewis Oleson, one of the lucky few who had been washed ashore the night before, dove in after the Lyle line and was battered to death on the rocks on his way back.

As the ruptured hulk groaned and settled on the rock, those aboard scrambled up on the roof of the saloon deck, then onward up the teetering mast, biting the lines when their fingers grew numb. Finally it snapped under the weight of some twenty climbers; they tumbled down on the deck and were swept away.

After the call from Cape Beale, Phil Daykin and two linemen set out immediately from Clo-oose. By late afternoon they were plunging through the rain forest, guided by the dim light of miners' lamps strapped to their heads. They waded some of the narrower creeks, hitched rides with Indians in dugouts over wider and faster streams. By ten o'clock next morning—after a grueling eighteen-hour trek—one of them saw a line lying across the trail just ahead. They reeled in a harpoon, one of those fired hours before from somewhere a hundred feet below. Crawling through the salal and dead falls, they peered over the cliff's edge to be greeted by a rousing cheer. But all they could do was wait and watch the deadly panorama unfold below.

Seaborne rescuers were every bit as frustrated as Daykin and the party of linemen watching from their balcony seats. When news first reached Victoria, there was some trepidation that the stricken vessel might well be *Valencia*. She was now thirty-six hours overdue. Her sister ship, SS *Queen City*, steamed out of the harbour and headed up the coast along with the tugs *Salvor* and *Czar*. As each passed Carmanah lighthouse, their lookouts saw through telescopes the signals Daykin had unfurled to tell them a wreck lay eighteen miles further on, off Pachena Point.

Captain Langley, on board a salvage vessel, was first to stumble upon the grisly spectacle while searching for another wreck to pick clean. He encountered the steamer *Queen City* nearby, hove to, and shouted up the *Valencia*'s position through a loud hailer. An officer came into the wheelhouse with the news. "Everyone on the bridge said 'My God! There is no saving of her!'" he recalled.

When they reached the scene, crews squinted through rain and spray for a glimpse of the crippled liner. Captain Cousins, aboard the *Queen City*, saw two masts and a funnel. Later he discerned some thirty people swaying from the rigging, and more clotted around the stern. By eleven o'clock another ship of the PCS line, *City of Topeka*, arrived. The company's manager was aboard and, for reasons never since disclosed, he ordered *Queen City* back to port.

The three remaining vessels, joined later by the *Queen* up from Victoria, ran in as close as they dared to *Valencia*. None put down a boat. The fate of the *Valencia*'s boats gave too clear an indication of what would happen to others once they were turned loose in those mountainous swells. So the remaining survivors were treated to the spectacle of salvation within reach but far beyond their grasp. Then to their utter dismay and disbelief, they watched the flotilla of would-be

The coastal steamer *Queen City*, sister ship to the *Valencia*.

rescuers steam away one by one, heading for shelter and help in Bamfield. The *Queen* kept up a lonesome vigil through the *Valencia*'s last night.

Once again men pleaded with women to take their places in two remaining life rafts and again the women refused, believing that their deliverance was finally at hand. Reluctantly Johnson explained that this was their last chance, but they all replied they would rather die on the ship than on the raft. The first raft was dropped into the surf with nine men hanging on, and disappeared across the white water. Nineteen others fled the wreck on a second raft after pleading in vain with the women one last time. Captain Johnson steadfastly refused his crewmen's entreaties to quit his ship. As the swells bore them away, the escapees turned and saw their captain clutching a revolver in his good hand and waving good-bye with his bloody fist. He turned away and took shelter with the women behind crates of cabbages piled around the wheelhouse, then joined them in singing "Nearer My God to Thee."

Valencia was already well into her death throes, even as the last raft rushed away on the crest of the waves. Phil Daykin and the shore party listened helplessly as the haunting hymn lilted up to them; then *Valencia* shuddered and broke up, bodies raining down on the deck. As if growing bored with its prize, the sea sent a wave crashing over the hulk, toppling it off its rocky perch and under the waves. A small whaler, *Orion*, manoeuvered close enough through the flotsam and bodies to see only the stern mast with the last of its grisly human trophies hanging like marionettes, jerking with every heave.

One of the escapees on the second raft left a hair-raising account of their flight:

> The struggle to get past the surf was almost too much for the exhausted men. We were like demented demons shouting and fighting to stay alive.... On the crest of each wave we could see the *City of Topeka* which was about a mile away. When we were in open water, we hoisted a man on our shoulders and with a flag made from a shirt on an oar, tried to signal the ship.

The *City of Topeka* had set out from Bamfield to relieve the *Queen* at noon. A lookout spotted the raft but, after steering toward it, decided it was just more flotsam from the wreck. The quartermaster altered course again. The captain went out with binoculars, rested his elbows on the rails, and "could hardly believe what he saw." The *City of Topeka* made full speed for the raft. "They found us just in time," a survivor related.

> We were almost paralyzed with cold, for the water had been washing over us for several hours and we had drifted about five miles from the wreck. Some of the men were mostly in the water, while others did their best to keep them from washing away....

As soon as they were hauled aboard they told the *Topeka*'s crew about the first raft. The ship lumbered around in ever-widening circles, searching throughout the area, and finally gave up; "it was presumed they all perished."[5]

Most of them did, one at a time, as the raft was borne west and north, well past the searchers into Barkley Sound. Hardier men pushed pallid corpses overboard to make room for the living. Finally only four remained. Each had his own private store of grief: a wife, children, parents, or mates who had died under his very eyes. With each hopeless mile their sanity slipped away. One tried to strangle another, raving about finding a dog to eat. When they landed on Turret Island, one man fled into the bush and disappeared. Fortunately, local Indians discovered the last three and took them to Bamfield in their dugouts.

Together with those who languished numb and desolate around Tom and Minnie Patterson's parlour at Cape Beale, with "shipwreck" stamped on their anguished faces, they made thirty-seven survivors. Not a woman or child among them.

For days afterward Phil Daykin, two linemen, and a diminishing crew of squeamish Indians joined a fleet off shore in the search for bodies. Wading into the surf, they dragged the bloated remains up the polished pebble beaches above high water, then knelt to scoop gravel over them while gulls, crows, and eagles shrieked "foul" overhead. Leaving crude markers behind, they tramped onward for miles, stopping at the cry "There's another!" to retrieve a faceless blob of flesh. Some were pried or dug out of rock fissures with shovels, ham-sized pieces carried away in blankets. The Bamfield freight shed was transformed into a temporary morgue where cadavers were pieced together and laid out for identification while *New York Times* reporters added to their grim tally. They could

Wreck of the *Valencia* at low tide, 2 February 1906.

never get them all. Of the original 154 aboard, 117 were eventually listed among the dead and missing. Of the ninety-four passengers, fourteen were saved while twenty-three of the sixty officers and crew survived. The bones of many who booked passage on the *Valencia* must still litter that forbidding shore, ground and polished like sea-glass over the decades.

With an enraged U.S. public demanding answers, a high-profile Presidential Commission of Enquiry convened in Seattle on 27 January 1906. The commissioners filed in, the chairman pounded his gavel, and survivors, would-be rescuers, and witnesses revived the horror at Pachena Point for a packed and hushed audience: placed them in that lost wheelhouse, helped them into the lifeboats, shared the futility of the feckless Lyle lines, thrashed through the forest to Cape Beale, set them adrift on the cockle-shell rafts, left them numb with rage, grief, and shock.

It was a nightmare for the Department of Marine and Fisheries, and for the mandarins who had long placed economy before humanity. Although in their final report the investigators affirmed, "The Commission does not deem it proper to criticize the conduct of other than American citizens," witnesses were certainly unintimidated by any such diplomatic courtesies. The counsel for the commission took great pains to draw out their opinions about how the tragedy could have been avoided, or the appalling loss of life curtailed.

With one notable exception the response was unanimous. From the lowliest deckhand to the masters of the largest rescue vessels involved, all were of one mind. "Suppose there had been a good life-saving station with a properly equipped surf boat there, what is your opinion?" Captain Wallace Langley of the tug *Lorne* was asked. "I am perfectly satisfied she could have rendered assistance," he declared. Captain Troup, general superintendent of the B.C. Coast Service of the CPR (who had watched it all from the *Salvor*), agreed: "Yes, Sir, I believe that a self-righting, self-bailing lifeboat might have done some good that day." Most damning was this exchange between a commissioner and Captain J.B. Patterson of the Pacific Steamship Company:

> Q. I would like to ask you, Captain Patterson, what would be the aids to navigation to be provided by . . . the Canadian Government in that vicinity.

> A. They want some thoroughly good life-boats . . . and a properly equipped station and crew of paid men, not volunteers. They have an excellent place on the British side, Port San Juan, to have a station there, they have another place inside of Bamfield.[6]

The only dissenter was the lone Canadian government witness, Phil Daykin. As far as he was concerned, with an experienced crew he could easily have picked everyone off the *Valencia* and brought them to shore and safety. "Have you considerable experience in the surf?" the incredulous investigator asked. "I have, ever since I could walk pretty well," Daykin replied. It would have been no more difficult than going out for mail and supplies from Carmanah.

It would never be the same after *Valencia*. The humiliation of being called to account in a foreign country, of having their noses rubbed by the press in the consequences of their "cruel" economy, must have been agonizing for Anderson and his fellow politicos in Ottawa.

The Canadian government appointed its own, rather lame commission of enquiry into the *Valencia* tragedy, headed by James Gaudin, on 5 February 1906. A month later the *Vancouver Province* revealed the commissioners' findings and recommendations, which were then "in the hands of the Minister." Unfortunately, there is no way of knowing where the report went after Louis Brodeur read it. No copy has survived.

The *Province* reported that, "owing to nearly all the officers of the *Valencia* having been lost," the commissioners confessed they were unable to determine "whether the present aids to navigation on the west coast [were] sufficient to prevent a recurrence of other accidents under similar circumstances."[7] This was a deliberate smokescreen. Gaudin had surveyed facilities at Anderson's behest twelve years before, and had found them lacking. Even if one concedes a failing or faulty memory to a man carrying the can for the department, anyone who had read the U.S. report, or even the Seattle papers knew the whole story from surviving officers like Peterson, who had stood at Johnson's side in the wheelhouse that fateful night. Indeed, twenty-six officers and crew *had* survived, along with only eleven passengers. All the women had perished—a result which sparked early rumours "that Americans forgot their manhood and left the women and children to their fate"; rumours quickly retracted when the women's hysterical refusals to quit the wreck were fully documented.[8]

Even so, the Canadian commissioners' recommendations certainly dispelled the last lingering notions that existing aids were in any way adequate. They called for a new light and fog alarm on Pachena Point near the site of the wreck, and another at Sheringham Point in the Strait between Carmanah and Race Rocks, in addition to improvements at Carmanah, a fog alarm and more powerful beacon for Cape Beale, and "first order lights and fog alarms on the more prominent headlands from Triangle Island (Scott Islands) to Lennard Island." At long last they insisted that "self-propelling, self-righting and self-bailing lifeboats" be stationed at Bamfield and further north at Ucluelet. The commissioners also recommended upgrading and extending the West Coast Trail from Port San Juan all the way through to Cape Beale, with huts equipped with provisions and wireless sets six miles apart. The trail was to be patrolled by full-time linemen "at least once a day in all sorts of weather."

Five months passed. While Minister of Marine and Fisheries Brodeur, and Anderson, chairman of the lighthouse board, brooded over the costs of their commission's recommendations, James Gaudin underwent the humiliation of apologizing for their foot-dragging in Victoria. Hunkering down under the poisonous fallout of public outrage, the beleaguered agent warned Anderson, "The public generally blame the Department that work has not been started." Templeman, the acting minister, had better get home fast and mend fences. And when he did, Gaudin forecast, "Such pressure will be brought to bear on him that he will be compelled to give some reason why his pre-election promises of last winter are not carried out."[9]

The British Columbia Board of Trade, which politicians ignored at their peril, was adamant that the telegraph trail be extended all the way through from Carmanah to Cape Beale. Gaudin subtly turned the screws ever tighter. In August he wrote directly to Deputy Minister Gourdeau, recommending the telegraph trail be extended at once beyond Carmanah to the proposed lighthouse at Pachena Point, a link which would prove an "immense benefit in the recurrence of a similar accident to that of the *Valencia*." If the Canadian government balked at that, the agent blithely offered to apply instead to the province to complete the trail.

W.P. Daykin, who had long fancied himself the *Colonist*'s "West Coast correspondent," telegraphed his editor in August with a "scoop"—a macabre postscript to the *Valencia*'s demise. A party of beachcombing Indians had discovered a cave somewhere down the coast with its mouth high above the tide line. They clambered up and peered inside. There was a sharp drop beyond its mouth. A fetid stench rose up from the cave, along with the patter of hundreds of fleeing paws. When their eyes grew accustomed to the Stygian gloom they saw a white boat lying down there in a pool of stagnant water. It bore the name *Valencia* on its bow and was manned by skeletons, all a-quiver with layer upon layer of maggots.

Sputtering with rage, Gaudin slammed the paper down on his desk and roared for his secretary. Twice already he had ordered Daykin to cease sending his damned "telegraphic news to the local press." Of all things he had to dredge up the *Valencia*! "This official has been besieged since the news you published in the newspapers," he snarled, "it places this Office in ridicule, that a subordinate should spread or broadcast such reports as those recently published in the local press."[10] This time he had gone too far, and the agent intended to report his conduct to the department. Daykin might well have laughed off that threat, knowing that the department would face no end of problems enticing someone to take *his* place.

By summer's end the mood in Victoria had turned downright ugly. The *Colonist*'s editor captured it in an article decrying the delay. Though stopping just short of naming Anderson, he printed a rumour that "one of the permanent officials of the Department" had the nerve to suggest on his last visit that Victorians "were a good deal carried away by sentiment" in their "demands for appropriations." True or false, "the Department has acted very much as if it thought we were," the editor charged, "for a summer has been allowed to pass and very little has been accomplished."

He exhorted his readers (and voters) to demand their MPs give some rational account of why officials, who defied public opinion "with impunity," had delayed

Last liferaft of the *Valencia*.

or defeated "well considered plans pressed with so much earnestness . . . and proved necessary by more than one tragedy of the sea."

It is no answer to say that this, that or the other official reported so and so. Official inspections on a fine summer day from the comfortable deck of a government vessel which dodges into port "whenever the breezes blow" give a very poor idea of the conditions to be encountered by mariners during winter storms and of the sufferings certain to overwhelm those who escape the merciless sea only to be cast upon a merciless shore. We look to our representatives to protect our interests and to remove the reproach arising from insufficient coast protection, and they will not be allowed to take shelter behind official indifference.[11]

There was only one consolation coming from Ottawa: Captain J.W. Troup, head of Canadian Pacific Steamships, had just been appointed to the Lighthouse Board, an occasion of "very great satisfaction for shipping men" and the general public. Now an eyewitness to the loathesome spectacle at Pachena Point was about to entrain for Ottawa to take his seat at the same table as Anderson. Troup was a man of boundless influence, "able to present the case in a manner that will command attention." Needless to say, he would also present the CPR's demands with similar gusto. The lobbyist who had hovered so long in the corridors of power was through the door at last, within easy reach of the levers which drove the Department of Marine and Fisheries.

The combination of the festering mood of the public, the intransigence of the Victoria Board of Trade, Gaudin's hint of humiliation, and Troup's appointment all served to spring the lock on the Treasury.

But the *Valencia* continued to haunt the coast. Four years later the *Seattle Times* printed accounts from "sailors on vessels frequently in and out of the Cape," who swore they had seen a phantom ship which seemed to dog their course. "They said it resembled the ill-fated *Valencia*...and that they could vaguely see human forms clinging to her masts and rigging." The *Valencia*, it seemed, was assuming a place in seamen's overripe imaginations akin to the *Flying Dutchman*. In 1933 a more tangible ghost was found adrift in Barkley Sound: her old No. 5 lifeboat with its paint still in prime condition after a quarter century.

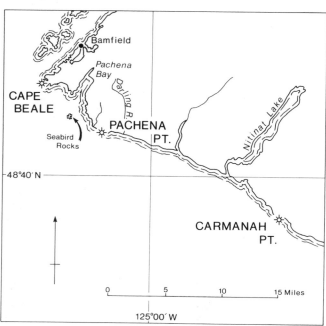

Pachena

The lighthouse and fog alarm at Pachena Point would be a marker over the *Valencia*'s grave, linked by telegraph and trail to Carmanah, then through Cape Beale to the new lifesaving station at Bamfield. Full-time linemen would patrol the length of the trail as lookouts, charged with maintaining the shelter shacks and getting word out fast over the wires in the event of the dreaded "similar accident."

Pachena was not to be graced by one of Anderson's concrete sculptures. There was no sand nearby, and the site itself was too precarious, a hundred feet up. In February 1907 a landslide swept away "the work of weeks." The dispirited construction crew salvaged lumber, surveyed a second site, and began all over again. By late May the tower had been completed, treated with linseed oil, and given its first of many coats of white paint. The *Cascade* was bound up the coast with more lumber for the fog alarm building. By mid-summer Montgomery, chief engineer of the Victoria agency, had installed the engines and run them in. In January 1908 a signal mast was erected. John S. Richardson, Pachena's keeper, received a set of flags and a Commercial Code Signal Book, along with instructions to answer signals from passing vessels and to report their movements and messages to Victoria three times a day. He also unpacked a Lyle gun, its shells, and lines to be "kept in readiness to be used in case of shipwreck." Gaudin promised to ship Richardson's piano up with the remainder of the lantern apparatus.

Up in the tower technicians painstakingly pieced together the very latest lens of dioptric design, a monster even larger than Lennard's light, which shot a four million candle power beam through its crystals out to sea, visible from Carmanah fifteen miles east and Cape Beale six miles west. With its lens floating on a nine-hundred-pound mercury bath, the Pachena assembly weighed all of thirty-eight tons and was featured as an illustration in that year's *Encyclopedia Britannica*. "Its light will...extend beyond lights on all those points," the *Victoria Times* boasted, "and as a guidance for navigators entering the straits is unexcelled." When the beacon was lit up for the first time after nightfall on 21 May lightkeepers *thirty-five miles east*, at Tatoosh on the American side, were astonished to see the flash, and radioed their congratulations to Gaudin in Victoria.

Richardson was a bachelor. His sister Gertrude came up to Pachena with him as an assistant. By the autumn of 1908 she began to succumb to their racking solitude, "suffering from strange hallucinations." On 1 November she fell in the tower "and struck her head badly." Richardson wired Victoria seeking permission to take her home to England. "It would have been necessary for me to go with her as she was in no condition to travel alone," he explained, asking for three months' leave. It wouldn't be necessary after all. She found a faster way out.

"On Saturday morning she was somewhat depressed, so I took her with me to the engine house so that I could chat to her while I was cleaning things up there," he wrote Gaudin ruefully on 6 November. "As soon as we reached the wooden steps she darted from me and jumped over the cliff just against the lower derrick. Her action took me completely by surprise as I never had any reason to fear such an action on her part. She fell on her head and was instantly killed." Richardson clambered down the rocks after her, knelt down, and felt in vain for signs of life. "The sea was too rough to land at the Point," he continued, "and as we had many kind offers of help we carried her remains over the trail to Bamfield and I am going to bury her in Alberni tomorrow."[1] Richardson could not bear to return to Pachena, and Gaudin wrote Sloan, the local MP, lamenting the loss of "a good and faithful servant."

The records of Pachena after Richardson's tragedy are fragmentary. None of the lightkeepers' logs prior to 1923 have been found. A man named Irwin replaced Richardson and it was he who, in 1909, witnessed the long-anticipated "similar accident," and set the elaborate new West Coast lifesaving network into motion.

If ever a man had ample reason to be chary of misreading the West Coast lights, it was Captain Charles Henningsen. Ten years before, at the helm of the 273-ton barkentine *Uncle John*, he mistook Cape Beale for Carmanah and swung round to enter the Strait, realizing his folly only when the sea-roar of the breakers came at him out of the darkness. He dropped both anchors. The tumultuous groaning sea soon snapped their chains and bore the *Uncle John* up on the rocky shore.

That time, though, luck had been with him. The first lifeboat lowered was smashed against the hull, spilling out its occupants, but all scrambled back aboard. The swift tide dragged *Uncle John* along over the rocks and finally lodged her up on an outcropping. Her crew had only to slide down ropes and spent the night shivering on the rock. Next morning a sailor swam ashore with a rope around his waist, rigged a block and pulley, and all hands were hauled ashore. The captain of the *Willapa* spotted the wreck and their signal fires three days later and flew signals for them to hike to Clo-oose where he took them aboard.

But in January 1909, almost three years to the day after the *Valencia*'s luck ran out, Henningsen's left him. He had a much larger and finer vessel under his command this time—a stately four-masted coaster of 767 tons called *Soquel*. Only seven years old, she might more aptly have been christened *"Sequel."* Incomprehensible as it may seem, with four lights burning now between Flattery and Cape Beale, each with its unique sequence of flashes and horns shown clearly on his charts, Henningsen steered once again between Carmanah and Cape Beale,

Above: Bamfield Lifeboat.
Below: West Coast Telegraph Trail near Pachena Point.

on a collision course for Seabird Rocks, only a few miles from his earlier wreck.

He may have been distracted since this voyage was something of a celebration: his last. Upon his return he would be home to stay, so he had brought his wife and child with him. They were sleeping soundly below decks when the collision jarred them from their bunks. Henningsen came below and advised them to stay put until he had a damage report, but his wife wrapped their three-year-old daughter in a blanket and climbed topside a few minutes later. Henningsen ordered a lifeboat cleared and helped her in. "This is death," she wailed. "Kiss me, Carl."

A week later there was hardly a dry eye behind the *Colonist* when Victorians read its account of what happened next: Henningsen

> took the child and held it in his arms, while the pounding of the seas and the whistling of the wind through the cordage accompanied by sharp reports as the sails snapped drowned the voices of those who shouted all manner of commands as they ran about the decks. Then the mizzen and jigger masts snapped and came down with a crash. The big spar fell on. . .the little girl, knocking her from her father's arms, while he was knocked to the deck with a badly bruised back. As he scrambled to his feet, he saw the end of the big spar fall across the lifeboat striking his wife. He ran to her just in time to see her expire.[2]

Henningsen was useless after that. Doubled over in pain, he wandered the decks wailing, wringing his hands, his bleak and undone mind in a daze. The first mate, C.E. Svenson, quickly took command and brought order out of the bedlam. He ordered five crewmen to help him launch the captain's gig and they pulled away, tossed like a peanut shell in the surf. The little boat flooded, but before it sank the swell carried it up onto a reef halfway to the shore. Back on the ship it seemed like suicide to press their luck and launch another boat. The remaining crewmen scrambled up the rigging. "She's going any moment!" sailor John Herman hollered. "I'm not going to drown like a rat when I can make a fight of it! Who's with us?" He and another sailor straddled the spinnaker and inched their way along. Before they could jump onto the reef a giant comber careened broadside into the *Soquel*. Her mast splintered and they fell to the deck. Herman's leg snapped under him.

Svenson and his mates managed to light a fire over on the reef. Lightkeeper Irwin spotted the feeble light and ran up the tower with his spyglass. In that wild pre-dawn blizzard it was like deja-vu: a ship impaled on storm-swept rocks, with men writhing and screaming in the ratlines. He bolted for the telephone, turned the crank, and put all the post-*Valencia* preparations to their first great test.

Irwin's distress call went up the wire through Carmanah and Cape Beale to Bamfield. Shaken awake, the lifeboat crew and its leader, Captain W.H. Gillen, pulled their lifejackets, gum boots, and slickers over their longjohns. Their motorized surf boat had been wrecked only days before so they jogged down to the

Wreck of the *Soquel* on Seabird Rocks January, 1909.

Leebro, lying at anchor with full steam up. Captain James Hunter made straight for the wreck and ordered an eighteen-foot boat swung out for Gillen and his men. They pulled away to the wreck, disappeared down the troughs between the roller-coaster swells, then shot up their crests trying to find water with their oars as the *Leebro*'s crew leaned breathless on the rails. But muscle was no match for that high running sea. Gillen ordered them back.

The CPR's *Tees* came steaming up at two o'clock and Gillen went over the side again with his crew in *Leebro*'s number two boat. They tied their boat to one of the *Tees*' boats and, with half the crew in each, set adrift downwind for the Seabird Rocks, keeping a line to the larger ship. This time the surf swamped clear over the gunwales of one boat and capsized it. Some of the crewmen were hauled back aboard the *Tees*. The remaining crew bailed it out, then went out a third time.

This time they swept in close enough to the reef to cast a line over to the five men and haul them out. They shouted out there was no way to come alongside the wreck until the sea ran down, but Svenson steadfastly refused to budge until all his mates had been taken off the battered *Soquel*. The rescuers tossed some provisions over to the plucky Swede. Throughout the day he shouted encouragement to the seamen hanging above him. The *Leebro* followed in the *Tees*' wake back to Bamfield at nightfall.

As darkness fell the six men left aboard huddled against a gunwale out of the spray. The wind roaring through the crosstrees was punctuated by Herman's howls of pain, Henningsen's hysterical keening, and Svenson's exhortations to keep their courage up as he squatted beside his fire on the reef. Suddenly they were bathed in a blinding light and stood up to see the U.S. revenue cutter *Manning* lying off them, plying her searchlights over the listing *Soquel*. It was a welcome relief from their desolation and quelled their despair of ever seeing the lifeboat again.

Sunday morning the tide ran out. Looking over to Svenson on the reef, the remaining crew concluded that if the lifeboat had plucked four mates off it the day before, it could surely save them all today. They clambered down the hull and waded over, dragging Herman and Henningsen with them. The lifeboat came back and took them aboard. In Victoria the *Colonist* heralded this first test of the West Coast's lifesaving network:

> They waited confidently feeling that rescue was certain when the lifesavers returned. Not far away lay the wreck with the mizzen and jigger gone, the standing yards away. . . listed with spray breaking over as the seas pounded the impaled craft. Nearer the two boats lifted and fell in the long-lipped waves, standing in as close as possible while one by one the eager lifesavers hauled the worn-out seamen. . . from the rock. One moaned with pain of his broken leg, another lay helpless in the bottom of the boat with a badly bruised back; all were worn to exhaustion."[3]

But all, save Henningsen's wife and daughter, were alive and safe. The investment in the Pachena light, the wireless, and the surf boat had reaped its first great dividend.

Richard Clark came to Pachena after Irwin left for the trenches in 1918. G.A. Couldery took over from him in May 1919. Wishart, postmaster at Bamfield, and many other citizens of the outport resented the appointment of this "outsider" over one of their own. Right from the beginning they made life miserable for the new keeper. "For the sake of peace, I have overlooked more than anyone could believe a *man* could stand," Couldery grumbled to Wilby. "The task here has been tough enough in all conscience without this continual undercurrent of enmity." Wishart, who was also a lineman, packed mail in for the wireless operators at Pachena but spitefully refused to carry Couldery's letters, claiming he wasn't paid "for carrying any but the wireless' mail anyhow." Couldery fumed, "I shall have to take this & the other letters myself tomorrow & I have enough to do without a 21 mile walk added to it."

In June 1921 Couldery was greasing the aerial hoist when he heard his wife's screams up at the house. He turned, saw a pillar of smoke coiling up, and came on the run. His wife pulled up her skirts and dashed over to the wireless shack, returning with the operators who found Couldery throwing buckets of water through the kitchen window, the house "a mass of flames." For twenty minutes the Pachena crew fought a one-sided battle against the hungry fire, then retreated to protect the other buildings. The Coulderys were ruined. They had been unable

Landing supplies at Pachena Point.

to purchase insurance due to "the large quantity of inflammable material which was kept by the Government in proximity to the house."[4]

A. Gorden replaced the Coulderys. Can openers were indispensable in those days before refrigeration. When Gorden took one and wound it around the lip of a tin on 25 June, he had no inkling anything was wrong until he doubled over hours later in the throes of ptomaine poisoning. The *Estevan*, alerted by the radio operators, called and took the stricken keeper away to Port Alberni. Dr. C.T. Hilton (who diagnosed Gorden's symptoms as "Abdominal Influenza. . . aggravated by some canned stuff he had been eating") discharged him from hospital though his patient was "still weak," and his hands had not "recovered their normal tone." Gorden died two days later. Trowsdale, one of the radio operators, wrote Wilby to ask that he send up a cook since none of the men at Pachena could "bake bread or even cook properly for themselves." He also needed "some Cabbage & other Vegetables to help out the potatoes," because "there was a lot of waste due to them being bad."[5]

In February 1925 Marine Agent Wilby laid down precise instructions for co-ordinating lifesaving services along the West Coast. All that outlay for men and equipment would be wasted without a "regular or fixed procedure as to taking advantage of this communication." Pachena would be the nerve centre, the brains of the entire apparatus, since the light was in communication with Carmanah, Cape Beale, and the lifesaving stations at Bamfield and Clayoquot, as well as having a direct link to "officials controlling the situation in Victoria." Wilby ordered the keepers and coxswains to notify Pachena's officer-in-charge "on receiving any sort of notification of trouble." Then the lightkeepers would dispatch patrolmen to the scene. The lifesaving stations were to advise Pachena of any action taken.

Jack Hunting, Pachena's keeper, translated Wilby's orders into a set of "Instructions to Patrolmen" in 1931, headed "Please keep these instructions clean and for future reference":

> Whenever stormy weather prevails carry out work in the vicinity of some method of communication and report to me daily, should the telegraph line be down report to the lightstation without delay. In cases of vessels appearing to be in distress, drop whatever work is in hand and notify me without delay. If in the case of Hillis, the telegraph line is broken *WEST* of him, try and get in touch with the lightkeeper at Carmanah, asking him to forward information to Pachena by radio.
>
> In the case of patrolman Macdonald should there be a break *EAST* report at once to the lifeboat station, and inform me also by radio, in cases of emergency patrolmen must at all times act quickly and make sure their reports are understood correctly.

Hunting's instructions reflected the West Coast lifesaving network at the peak of its effectiveness. With six lighthouses and fog horns scattered over 180 miles from Pachena to Kains Island, two lifesaving stations at Bamfield and Tofino, and regular foot patrols, the "graveyard of the Pacific," which Captain Johnson had blundered into with the *Valencia* nearly forty years before, had been transformed. If anyone ever questioned the necessity of all the expense, the war offered ample justification.

The whole West Coast was ordered blacked out after two vessels shelled the lighthouse on Estevan Point in June 1941. From Pachena to Kains Island keepers climbed the stairs and drew the drapes, turning the clock back seventy years. Then they set to work at a heart-rending chore: painting over their white and red trimmed buildings with a hideous coat of camouflage grey-green. This was a curious strategy at best; it had long been one of warfare's unwritten laws to use enemy aids to navigation. The American lights remained in operation so, once past Flattery, shipping faced the same blind peril that had struck terror into its ancestors.

Hunting and the others at Pachena were quickly caught up in the carefully orchestrated post-Estevan hysteria. In May 1942 Hunting got wind of a proposal to organize a local militia and coast-watching service to be dubbed the Rangers. He wrote Hartnell, Wilby's temporary successor, asking to be included. "I have a very good 30-30 Savage rifle," he boasted, "and I think I know this part of the country as good as anyone. . . ." He and the operators had already assembled a motley arsenal of shotguns and a 25-20 rifle, "all of which would give a very good account of itself. . . to take care of enemy infiltration parties."

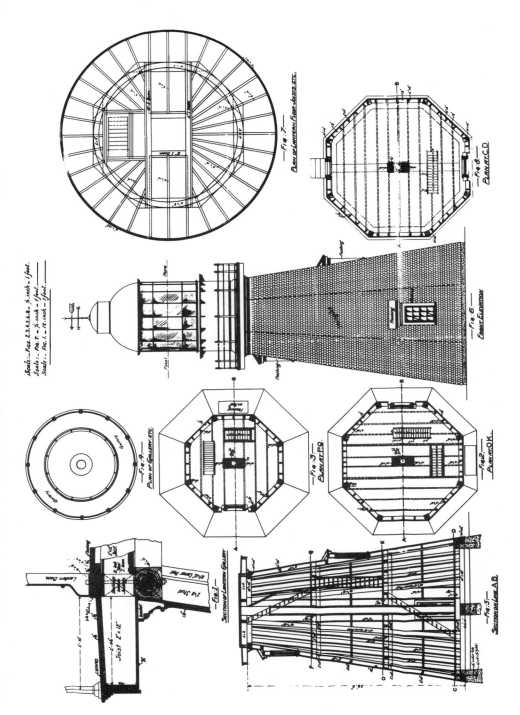

1908 plans for Pachena Point Light, the only wooden tower still serving in 1985.

Infiltration parties would have been somewhat conspicuous—the only Japanese on the coast after the forced evacuations of the previous year. Nevertheless, by October the men had joined the British Columbia Militia Rangers and had set about playing at war. They were issued 30.06 rifles and bayonets as well as a Sten gun which Hunting appropriated, keeping it always "at hand and ready to use." The lightkeeper planned to muster his battalion soon "for some practice with the arms... supplied, and," he said, "we hope to become an efficient group." Though it's doubtful that Canadians slept much easier knowing the fearless band of Rangers stood guard against Axis hordes night and day, Jack Hunting certainly performed sterling service as an aircraft observer and was awarded a plaque after the war for his diligence in reporting aircraft movements.

In April 1943 the war finally came to Pachena with the fearsome pounding of deck guns and star-shells ripping through the night sky. It was no party of crack Jap commandos but some of "our guys"—a bizarre and befuddled crew of Russian men, women, and hogs who stormed ashore a mile east of Pachena. Though originally of Russian registry, the SS *Uzbekistan* was part of the vast armada of Liberty Ships slipping out of U.S. shipyards and ports to convoy Lend Lease supplies to the Soviet Union. Japan and the Soviet Union were not yet at war, and *Uzbekistan*'s hatchcovers were painted a brilliant red and white, with her name and "USSR" displayed prominently for the benefit of Japanese and American pilots hungry for targets.[6]

The 3039-ton freighter left Astoria on 1 April 1943, bound for Seattle to take on Lend Lease supplies for a run to Vladivostok. At 10:25 p.m. her watch officer mistook the Swiftsure Bank lightship for the Umatilla Reef light which was twenty-six miles astern, and her navigators overshot the Juan de Fuca mouth.

It was the same old mistake which had claimed so many ships and men. If Carmanah and Pachena had been alight, it would have been unthinkable. *Uzbekistan* plowed on through a forty-five knot gale, headed straight for the West Coast, her officers on the bridge oblivious to imminent disaster. At 11:10 the watch officer shouted down to the captain in the chartroom that he could make out a broken white line off to starboard. By the time the captain's eyes grew accustomed to the darkness and he heard the breakers, it was too late. He ordered the ship swung over, but *Uzbekistan* rammed the reef broadside. She was hoisted up and impaled by the swells.

The captain ordered all speed astern but the screws failed to shift the wreck. Water was already flooding the engine room. Seven minutes later the first distress call went out:

SOS SOS SOS FROM UVBY UVBY FLATTERY FLATTERY RKS FLATTERY RKS ALL STATIONS ALL STATIONS ALL STATIONS ALL STATIONS FROM UVBY UVBY UVBY SOS SOS SOS POSITION POSITION FLATTERY FLATTERY FLATTERY RKS SOS SOS UZBEKISTAN SOS SOS SOS SOS UVBY UVBY UVBY

But *Uzbekistan* was far northwest of Cape Flattery—pinioned off the mouth of the Darling River, a mere mile-and-a-half southeast of Pachena. Her distress call was immediately received and re-broadcast by radio operators at the Estevan Point light. The U.S. Coast Guard cutter *Wellwood* veered away from her patrol in the Strait, steered at once for Flattery, and searched in vain for the wreck.

Uzbekistan's crew elected to remain on board in spite of the swells clobbering her exposed starboard beam. The ship pivoted about on the rock, sending shudders along her entire beam, grinding plates and rivets. Seven hours of darkness stretched before them and the Russians clung to the hope that rescuers would surely spot them at sun-up. A naval lieutenant went aft with his gun crew and they began sliding three-inch shells into the breach, firing at random, sending off flares as well. MacDonald, the wireless operator at Pachena, had been monitoring the distress signal out of curiosity, unaware that it came from just below on the rocks. Suddenly he was jarred by the boom of the stern gun and its whistling shells. The lineman at Clo-oose, eleven miles south, could plainly see and hear the fireworks. He immediately rang up the lighthouse.

At Pachena they had no way of knowing the firing originated from *Uzbekistan*, supposedly aground down at Flattery. The Clo-oose lineman concluded that either another vessel was in distress or the Japanese had landed at last. He left Clo-oose with his son and brother-in-law, headed west. Following the same trail Daykin and the others took to the *Valencia* thirty-seven years before, they forded the Nitinat River and made their way to the steep banks of the Klanawa. MacDonald pulled himself across on the block chair; the others hiked back to the Tsusiat line cabin, planning to cross the swollen river by raft at dawn.

Meanwhile the operators at Pachena concluded that the gunfire originated from the Russian ship, and sent out a message giving her true position. The *Wellwood* made full steam for Pachena and came across *Uzbekistan* at 4:30 a.m. There was no possibility of coming alongside in the heavy swell, and *Uzbekistan* signaled that all her crew were now safely ashore. As the tide receded the captain had ordered a lifeboat lowered halfway down. His crew climbed into the boat, then down a rope ladder onto the rocks. They stood marooned on a flat shelf of rock, 150 yards from a beach littered with driftwood. The Russians lit a fire on the sand and began transferring supplies from their ship. At last the captain realized his position, so far from Cape Flattery.

MacDonald had been on the trail five hours. At 5:00 a.m., just as the sun began to illuminate the muddy sky, he topped the bluffs overlooking the Tscowis River, at one end of a suspension bridge. From there he could make out the *Uzbekistan* and the ant-like activity around her, nearly two miles away. He crossed the precarious bridge, went into the lineman's cabin at the north end, and rang up Pachena to relieve their fears of an enemy landing. After catching his breath, changing clothes, and wolfing down some of the rations stored there for ship-wrecked sailors, he hiked to the beach and shook hands with the Russians. Fortunately, the captain and some of the officers had a smattering of English and

Pachena Point Lightstation from the air, 1981. Jim Ryan photo.

the lineman managed to make them understand the lighthouse lay only two miles above and beyond the beach.

The tide was turning against them but the Soviet seamen had already carried away a supply of food, pots and pans, blankets, and their squealing pigs. They squatted around their roaring fire, sipping tea and watching the action offshore. The *Estevan* had joined the *Wellwood*, and RCAF planes made repeated overflights. The *Estevan* was by far the best equipped and most experienced vessel to undertake a landing, and her captain had made more landings at Pachena than any other officer on the coast. However, the wind was picking up, so he recommended that *Uzbekistan*'s crew be relieved overland from the lighthouse. Then the Canadian navy entered the drama.

Maritime Command in Victoria ordered the minesweeper HMCS *Outarde* to supervise the rescue operations. Breaking off her patrol in the Straits, she arrived off Pachena at 4:30 p.m., ordered the *Estevan* to stand clear, then sent off a lifeboat manned by a crew of eight men under command of a lieutenant. The lighthouse tender's crew shook their heads in disbelief as the whaler was swept past the stranded ship and hurled up on the rocks. The Russians ran over, tossed a line to their would-be rescuers, and pulled them ashore. They took their places around the fire with the Russians, then climbed up to Pachena to stay with the Huntings.

By five o'clock the tide was ebbing again and the Russians began transferring more stores from their ship. By this time *Uzbekistan* was well flooded and her keel broken. Bulkheads were buckling. The captain returned from Pachena after sending messages and stared sullenly out at his captive and crippled ship. Moscow would not be impressed. After a merry chase, the crew caught and slaughtered one of the pigs and were in high spirits at their impromptu barbecue.

Sated and relieved by their good fortune, the Soviets bundled themselves up and fell asleep. At dawn they began transferring more cargo. Later that day orders came for them to hike to Bamfield. The three-man naval guard that accompanied them was no more familiar with the trail than the Russians. The Pachena people watched the shipwrecked sailors tramp past the light, loaded down with personal possessions and other gear, most of which was cast aside within the first mile as they began to wrestle with the West Coast trail in a bout that went on for twelve miles.

They rendezvoused with HMCS *Allaverdy* at five o'clock. The patrol vessel carried them up the inlet and transferred the Russians to the *Outarde*, which set out at once for Port Angeles. While his seamen entertained their Canadian comrades down in the mess with an accordion, the captain, in halting English, soundly denounced his allies for blacking out their lights, and "commented on the difference between the American and Canadian practice at the time in this regard."[7]

On the beach near Pachena a three-man army party stood guard over the haphazard heap of supplies which included guns and ammunition. Five more soldiers from the Edmonton Fusiliers, under command of a sergeant deputized as Deputy Receiver of Wrecks, came up to Pachena, passing the exhausted Russians on the trail headed for Bamfield. They were later joined for a time by the B.C. Provincial Police. The police left 9 April and the soldiers began carrying the material up to the lightstation where Hunting put it under lock and key.

When her captain and crew returned to the wreck on 27 April, they were appalled to find that much of their ammunition had been fired at the ship. Someone had vandalized her interior and made off with fittings and personal property. Soviet authorities lodged a formal complaint with Ottawa while the sailors set about salvaging what little of value remained on board. Naval intelligence officers investigated the Russians' charges and concluded in their official report "that there was definite indication of improper conduct on the part of military personnel attending the wreck during the period the guard and carrying party were stationed there."

On 5 August a military court of inquiry convened at Esquimalt to investigate thefts, shooting, drunkenness, and other un-soldierly conduct at Pachena. Testimony revealed a carnival atmosphere at the site, with army and civilians alike using the ship for target practice while soldiers sold booty plundered from the wreck.

The *Uzbekistan* affair was a shabby footnote in Canadian military history. The *Outarde* had made a stupid spectacle of the navy by disdaining the *Estevan*'s advice and ordering her away, very nearly losing a boat's crew which had to be rescued by the very men they sought to save. The army party had behaved like a band of pirates. Both services must have been very grateful indeed that wartime censorship confined details of the scandal to a few citizens along the West Coast, who had souvenirs of Soviet Russia in their parlours.

But aside from revealing the ineptitude of the army and navy, the *Uzbekistan*, as it reeled and broke up before the surf on the reef off Pachena, underscored Gaudin's fifty-year-old claim that lighthouses and fog alarms were the keys to safe navigation.

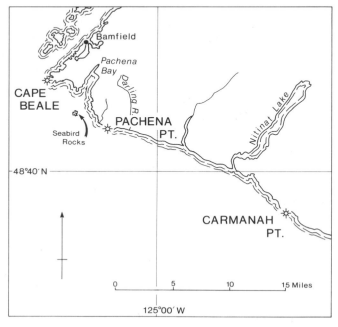

Above: Dioptric lens at Sheringham Point. Jim Ryan photo.

Amphitrite

Whenever seamen gathered in smoky fo'c'sles from Singapore to San Francisco, hunched in their slickers or hammocks under lanterns swaying eerily with the swells, they muttered ominously about the hazards of the "Horn," the Cape of Good Hope, and Vancouver Island's West Coast. And after Christmas Day 1905 they spoke in fearful urgency about the fate of the *Pass of Melfort* off Amphitrite Point at the northern entrance to Barkley Sound.

Autumn 1905 was bleak indeed for the ship's owners. Steamships were elbowing sail aside all over the world's sea lanes with the bullying force of superior technology. The *Melfort*'s master whiled away the torrid days and sweltering nights drunk in his cabin, and the 2341-ton steel bark sulked in her moorings at Panama, each day draining dollars away from her anxious owners. In desperation they approached Captain Scougall, a fifty-five-year-old retired veteran, settled at last into his own family and business affairs ashore. They implored him to sail the ship out of her doldrums. Scougall, "a kindly man of friendly disposition," agreed to take on one last voyage "out of consideration for his former employers." Like the road to Hell, his course to Amphitrite Point was paved with good intentions.

With Scougall at her wheel, *Pass of Melfort* weighed anchor and slipped through the locks, bound for Port Townsend in Washington with her thirty-five crewmen and a load of ballast. Captain Olsen of the *Broderick Castle* overtook her off southern California thirty-eight days later. "Whither bound?" he signalled, and advised he was himself headed for Puget Sound. Arriving in the Sound in a fearful storm, Olsen was surprised to miss the *Pass of Melfort*. "We must have been near each other during that storm off Juan de Fuca Strait," he later speculated. Olsen, however, was far too preoccupied with saving his own ship, "the toughest bit of sailing he had ever done."

As for the *Pass of Melfort*, she was swept helplessly northward, past Carmanah, Cape Beale, then beyond the curtain of darkness, driven remorselessly by the same monstrous seas which Frank Garrard and the stranded construction crew watched scouring the reefs off Lennard Island.

Amphitrite Light, like many on west coast, was built under trying conditions.

On Christmas Eve, Indians saw distress rockets arc and blossom in their dreadful, haunting brilliance across the blackened sky over the Uncluth Peninsula on the north shore of Barkley Sound. They pushed their dugouts into the raging waters and paddled along the shore to the village of Ucluelet to report a ship aground. Next morning all that remained was a sad, surging flotsam borne against the ramshackle lookout station at Amphitrite Point. Picking their way along the rocky shore, searchers found two bruised and torn bodies among the shattered hatches, fittings, furniture, and sea chests, and soon abandoned hope of ever finding more. W.H. Lyche, lineman at Ucluelet, tapped out the grim news to Captain Gaudin down at the marine department in Victoria:

VESSEL WENT ASHORE LAST NIGHT QUARTER MILE EAST OF AMPHITRITE POINT. ONE BODY RECOVERED DRESSED IN OIL-SKINS AND OVERALLS; TWO MORE WASHING IN THE SURF BUT IMPOSSIBLE TO REACH THEM. SEVERAL SHIP'S BUCKETS MARKED PASS OF MELFORT, A BAROMETER, SOME CABIN WRECKAGE, SMASHED BOATS, A WOODEN FIGUREHEAD OF A WOMAN PAINTED WHITE AND MUCH WRECKAGE IN ROCKY BAY. OPINION VESSEL VERY CLOSE TO SHORE. TWO SPARS VISIBLE WASHING ABOUT, EVIDENTLY ANCHORED. EVERY-THING POSSIBLE BEING DONE TO RECOVER BODIES.[1]

Like all mystery wrecks, the *Pass of Melfort* gave vent to an endless round of speculation which swept through harbour bars and ships' chandlers as every armchair sea-captain charted a better course with a gnarled, insistent finger

Amphitrite tower rising, 1914.

across the squeaky trail of beer on his table. Yet even ignorance can give birth to consensus if it labours long and hard enough. The influential Seattle sea captain E. Cantrillion expressed it best when he pointed to the lack of accurate charts, lighthouses, and lifesaving stations north of Cape Beale. As the lights crept up the coast they only pointed the finger to peril; each argued for the next, further west and north.

Captain Hackett of the *Quadra* steamed out of Victoria on the morning of 15 June with whistle fog alarms—"the first on the British Columbia Coast," costing "several thousand dollars"—to be installed at a new lighthouse on Amphitrite Point and at the existing lights on Lennard and Egg Islands. The *Colonist* advised that tenders would shortly be called for the construction of boilers and machinery at the new light over the *Pass of Melfort*'s tomb.

Lying off the north entrance to Ucluelet Harbour, the Point was named by Captain Richards of HMS *Plumper* for HM frigate *Amphitrite*. In late January 1906 Colonel Anderson authorized Gaudin to build a wooden tower on the outermost high rock at the point, a place "marked by a bunch of shrubbery and separated from the mainland by a gorge" that required bridging. A Wigham 31-day lamp with three wicks was installed. The Wigham lamp was an ingenious device. Mounted upon a full drum of kerosene, a belt wick driven by clockwork fed continuously into the flame. The coxswain of the lifeboat stationed at Ucluelet undertook to examine the lamp, top up its fuel, and change wicks. "The new lamp. . . should prove of incalculable value to a vessel drifting in close to the island shore on such a night as the one in which the *Pass of Melfort* went to her doom," the *Victoria Times* predicted.

The arrangement lasted eight years. On 2 January 1914 a tidal wave swept through the gorge and demolished the tower. *Princess Maquinna* radioed Victoria with the news: LIGHTHOUSE WASHED AWAY ON AMPHITRITE POINT YESTERDAY AND DRIFTED TO SEA. Next night a lantern was hung from the lookout station above and behind the bare rock.

In April the Ucluelet Development League sent a petition signed by six sea captains off to Victoria, requesting that the government "immediately erect an up-to-date lighthouse, a wireless station and a fog alarm at or near Amphitrite Point." It was obvious to all concerned, from subsistence fishermen on up to Anderson himself, that a permanent structure was necessary. The project would be a windfall to Ucluelet, a pioneer venture in "pump priming" public works. The village was one of those backward communities scattered along the West Coast, marginal and depressed, where residents eked out a stark, precarious living by fishing, trapping, and waiting. In the winter of 1914 William Thompson, coxswain of the lifeboat, wrote Marine Agent Robertson a letter that laid bare Ucluelet's grim social order.

"There is at present fifteen families (man, wife & three children) all on the verge of destitution; some are one & two hundred dollars in debt, some stand clear of store bills but no cash in hand," he reported. Fifty men were idle and without hope but if they left the place to look for work, they would "only jump from the frying pan into the fire." Thompson advised that a relief committee had recently been formed. "The only people drawing wages here are the lifeboat crew, telegraph operator, school teacher, doctor, policemen, and Indian missionary," he revealed, "and these people realize that they are faced with the necessity of providing all the others with the necessities of life." For his part, Thompson was out fishing from the lifeboat two days a week, and he delivered his catch free at both village stores. "You can then probably realize what a relief the construction of a Light would be," he wrote.[2]

Those fifty idle men were accustomed to hard labour under local conditions and could easily commute to the lighthouse site from their homes. He proposed a work-sharing scheme which would spread wages evenly throughout the community. Wives would "jump at the chance" to cook for the crew. Thompson pledged his crew's assistance. They had already begun repairing the trail connecting the lifeboat station with the site. A week later the local justice of the peace, the secretary of the newly formed relief committee, wrote Robertson to underscore Thompson's claim. "The condition of 15 families is nothing short of destitution & 50 men are out of work & with no prospect except the tower of getting any," he declared, imploring the agent "Do what you can to reduce the distress."[3]

How they voted determined whether they worked. H.S. Clements, the Conservative member for the constituency, wrote in confidence to the agent, warning him to insure "the boys would use every precaution possible, especially on the West Coast," to hire Tories. This was "one special place where I want to take care of my friends and not the enemy," he wrote. "There has always been a hive of dissatisfied ones there." Pledging to carry out the work "in a perfectly orthodox manner," the agent conferred with the president of Ucluelet's Conservative Association and left behind a list of positions required.[4]

Even if there was very little to go around in Ucluelet, they still had their politics—with as many layers and as much acid as an onion. Richard Johnson, a storekeeper, was secretary of the Conservative Association. No sooner had work begun on the project than he wrote Clements, the MP, charging that the labourers had been hand-picked by coxswain Thompson "and the rest of the liberals on the life boat," much to the disgust of Ucluelet's true blue Tories.

Johnson's charges prompted a flurry of correspondence back and forth between Victoria, Ottawa, and Ucluelet that threatened to hamstring the long-awaited construction bonanza. The foreman, H.L. Robertson, undertook "a quiet investigation," and labelled the vindictive merchant "an unmitigated liar." He was prepared to vouch for the political fervour of the men under him and sent evidence that Johnson and "some of his friends would like to control the job; but do not worry," he concluded, "they certainly won't; so long as I am in charge." The real reason for Johnson's meddling, Robertson discovered, stemmed from the workers' using their unaccustomed cash to purchase cheaper goods from Victoria rather than patronizing Johnson's store.[5]

As for the job itself, weather proved to be as vile as the oppressive political climate. The *Leebro* originally intended to land supplies at the site. High tides and heavy surf soon ruled out that strategy. During February the tender lay heaving off Amphitrite Point for five days and nights as workboat after workboat beat its way across the raging channel only to return fully loaded, crews panting over their oars. "In fact the last time they attempted the passage with a load in the workboat," Robertson wrote, "they nearly upset & that has put the fear of the Lord into them." Looking up from his report, the foreman saw "the surf was breaking right up against the base of the rock & sweeping clear over the top of [the] high rock to SE of site."

The 323-ton *Leebro*, built by Leeming Brothers in 1908 and periodically used as tender.

They decided to land at the lifeboat station and the workers would haul supplies over the road. All that February clouds dumped their ballast and hosed the West Coast with an average of two inches of rain a day. Robertson complained, "As I write this I can hear a good steady fall of rain on the roof." The road turned into "a mass of mud from one end to the other." Wheelbarrows sank up to their axles. Seven cursing Conservatives hauled all the gravel, sand, and cement up the hills in sacks, piled 450-pound loads on the sled, then harried the steaming draft horses, with traces and whips, to drag their loads through the quagmire to the hungry cement mixer waiting at Amphitrite. Within a week the "road" disappeared under six inches of sucking mud. Robertson assigned a man fulltime to lay corduroy poles and fill sink-holes with the precious gravel.

In spite of this wallowing obstacle the labourers stuck to schedule. By 8 February they had drilled and blasted 125 yards of rock off the point of the site, hauled seventy cubic yards of gravel and 420 sacks of cement, and were pouring one mix (six cubic feet) of concrete every three minutes of their fourteen-hour days. All the while the wind drove a horizontal blast of rain and sea-spray at them. "But we keep plugging along whenever possible & making fair progress," Robertson boasted. By the first week in March the bunker-like tower, resembling a squat Mayan temple, was virtually complete. Robertson turned the site over to Coxswain Thompson, sent the tired horses home, and paid the workers off.

The Ucluelet lifeboat crew ran Amphitrite light and horn until July 1918 when their boat was withdrawn from service, a casualty of wartime economy. James Frazer, watchman at the now vacant lifeboat station, took charge of the light as well for ten dollars a month. He had previously earned four times as much from the Naval Service Board for the same chore, and found that working for Marine and Fisheries hardly compared with the four dollars a day he could be earning at the Canadian Fishing Company nearby.

On 10 March 1919 the mistreated keeper wrote Marine Agent Robertson, telling him: "If $10 a month was your idea of what was fair and just, you might have let me know at once so that I could have resigned & taken advantage of the work in the neighbourhood & been able to earn a decent living." He pledged to keep the light going till the month's end but no longer.[6]

Frazer took up his grievance with Gordon Halkett on 23 March 1919. Halkett agreed he was "only asking what was fair and just," and promised to take the matter up with Captain Robertson. For his ten dollars Frazer had to tramp a mile at sunset to light up, return at midnight, "in all weathers," to wind the revolving machinery and trim the charred wicks, then head back again at sunrise to extinguish the light. Floors inside the tower were constantly flooded. Frazer hauled firewood to keep a fire banked to dry out the woodwork, and "kept the building decent." Anticipating a fair wage he had also "kept the brasswork and copper utensils as bright as when [he] was paid $40 per month."

The problem of manning a light with a caretaker a mile or more away, for wages far below even Ucluelet's prevailing rates, continued to bedevil the department. In August 1927 Halkett cabled Victoria from Ucluelet to advise that the fog horn had been blasting continuously for ten days and nights and warned it was "IMPOSSIBLE ONE MAN OPERATE FOG ALARM CONTINUOUSLY UNDER THESE CONDITIONS." A second man must be appointed to relieve him. The local Fishermen's Association insisted that the plant be operated "at once" by one man from 3:00 p.m. to 8:00 a.m., when the fishing fleet left and returned to their harbour. Vandalism and the need to wipe down the panes, since the tower was continually coated with spray, also argued forcefully for a man on the station full time. Moreover, Wilby, the new marine agent in Victoria, informed Ottawa that Amphitrite light was now "a most important one. . . greatly depended upon by the Trans-Pacific Liners making this Coast." Wilby realized that the salary level would have an important bearing on whether a permanent keeper could be employed. "There is practically nothing else that a man can do at this point," he explained, "and to live there by himself. . . is going to be a severe tax on the morale of the average man," especially when his only neighbours were Japanese fishermen a mile away.

Even if paying a fulltime salary was a deterrent for the department, Wilby certainly preferred that to the alternative: "Thick weather conditions may exist for two or three hours and clear off; the plant is shut down, the keeper takes the opportunity of getting some sleep; thick weather again sets in; keeper still asleep; plant not in operation." A scenario ripe for another disaster on the scale of the *Pass of Melfort*.

Amphitrite's accommodations were certainly no incentive for permanent occupancy. The diaphone took up half the living room. The only ventilation came through the floor, "and all the steam and foul air" passed through these quarters. The nearest drinking water was over a mile away. Routcliffe, Frazer's replacement, had wired his resignation after twelve hours of fog, though he had been persuaded to hang on by the promise of an assistant. "He is not a strong man," Wilby allowed, "in fact no man is strong enough to be relied on under the above conditions, and the station can never be properly operated until a dwelling is built to accommodate a man and his family."[7]

Routcliffe clung to Wilby's promise of a dwelling until April 1928 when he resigned again, claiming, "The present quarters at the station are unfit to live in in very wet weather." There was no escaping the suffocating din in the engine room, no means to find even temporary relief aside from quitting the station, hiking home, and sending his wife out for someone else.

A dwelling was finally put up at Amphitrite in 1929. In a fashion reminiscent of the 1914 patronage wrangle A.W. Niell, MP for Alberni, balked at a proposal to send up a foreman from Victoria. "Absolutely no," he wrote Wilby, threatening to "go down myself, little as I can claim to be a practical carpenter," if a party man from his district could not be found for "an ordinary hammer and nail job like that."

Today Amphitrite ranks as one of the "in stations," lying only a few minutes of good paved road from the burgeoning modern town of Ucluelet. It affords a nice

"Like a squat Mayan temple. . ." Amphitrite tower has lines unlike any other.

finale for the camera-clicking army of tourists on their way home from Long Beach. Local divers have found the *Pass of Melfort*'s ruptured hull and anchors under thirty feet of water near the light. Though they are determined to salvage an anchor for a memorial to her lost crew, its sheer weight and the wretched sea conditions off Amphitrite Point pose too great a challenge today, just as they did for Captain Scougall at the end of his last voyage on Christmas Eve.

Early lookout on Amphitrite
Point.

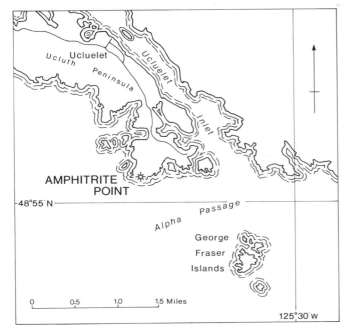

Kains Island

Quatsino Sound, like Barkley Sound sixty miles southeast, was another harbour which never lived up to the imagination of its boosters. In August 1904 the British Columbia Board of Trade applied to the Marine Department for a light on Entrance Island off the northern tip of the Sound, "owing to the establishment of sawmills and the development of mining industries" along the splayed fingers of Holberg, Rupert, and Neroutsos Inlets.

Once informed of the board's proposal, Gourdeau asked Gaudin to consider whether an unmanned gas beacon would suffice. The agent told the deputy minister, "The commerce of Quatsino Sound is increasing, and. . . this light may almost be considered as a leading coast as well as a harbour light." It was the consensus among developers and mariners alike that "there should be some person constantly residing at the station to operate a mechanical horn in foggy weather."

As a temporary measure, Gaudin installed a Wigham lamp on Entrance Island, later renamed Kains to avoid confusion with the Entrance Island outside Nanaimo. In the summer of 1906 the part-time keeper smashed his boat while landing at Kains to tend the light, and was marooned. Fortunately he was spotted and picked up in time. He returned and built himself a rude log hut, ten by twelve feet. The shack at Kains affronted Colonel Anderson's aesthetics; he ordered it torn down as soon as he came ashore. "It is very rough with log sides spaved too wide, a roof of shakes and a rough door," he wrote in disgust. "It has no floor yet and is neither secure nor habitable."

Work commenced on a more permanent and pleasing structure in the summer of 1907. It was a vile place to land supplies. "As white men were scarce, Siwashes were hired to freight lumber and building materials to the island." The project dragged on into fall, then the November gales pounced upon Kains. "A more disagreeable time of the year could hardly have been chosen for the work," E.P. Kelly, the construction foreman, told a reporter for the *Colonist* afterward. "The North wind blew with such violence at times it was impossible for anyone to work on top of the light house some twelve feet from the ground."[1]

On 8 October Gaudin predicted the work would be complete by mid-November, but the project ran a full month behind. In December, as the gales steadily mounted in their ferocity, even "Siwashes" steadfastly refused to venture five miles out of Winter Harbour, leaving Kelly and three labourers marooned "in a serious plight for days." The distraught workmen crowded into the tower for shelter and "were in a bad way as provisions were rather low." They "had no boat save a little Siwash canoe. . . kept in reserve in case of emergency." Fortunately, George Jackson, "an old veteran of the sea," sailed by Kains, spotted the four men, and reported their plight in Winter Harbour. He sailed back next day and tacked back and forth out beyond the breakers for a day and a night while "a terrific north wind was raging making it impossible for any small craft to land."

Next day Jackson rowed for over an hour to manoeuvre his boat into the entrance of the bay. The carpenters dumped their bedrolls and tools into their canoe and two men shoved out into the receding swell. They hastily transferred their cargo to Jackson's skiff and the "cranky craft" came back for the two men waiting ashore. "This second trip was also made in safety, but the canoe was half-filled with water," Kelly related. "After several hours hard rowing we finally arrived in Winter Harbour."

The tower they left so happily behind on the beleaguered island rose eighty feet above sea-level. The lantern sat on the red roof of a square white wooden building. Nels C. Nelson, a Danish settler from Holberg, was appointed Kains' first keeper and issued with a hand horn. In July 1911 Nelson scissored out a newspaper clipping and mailed it off to Gordon Halkett in Victoria:

> Shipmasters on this coast are hereby informed that all lightkeepers on the coast of British Columbia are permitted to fly at their respective stations the British ensign with the arms of Canada thereon between the hours of sunrise and sunset on any day of the year. Should the lighthouse require assistance from any vessel the said ensign will be flown with the union down. Mariners will govern themselves accordingly.

"Please let me know if the Department will furnish the station with a flag," he asked. Halkett noted in the margin of Nelson's letter that no flag had been supplied and sent one up. Though it seemed a minor bureaucratic exchange, the Sadlers, who came after Nelson, owed their sanity, if not their lives to his request. Petersen, Nelson's brother-in-law, drowned when his skiff capsized offshore. The keeper resigned in November 1915.

In December James Henry Sadler received a telegram from Captain Robertson advising him of his appointment to succeed Nelson. It must have been welcome news. Like most men seeking a new start on the lights, Sadler was somewhat out at the elbows. He confessed, "I haven't the means to furnish myself with a six or even 3 months' supply [of food] to take to the lighthouse."[2] Robertson advised Sadler to order from a Victoria wholesaler and send them an authorization to cash his quarterly paycheques. According to regulations, government steamers called at Kains Island once a year, he explained, "But I try to arrange the work so it will

call twice a year or oftener if possible." The agent also informed Sadler he would
have to row seventeen miles to Winter Harbour for his mail, "or anywhere else in
the vicinity where you wish it addressed."

Sadler arrived at Kains with a one-year-old child and began setting up house for
his wife, Catherine, who stayed behind at Quatsino village with a three-day-old
infant. There was bad news in the first mail bag. Rumour, obviously unfounded,
had hinted that Nelson came away from Kains a wealthy man, but Sadler slit open
an envelope from Ottawa and read that he would be paid a mere $40 a month. It
was a cruel blow, but the new keeper and his wife elected to try it for two years.
After all, he had sought the job; the government hadn't forced it upon them.

In 1917 the CPR cut out its service to Winter Harbour, shattering the once-
vaunted dreams for another busy port on the West Coast. Now there would be no
mail dropped off at the light. A local merchant wrote H.S. Clements, his MP in
Ottawa, on Sadler's behalf, asking the government to pay Captain Henry Peterson
five dollars to ferry mail out to Kains Island. Sadler could hardly afford the service
with his meagre pay. "Please, Mr. Clements, fix this thing up, the keeper is
entitled to mail, he has a wife and three small children," the writer implored. "I
feel quite sure that you will see the justice of giving this man a chance to remain
in touch with the outside world and I will also consider it a personal favour and
thank you in advance. . . ."[3]

Always cost-conscious, the department refused to pay to have Sadler's letters
taken out to Kains. When the mail came, it arrived tucked away in the bow of his

Aerial view of Kains Island Lightstation, 1978.

fourteen-foot boat after a grueling round trip of ten miles, while his wife wondered when, if ever, he would be back. Catherine had landed with their new baby three weeks after Henry came ashore. The father delivered his third child by lamplight a few days before Christmas but the event only underscored their peril. All their provisions were gone except for flour and a few limp root vegetables. The *Cape Scott* came out twice with supplies on board but heavy winter seas made landing impossible. Post-partum depression combined viciously with isolation and fear of starvation. Every night Sadler prayed for the sea to simmer down, "yet each day the breakers came rolling in as high as the day before."[4]

Early Christmas week he spotted a vessel some four miles off. He told his wife he was just going out to the garden for a few minutes, slipped outside, and bolted for his skiff. "It was a fool thing to do, perhaps," he admitted, "but I felt that if I had any possible show I would take the chance to reach that steamer." Three times he pushed off and each time the ten-foot waves flung him back onto the rocks and piled into the skiff. The steamer was slipping away. Finally Sadler mounted the crest of a swell but collided with a log.

> The skiff turned completely over and I was pinned underneath. I remember grabbing a cleat in the bottom of the boat and tugging myself free again, although for a few moments I was stunned by striking a log. For an hour I was washed back and forth, now towards the rocks, now into the open.

Finally the log drifted close enough to the rocks for Sadler to shove off and grab a handhold. He staggered up the cliff, his "heavy water-filled clothes seeming to weigh a ton."

But the worst trial lay ahead. Sadler slogged shivering up to the house, knowing full well that Catherine "was just in that state of mind and condition" where the sight of him "all wet and bruised and fagged out might completely unnerve her." He saw her through the window rocking the baby in the sitting room. Sadler stole around to the back door and tip-toed squelching into the kitchen.

> I tried to be as quiet as possible, but she evidently heard me, for she called out and asked if I had been in the boat. I don't know what it was; perhaps it was my voice when I answered her, but she came rushing towards me as though in a delirium.
>
> She couldn't seem to speak. For nights after that she could not sleep. She was constantly worried and watched me all the time. She made me promise again and again that I would never take the boat out in such a sea. Whenever I left the house, I had to explain where I was going, what I was going to do and how long I would be away. "Where are you going, daddy?" she would ask me every time I moved. And I can tell you I did not move much for three days after my experience in the boat.

Catherine also wrung another promise out of him: this would be their last winter at Kains Island. In April Sadler wrote Victoria asking for a transfer to

Green Island, a station in the fairway of Alaska-bound steamer traffic and within rowing distance of Port Simpson. He couldn't just quit, after all, not with three children. Besides, his wife was pregnant with their fourth. Shortly after the delivery Sadler flagged a passing Seattle fishboat and explained his plight to her captain and crew. They could scarcely believe the conditions at Kains and pressed the lightkeeper "to take his family and leave at once." But Henry Sadler "was too faithful to his employer, the Dominion Government, to quit without giving notice."

They watched and waited instead. Henry desperately tried to buoy Catherine's spirits as she sank into a morass of despair, discoursing for hours upon "things that otherwise would have seemed the most commonplace events imaginable": a Siwash canoe or whales blowing off in the distance, and the weather, always the weather. "If a boat passed, we would watch it until it disappeared and all the while we would talk about it, remark on its appearance and when we saw it before, speculate on who might be aboard and where it might be going," he recalled. "Those boats that passed by often miles away were the only company we had and we made the best of it."

But they just kept steaming right on by all that anxious spring. Mother and baby fell sick and Sadler "began to think that [he] would have to do something, even if it did mean breaking the contract with the Government." When the next steamer came over the horizon, Sadler launched his skiff and rowed hard in pursuit while his wife pumped feverishly away at the hand horn. The wind blotted out the blasts. After an hour's fruitless rowing Sadler turned back, crawled up the rocks, and found Catherine collapsed beside the horn. "For days afterward my wife was white as a sheet. I couldn't get her to smile. She seemed to have lost all her spirit. The child was on her mind."

Then, in July, they looked out and saw the *Leebro* coming. At long last their nightmare seemed near its end. Her captain rowed ashore and was astonished to learn that the lightkeepers expected to leave on his ship. He had no notice of any move for the Sadlers, not to Green Island nor anywhere else. "Practically the whole conversation I had with the captain was devoted to our troubles on the island," Sadler remembered. "My wife cried when she learned that the *Leebro* was not going to take us away." When he returned to his ship, though, the captain sent off a message stating "everything OK" with the Sadlers.

5 September 1918 promised to be the long awaited day of delight at Kains. A launch anchored off the island and Henry rowed out for the mail. He tossed the sack to his wife and went to hoist up the boat. Catherine rummaged through six months' mail, searching for a letter from the agent. Nothing. "After all these months," she sobbed, "there has been no letter from the department." Sadler flipped through the post, putting the bills aside, and confirmed it. At least they had mail from "somewhere in France," from Catherine's younger brother. When she opened it she learned there would never be another letter from him. Her sanity, stretched like a rubber band to its outer limits, snapped.

"From that time on she was completely out of her mind," her agonized eyewitness related:

> Sometimes she would begin screaming and calling for help. She repeatedly talked to herself and often recalled the time I was nearly drowned when the skiff overturned.
>
> Her mind sometimes went back to her home in the Old Country, to her girlhood days in Stirling, Scotland. I was forced to tie her to the bed-posts at times, fastening her hands above her head. When she was free and I was not watching her, she would tear books to pieces and throw plates and tableware on the floor.
>
> Once I just caught her as she was about to leap over the verandah. At the time she appeared to see a vision of her father and she was calling to him. I couldn't get her to eat. Goat's milk, half a cup at a time, was all she would take. The children languished also from lack of nourishment, especially the little ones.

"We spent a whole week like that," Sadler related. "I began to feel that I was beginning to lose control myself." As if to torment him further, several fishboats passed close by that hellish week, but the horn never carried over the noise of their gas engines. Nor did anyone notice Nelson's red ensign unfurled upsidedown at half mast. "As for me," Sadler declared, "my sole object in life became the discovery of smoke or a sail at sea. I would stand watching the horizon until my eyes pained and filled with water."

Sadler's vigil promised to pay off one day when he saw a steamer, the *Malaspina*, nosing through the haze toward him. He bolted like a madman for his horn, gave four quick blasts—the distress signal—and saw an officer step out on the bridge. The ship turned toward the tower. Sadler scrambled down the rocks and unleashed his skiff. But when he looked up the *Malaspina* was steaming back into the fog.

On the eighth day he saw a whaler heading past. Sadler lashed his wife spread-eagled to their bed, locked up the children, and sprinted for his horn again. As usual the whalers seemed eager to get home and away for a while from the offal and stench of their gory calling. If they saw or heard Sadler they gave no sign, and their craft shrank toward the horizon. Luckily, one of them had a telescope on deck, sweeping the horizon for a blow spout. He passed it over the island, then swung it back in surprise. They were a long way off but he swore he saw a man lying motionless on the rocks. And there was something wrong with the flag.

Sadler came to his senses an hour later with strange voices buzzing in his ears above a forest of gumboots and oars. He couldn't speak. One of the crew rolled him over, picked his pocket, and called him by the name in his wallet. When the lightkeeper finally blurted out his lurid tale the men tramped up to the house with its mad matron and scrawny, cowering children—a literal bedlam. They rowed back to their ship and headed full speed for Port Alice. The whalers came ashore again in the night with Dr. O.M. Lyons. As soon as he had arranged for safe confinement of the raving mother and her youngest children, Lyons, muttering in rage and disbelief, went to the cable office and wired Captain Robertson in Victoria:

WHALER ST. LAWRENCE CAPT. OVERSEN ARRIVED SAT. NIGHT REPORTED HAVING ANSWERED THE DISTRESS FLYING FROM ENTRANCE IS. LIGHTHOUSE QUATSINO FOR THE PREVIOUS FIVE DAYS. FOUND KEEPER AND FAMILY IN VERY GREAT TROUBLE BUT STILL KEEPING LIGHT BURNING. STARTING IMMEDIATELY REACHED LIGHTHOUSE MIDNIGHT FOUND KEEPER WIFE SICK TWO WEEKS VIOLENTLY INSANE LAST FIVE DAYS FOUR CHIL- DREN PRACTICALLY STARVED HUSBAND EXHAUSTED FROM RESTRAINING WIFE FROM SUICIDE FOR FIVE DAYS AND HIMSELF ON VERGE OF INSANITY BROUGHT WIFE AND TWO CHILDREN TO PORT ALICE AWAITING FURTHER RELIEF SADLER STILL TENDING LIGHT IN CRITICAL CONDITION WOULD RECOMMEND INSPECTION OF SADLER'S CONDITION.[5]

Robertson immediately radioed Gordon Halkett aboard the *Leebro*. The captain altered course and made full speed for Quatsino. Halkett came ashore a week later. Sadler was "very excited and despondent and worrying over his wife's condition as he had heard nothing of her since she was removed.... He informed me that his wife had been poorly in health for some time worrying over their financial condition," Halkett continued, "his wages even by close economy not covering the cost of living." The news that her favourite brother was killed in action "caused despondency and she became mentally unbalanced, continually trying to commit suicide, and fighting fiercely."[6]

Halkett stayed behind for two days (literally superintendent of a light for once) and ordered the *Leebro* to take Sadler away to Port Alice. The lightkeeper found his wife reduced to a raving lunatic and signed papers committing her to the insane asylum at New Westminster. He returned two days later with Fred Christensen who agreed to keep him company for three dollars a day. Sadler wanted off—he could no longer live at the island. Halkett had his remaining children removed at his request, "placing them under the care of settlers at Quatsino village."

While admitting that labour conditions were "acute in this district," where lumber companies paid out between $4.50 and $6.00 a day in forest camps and pulp mills, where even Indians were "making high wages fishing for the canneries," Halkett concluded that Sadler should have sent his wife on holiday rather than stretch his $40 a month (less than a quarter of shore wages) to buy goats.[7]

For two weeks Robertson tried in vain to find a replacement. Finally he recommended automation in place of a living wage, arguing, "The question of remuneration for these small lighthouses is a serious one on account of... high wages that the labourmen now have offered to them." It was a situation ripe for scandal, one that threatened to expose, for the first time, the horrendous working conditions on the lights to an aroused, outraged public. Halkett and Robertson knew, the whalers aboard the *St. Lawrence* knew, and (worst of all) so did Dr. Ormund M. Lyons.

A medical man in a place like Port Alice was a pillar of the community, a scion with prestige and ready access to journalists and politicians: a force to be reckoned with. Predictably, Dr. Lyons was disgusted at what he found when he came ashore at Kains that crazy night. "It is a pity that such a calamity should befall a family in the midst of civilization," he declared in a stern letter to Robertson. "It seems that this Light tender was receiving only $40.00 per month and with this meagre amount was attempting to support a wife with four small children. Isolated as they were from the world at large & having insufficient food to sustain the family for the winter & much more, no money to buy food, it is not surprising that the Mother became insane." Dr. Lyons trusted the marine agent would inform the proper authorities at once that lightkeepers' wages "were absolutely insufficient to support a family at these times." Robertson should seize upon the "dire need of this family" as an example, "in order that prompt action may be taken to advance these salaries at once, before another similar calamity occurs." He advised that Mrs. Sadler was now in the Westminster Insane Hospital, her children having been placed in the care of neighbours, and he enclosed a bill for his services.[8]

Robertson replied 11 October, thanking Lyons for his help. Affirming he did not "hold a brief for the Government of Canada," he thought none was necessary "in this case." Then the agent set out his position on wages and working conditions, crawling around on top of the truth:

> The lightkeeper at Quatsino is far from being what you would call isolated, the conditions there being as good, or better, than a number of our lighthouses both in regard to the pay and the work etc., and by me being able to get a man to take the vacancy at the salary Mr. Sadler was getting, goes to show that there are worse jobs than that of a lightkeeper.
>
> I might also say for your information that lightkeepers are appointed by the Government of Canada and their salaries are passed by the Parliament of Canada which is the voice of the people.
>
> The salary paid at Quatsino is $40.00 per month, and everything found, a home, and in this instance a two acre garden, in addition, as his duties are so very light he is allowed to earn money on the outside if he wishes, and this I believe he could have done if he had wanted to work at the cannery.[9]

As for Lyons' bill, Robertson deemed it "only right" that Lyons "should look to Mr. Sadler for his wife's hospital expenses while in Port Alice." The bill went back and forth between Lyons, Robertson, and Sadler (himself now in hospital), and finally wound up with the provincial secretary. White, the deputy provincial secretary, advised Robertson, "It appears to me that the Dominion Government no doubt provides for the maintenance of the family of this Lighthouse-keeper," and asked if they would assume "the liability." But the department refused to reimburse the province in spite of "the sadness of the case."[10]

For his part, Dr. Lyons regretted the department's attitude. Try as he may, he could not "quite appreciate how they could disclaim. . . the expense incurred." He hoped the department would never require his services in future. Finally, on 26 June 1919, Lyons received a cheque for $125 (three months' pay for the Sadlers) from the department.

There the matter might have rested if Sadler, "broken in heart and spirit," hadn't walked into the offices of the *Colonist* the following January, and poured out his soul. Everyone from editors to copyboys milled around, silent and shaken, as Sadler relived his Kains Island nightmare, close to tears, while pens flickered across notepads. He had come to Victoria looking for work but "internal injuries sustained while at the lighthouse" rendered him unfit, "a mere shadow of the man who went north to serve the government several years ago." At least he hoped he might see his wife again in the asylum. "If they won't let me meet her face to face," he said, "perhaps I can get a glimpse of her anyway. I hope she will be better soon, so that we can start all over again."

It was a scoop, no doubt about that, and when the full page spread hit the streets, telling how the Sadlers were "LOCKED FROM WORLD ON NORTHERN ISLAND," it peeled back the romantic veneer from the harsh reality of lightkeeping. Victorians set up a relief fund for the impoverished family. Robertson desperately tried to lance the festering scandal by assigning Gordon Halkett to rebut Sadler's claims with a lame excuse: "The man accepts the position knowing the conditions and is at liberty to resign any time, when the lighthouse steamer will take him and his effects away." He boasted that his keepers even received extra pay for the hand horn, could grow their own vegetables, and blithely suggested again that Sadler's wife might be sane today if only he had sent her on a holiday.

Incensed, Sadler went back to the newspaper and took up cudgels with Halkett point by point. The soil was poor at Kains. Moreover, gardens were out of the question at many other stations. At Triangle Island, for example, "they can't keep chickens because they blow off, the winds are so strong," he explained. "Even a cow was hurled into the sea by a gale." They had no friends to put them up in Quatsino so holidays were out of the question. Besides, if they left the station they would have to find and pay someone to relieve them. If Catherine had gone over alone, Sadler would have faced regular hotel or boarding rates, "and on a salary of $40 a month from the government that would be a rather hard thing to do."

The next keeper, Robert S. Nosler, stayed only long enough to give the lie to Robertson's claim that Kains Island was some sort of worker's paradise. The proof Robertson had advanced that the salary would soon entice a man to replace Sadler wore threadbare within a month. For two weeks Halkett tried in vain to find a replacement while Nosler took over Sadler's job for $4.00 per day. Three weeks

Kains Island dwelling and tower, 1946.

later, with the wage bill mounting, *Leebro* dropped off two "Russian Finnish sailors" willing to work for less, and ferried Nosler back to Sea Otter Cove. Shortly after, the tender visited Kains and a shore party found the two Finns chasing each other "around and around the tower," one brandishing a knife.

Nosler still wanted the work but advised, "I will not accept for less than 650 dollars a year. . . as it is not possible to live on the former salary." Robertson had coaxed an extra temporary allowance out of Ottawa, enabling him to up the pay to $600. In March 1910 Nosler allowed, "I like the position. . . I have no objection to the place," but was resigning "since the mail boat has stopped coming." Nor could wages keep pace any longer with the "high cost of everything." Sugar cost twenty-two cents a pound, flour and potatoes eight cents a pound, and post-war inflation had driven prices up "20 to 200 percent in six months." He asked permission "to go out to work or fish." Robertson refused. Instead the agent suggested he take a holiday but Nosler replied he could find no relief keeper to work at those wages.

Colonel Wilby, who took over from Robertson at this time, wrote the deputy minister to advise that Nosler's resignation presented something of a quandary: "This being one of the lowest paid stations, there is no lightkeeper in British Columbia willing to take same."[11] Nosler reminded Wilby that both Sadler and Carl Quick, one of the Finnish seamen, "went insane here owing to no mail, and no pay," and suggested the salary be doubled.

In late June Wilby discovered Nosler was right; when the keeper quit he could only secure a temporary relief for $100 a month. The rate "seems high," Hawkes, the assistant deputy minister, pointed out. He ordered his agent to visit the area and seek out someone willing to work for less. Reclassification for Kains Island was under serious consideration, he advised, and might result in a salary scale somewhere between $650 and $750.

Wilby placed R. Allan, his wife, and four children in temporary charge at Kains on 22 June and wrote Hawkes that, if the reclassification were approved, it would actually entail a cut in pay rather than an increase at the temporary $1200 salary. He made "a strong plea for a real betterment of the salaries of the stations." The agent then asked Toivo Aro, keeper at Pulteney Point, to tack up a notice in Sointula's post office, advertising the permanent position at Kains. Aro replied, "They think the salary is too low for such a lonely and rough place." Allan quit December 16.

The department finally found a permanent keeper in James Quinn, a seventy-year-old ex-sailor whose two long-service pensions would stretch the pay toward subsistence. He was senile and slow, given to "rambling inaccurate statements," but he kept the light "faithfully." Gordon Halkett visited him in October 1921 and was appalled when Quinn complained that he had yet to receive his pay, but later he turned up $700 in cheques stashed in the "dirty and unsanitary" house. Quinn, in Halkett's estimation, was hardly a satisfactory lightkeeper. "I believe it is only a matter of time before he will be unable to look after himself," he stated.[12] Halkett persuaded the postmaster at Quatsino to pay Quinn regular visits to check on his condition. When he learned of his superintendent's critical report the indignant Quinn reminded Wilby he had sailed the Mediterranean "while these people in Ottawa were in the Blankets." "I will never leave my post. . .I hold the keys of life and property while in charge of this station," he declared. "Was I in Victoria or Vancouver I would put this letter in print so all seagoing Mariners could see it."[13]

In March 1922 Alexander Johnston, the new deputy minister, received word from a medical examiner that Quinn "should not be left alone as he may develop cerebral hemorrhage at any time." In spite of his precarious condition, Quinn set to work single-handedly to rebuild a post and plank bridge which had collapsed in a storm the previous winter. He was hard at it, driving spikes, when Robert Nosler came ashore to visit March 31. Nosler reported the old salt was quite agitated about having to submit to a medical examination "and other minor troubles." He should be transferred to a more accessible station. For his part, Nosler was willing to help the department all he could, and promised to call at Kains Island once a month. Much to his disgust, Quinn was pensioned off that April.

Alfred and Annie Dickenson took over Kains Island light from the doddering Quinn. They carried their crates into a dwelling that was "in a very poor, neglected condition" (Quinn having regularly entertained goats and chickens in his parlour), and the two set to work. By November they had transformed most of the station, repainting every building from top to bottom, and had resurrected the weed-choked garden.

Quinn had been the last keeper at Kains to turn out of bed at the sound of a steamer's whistle and drag the hand horn outside. As early as August 1911 the Wallace Fisheries at Claxton up the Skeena River had asked Robertson to install a foghorn. In July 1920 the Whalen Pulp and Paper Mills at Port Alice wanted a horn. Shipping was booming around the north end of the island and they insisted, "It is essential to our interests, as well as to the safety of vessels that these signals be given your prompt attention." So the Dickensons fell under the fog alarm's unbending regime of vigilance and toil, though diesel engines had by now replaced steam, eliminating the endless hauling of kindling, coal, and water.

At first the new keepers seemed possessed by a reverence, verging upon addiction, for their natural surroundings. They combined this with the resourcefulness and unflagging patience which have always been the hallmarks of successful lightkeepers. Rather than poring through the usual letters crammed with complaints and saturated with misery over wages and isolation, Wilby began to read letters from Kains which must have left the crusty agent somewhat envious behind his cluttered desk with its pestering telephone.

"This island, sir, is just an island of song birds," Dickenson wrote ecstatically. "I have never seen so many, and they are so tame we can nearly pick them up, my wife feeds them twice a day and it is kind of recreation to watch them." Deer wandered freely, brought their fawns into the yard, and nuzzled Annie when she pegged up the laundry. "There is no excuse for sane healthy people being lonely at this station," Alfred declared.

But loneliness did creep up on them. In April 1925 Dickenson applied for a month's leave. "My wife has not seen another woman since May 23 last year," he confided. The society of songbirds was no longer enough. "She is getting kind of restless, and she will not go away without I accompany her." He asked Wilby to send up a relief, preferably an older man because, he warned, "It is too quiet and dreary here for young blood, they soon get discontented and quarrelsome."

Dickenson's letters are a sterling example of the wildly shifting moods brought on by isolation: ecstatic one day over a pod of killer whales or the grandeur of a wild ripping storm; sullen the next at the prospect of weeks piling up with no prospect of mail or social exchange. As time collapsed around them, recreation in its literal sense was short-lived, for they relied always on the same raw material to recreate.

A rumour reached Kains that spring that there might soon be an opening at the Capilano light in Vancouver harbour. If so, Kains' keeper wanted it. "Have you any idea, sir, when I shall make the change?" he asked Wilby. "My wife is all anxious now to get away, she passes hours away looking through my binoculars for to sight a vessel."

By June Dickenson had still not heard if a relief was on the way. He wanted to send Annie away. As for himself, "I can go out in my boat and have a talk with the halibut fishermen, if they come near enough, also the mail man I talk to him twice a month anyway, also I get recreation fishing and going around these little

Five little Warrens at Kains Island, with pet chickens.

inlets." But Annie had no stomach for boats. "Think a woman needs a change more so than a man," he explained.[14] Their exile ended that fall when word came of the long-sought transfer to Capilano.

Sydney Warren had been six long lean months out of work before he got wind of the upcoming vacancy at Kains Island. Unemployment was a dreary prospect indeed for the burly ex-navy officer and qualified engineer. He and Jessie had six children, all girls, and no brighter prospects in life than the impending arrival of a seventh. Syd mailed in his application for the post, sent Jessie away to stay with her mother in Vancouver, then waited, hoping for a son and a job.

Colonel Wilby was of two minds about Warren right from the start. His experience certainly impressed: seaman, ferry master, engineer. But how could that many people possibly cram into the house? Given time, might he become another Sadler with a crazy wife and a big mouth? The agent tried to scare him off. Kains Island light was "a particularly lonely one, having practically no intercourse with the outside world," Wilby warned. "I am of the opinion that your wife should be acquainted with these facts as this station is particularly hard on women."[15]

Hard as it was, however, a lightkeeper's life out there was still a cut above feeding seven mouths on savings, then charity. Syd Warren coolly brushed Wilby's warning aside. "[I will] always endeavour to do my duty conscientiously, and keep the buildings and equipment creditable to myself and the Marine Dept," he promised. Whatever his forebodings, Wilby could hardly turn down an offer like this. He didn't even mention the pay!

Syd and his six girls boarded the *Estevan* at Quatsino wharf in September. As they neared the island, one of the girls pointed out a cross surrounded by the picket fence. Gordon Halkett explained it was a marker for a safe approach in deep water. Weeks later she hiked over and discovered the grave of Nelson's brother-in-law, Petersen.

The family followed Halkett up the "raggedy trail" to the house where Alfred and Annie waited with their crates. The Warren girls were taken aback by Annie's effusive greeting—they were the first females she had set eyes on for a long time. She fussed over them, babbling on about how cute they all were in their cotton dresses, and plied them with jelly "so hard it bounced off the floor." The silent sisters looked at each other in turn, thinking the Dickensons "weren't too bright, maybe it was time they were getting off."

Just as Wilby had predicted, the house was packed to the walls. The girls slept cross-ways, three to a bed. The kitchen floor was constantly swamped with mounting piles of laundry. The narrow hallway leading to the lantern room was transformed into a one-room school, with books stacked high up the walls and pencils rolling on the floor.

There was good news and bad from Vancouver. The law of averages finally caught up. Syd had a son, born the day after Jessie's mother died. She brought him to the island six months later.

The Warrens loved Kains, and their tenure marked a radical departure from the light's twenty-year tradition of discontent and despair. Jessie led a children's crusade into the bush, transforming an unruly patch of salmonberries and runaway foxgloves the Dickensons left behind into vast, lush gardens which mocked Henry Sadler's claim that the soil at Kains was poor. It proved rich enough with tons of kelp, compost, and chicken manure spaded in.

They soon learned the harsh lesson of *never* depending on tenders for supplies. Chicken feed ran out weeks after the *Estevan* was due in one autumn. Reckoning they would hear her whistle tomorrow or the day after, Syd and Jessie elected to feed their diminishing stock of dry goods to the gaunt capons and hens. It was all gone in a month, even the macaroni. The girls gathered up the emaciated chickens, put some by the stove, and the house echoed with pathetic squawks as they thrashed about in their death throes. The birds must be slaughtered fast so the girls brought them, two at a time, hanging by their scaly legs, to the boardwalk where they pressed their heads through knot-holes and held on as their father passed by below with his knife and life drained out of the feathered skeletons.

Once the hen-house fell silent and the soup became so thin it only quenched their thirst, the Warrens ate their way through all the home canning until nothing but flour and scarlet runner beans were left. The girls scampered along the rocks with pails at low tide, pulling clusters of metallic blue mussels off by their beards. Famished though they were for anything fresh, only three mustered the courage to try the "poor man's oysters" set before them that night, all orange and shriveled. Next morning Marjorie and Daphne climbed out of bed, collapsed, and dragged their useless legs across the floor, numb from paralytic shellfish poisoning. Doris, the eldest, felt a queer buzzing sensation in her mouth and at her fingertips. "It was a bit drastic there for a while," Violet remembered sixty years later, "you couldn't get away anywhere." Syd and Jessie poured pints of canned milk down their throats to flush out the bacteria. Luckily, they all recovered over time. After that, shellfish was taboo.

When the *Estevan* finally appeared offshore, they were subsisting on bread fried in melted suet and Bovril. It was a close call, and Jessie redoubled her work in the garden.[16]

Jessie Warren's diary is an incredible record of one woman's strength of body and will. Every night in the precious lull after the dishes were done and all seven children had been tucked in, she sat by the coal-oil lamp and set down her private thoughts and the highlights of the waning day—anything which stuck out from the regular tapestry of the weather out the window, the stacks of laundry all around her, and the weeds invading her garden. Nineteen twenty-eight was typical. Syd knocked the pins out of the storm door hinges in April and wrestled it back into its jamb in October, and Jessie's account of what went on in between is a moving record of a contented woman's life on the lights—a woman whose only window on the real world was the radio:

6 Jan. 28 Clear, cold, east wind. Big freighter passed in today. Got first egg today (old hens) Syd wrote about radio.

9 Jan. 28 Swell day, saw spouts from whales, got another egg but Daphne dropped it. Fog coming out of the sound tonight.

11 Jan. 28 Overcast. Rain & fog horn going s.w. all day. Heavy swells. Lilly [a rabbit] had 12—but one dead good size tho. Cleaned out chicken house 6 eggs.

21 Jan. 28 Part cloudy, some rain. Cold. Emptied can today. Saw some lights? tonight about 8 o'clock. Big bunch of porpoises or black-fish passed here this aftnoon at a great speed 1 egg.

25 Jan. 28 Rain, strong. S.Wester. Rough Sea. Maquinna went down this afternoon but turned back to Forward Inlet. The big freighter (City of Victoria) also passed out & blew 3 blasts to us. Syd returned same. She was headed straight out to Japan. Billy is one year old today, started to wean him. Horn going this afternoon till 8 p.m.

31 Jan. 28 Clear & bright sunshine, pretty cool tho. Strong easterly all day calm & s.w. swells coming in. Working in garden. Got 7 trenches done. *89 eggs for the month*.

18 Feb. 28 Rain & very heavy swells broke boat landing away. The worst yet. A gasboat came down the sound this afternoon & went up the Inlet. 2 eggs.

13 March 28 Lovely day an ideal washing day so we got busy. Nearly everything dried just some coloreds left. Fishing boats out today. Fishing cruiser out this morning. 2 eggs.

14 March 28 Clear then squally. Tried twice to get out the gap. Got "ducked" second time but third time they made it. They got a tow home. (Doris didn't get wet just Syd) Got parcel from Watson also pictures & other letters one from Dave, Dot & Pa. 8 eggs.

19 March 28 Rain scotch mist, horn going for awhile. Syd charged B battery today radio going strong tonight. No crackling noises now. Van. came in good and clear. Mrs. Elsie Woodall sang the Holy City C.F.Y.C. Heavy hail storm this aftnoon. 9 eggs.

26 March 28 Lovely Day. Slight northerly wind blowing. Several gas boats came in today. Radio clearer tonight. Syd charged A battery for a little while. Kids were down to the Pond all afternoon. Had a great time. 9 eggs.

4 April 28 Another wild day, rain, wind & rough westerly very cold wind. Boat was out fishing round here today got quite a few fish. Syd gave A battery a good charging.

Jessie Warren's lush vegetable garden defied claims nothing would grow on Kains Island.

Jessie Warren's livestock "ledger." She liked to show how much they were saving.

8 April 28 Pt. cloudy. Easterly then S.W. Painted lower part of tower. Syd planted seeds today also transplanted cabbages. Broad beans up. Indian here this morning gave us 2 cod (potlatch) 14 eggs.

15 April 28 Pt. cloudy S.W. choppy. Working in garden, planted runners, lettuce, chicory, onion sets & shallots also transplanted onions & weeded out lettuce bed. Set a black hen tonight on 13 eggs. 13 eggs.

3 May 28 Clear a little westerly to calm. Occasional showers. Washed today & all got dried & ironed. Great northern light display tonight at 10 o'clock. 4 eggs.

4 May 28 Helluva day. Horn going a short while. H. rain all day lt. westerly. K.K. round tonight so Syd & Doris got out for the mail. Sent lessons & letters of Daisy, Dot, Mrs. B & Mrs. P. also reports. Got magazine. 17 eggs.

12 May 28 Clear, calm, smooth, lt. northerly. Did the washing & got them all

dried. Planted 6 rows turnips 8 beets 6 carrots 6 onion 3 radish 9 corn. Milked Nanny tonight & got 1 pint. 12 eggs.

18 May 28 Rain & stormy. Princess Ena passed out but had to turn back to Forward Inlet. Big hen has got 3 chicks hatched. Ravens got away with 4 chicks today. 6 eggs.

19 May 28 Clear westerly light swell. Heat fog from 11 am 1 pm horn going. Kids at beach today bathing. Cut down some more bush. Got nearly 2 quarts [goat's milk] today. 10 eggs.

20 May 28 Clear very warm forenoon. Fixed the dahlia patch. Syd whitewashed (sprayed) the chicken & goat houses. Lilly had her batch this aftnoon. Fog very thick came down this afternoon so horn going and still going. Had roast kid for dinner! Had to get my ring sawed off. 8 eggs.

26 May 28 Overcast rain off & on all day. S. to S.W. choppy. Freighter went out this am. Busy getting lumber off beach to make chicken coops. Syd got 3

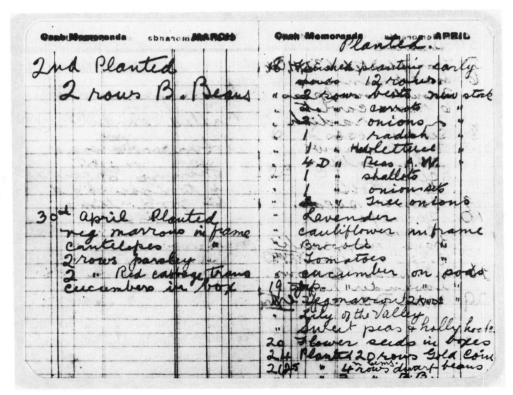

Jessie Warren's garden notebook.

made. 47 chicks final total. Several were dead in shell & 7 addled eggs. Nanny not feeling well so didn't milk her. Bunnies are O.K. 7 eggs.

5 June 28 Very hot today. Did some painting. Estevan went up the sound & came down again this afternoon & landed stores. Col. Wilby & Mr. Halkett came ashore & gave a great inspection! Maquinna down tonight. 7 eggs.

20 June 28 Clear calm in morning turned to westerly in aftnoon then to NW by N. Canning today got 8 quarts venison. 6 eggs.

27 June 28 Overcast slight S- fog first thing & horn going. 3 baby rabbits died. Had swell soup. Transplanted some savoys and red cabbage. Picked 3 buckets peas. Painting inside of tower & outside window frames also finished east side of power house. Kids all bathing again.

8 Sept. 28 Clear slight westerly. Fog up Sound & Inlet first thing this morning. Horn going. "Estevan" went up the Sound this forenoon & set a spar buoy on the way. Canned 4 quarts beef. The little rabbit died this a.m. The Hoot Owls on tonight for the first meeting.

5 Oct. 28 Terrible day. Heavy rain all day. Strong S. to S.E. Rough Cleaned the tower today & canning 3 qts. rabbit, 3 qts. chicken, 1 qt. giblets, 2 pts. cauliflower & 5 qts. veg. marrow. 2 eggs.

6 Oct. 28 Pt. cloudy, showering. S.E. quite rough. Boats busy up sound. My birthday today! 1 egg.

1 Nov. 28 Some day! Raining like H. & blowing. Strong S. with Easterly. Syd pulled up the boats in time.

4 Nov. 28 Lovely day calm as a mill pond no wind only very light northerly. Kinky Kid passed going up so blew to her & Syd rowed out with the mail & got a sack of mail off her. Got nightgown from Pa & 3 letters one from Daisy & Mrs. H. & a note from Nan. The films and lessons "everything."

6 Nov. 28 Pt. cloudy. Lt. S.W. calm. Clearing up yards & dumping the rubbish. Was going to paint oil shed but rain came on. Saw 2 great big whales out in front of derrick. Finished Billy's rompers today they look cute on him. Heard that the Maquinna was at Nootka S.-bound.

15 Nov. 28 Rotten day strong S. & rain. That boat finally went up the sound slow as a snail. Awful mess on the deck with the rain & wind.

23 Nov. 28 Pt. Cloudy. Clear in the morning. Some rain. S.W. wind. Mod. swells saw a light over by surf islands tonight. Syd made a "horse" for Billy he sure likes it.

29 Nov. 28 Pt. cloudy lt. easterly. K.K. down first thing & got over mail— Woodwards parcel! John called this afternoon so Syd and Doris managed to get out & get more mail Eatons things etc. a goose a fish & some tea and butter. Great excitement today. Rochelle up tonight.

17 Dec. 28 Pt. Cloudy with some fog. Horn going from 6:30 till about one oclock. John fishing again. K.K. down first thing & we got our MAIL! Needed a wheel barrow! Wesley Church box, Spencers order Simpsons & mail. Quite a day.

21 Dec. 28 Pt. Cloudy lt. swell. No boats around today. Made 2 Puddings, gave them a good boiling! Syd made the addition for the table. Heard episode 6 of the serial over K.G.O.

23 Dec. 28 Clear Mod swells lt. easterly 2 boats came down the Sound & went into Forward Inlet. Syd got and put up the tree. All the decorations on now. Cleaned the chickens tonight. Had corned beef & cabbage for supper sure was good. 2 of Flopsy's bunnies dead today. Syd fixing up the Evinrude.

"The lightkeeper, wife and seven children are all well and happy," Halkett recorded in his cabin aboard the *Estevan* after his "great inspection" that June. Every building on the station boasted a fresh coat of paint. The sheen of the machinery and its myriad brasswork bespoke the hours of care and attention Syd lavished on his diesels. According to Violet, "Those engines were his pride and joy." A year later the superintendent discovered Syd Warren had renewed the flooring in the house, laid new linoleum, and rebuilt the balcony and steps, all "in a good workmanlike manner." Again Syd, Jessie, and their brood were hale and hearty. "Their garden has done very well this year," Halkett marvelled, "40 lbs. of green peas being picked and canned the day previous to my visit. Practically all vegetable truck is now grown on the island."[17] Jessie kept careful track of current market prices for produce and entered the fruits of her toil as "profits" on her diary's back pages. Chickens, rabbits, and fish supplied protein. They ate "Lilly" one night, "Flopsy" later in the week, and anonymous chickens in between.

The Warrens seemed to have banished the frightful spectres of starvation and madness from Kains Island. If only all the keepers could copy them! Still, on those wages they worked only to eat. A cheque bounced at the grocers and a "dirty letter" arrived in the sack from Wilby shortly after, castigating Syd "to change his ways" because the department would never "keep anybody whose wages were garnisheed." Jessie spread out her ledgers that night and ferreted out the only

Syd and Doris Warren going for mail through the gap, a few feet from where the wave hit.

explanation possible: the agent had forgotten to mail their last pay voucher to the bank in Victoria.[18] In September 1928 Syd had to borrow money to pay up arrears in his life insurance premiums.

Gene Faulk always looked forward to dropping the mail off at Kains. Whatever tidings he brought in the fat satchel lying on the wheelhouse floor, there was no warmer welcome to be had anywhere. He set out from Quatsino on the morning of 23 October 1929, but his mood turned sour when his engine "acted up." He was halfway out though, and if whatever was wrong proved too much for him, Syd was nothing if not a sure-fire mechanic.

The mechanic was already at work, with his wrenches, oil, and pistons all over the engine room floor, when one of the girls came running with the news that the *Kinky Kid* had just rounded the shore. Syd wiped his hands, picked up the out-going mail at the house, and hurried down to the narrow cut of a landing. He flipped over the skiff, climbed in, and shoved off. The tide was out, leaving the gap so narrow that Syd had to stand up to make the first hundred yards or his oars would only scrape the rocks. Then the wave hit him, smashing the boat into the rock wall and pitching him overboard. Faulk was below decks puzzling over his afflicted engine and heard none of the commotion near the shore.

Heavy-set and overweight, Warren clawed at the overturned skiff for a few gut-wrenching moments while the sea filled his boots and clothing like cold concrete. Try as he might, he could not hoist himself up. A few yards away on shore Jessie and her daughters "hollered to the mail man to come and help, but he was down fixing his engine & didn't hear [them] calling until ten or fifteen minutes." After one last, futile heave, Warren lost his grip and slid under.

"Doris swam out to try & save him but I think he must have been dead when she got there," the widow Warren wrote Halkett. Her daughter swam in circles, peering through the kelp until she saw Syd wafting past in the undertow below. She dived down, seized him by the hair and, kicking furiously, brought him up.

"Marjorie ran over the rocks and threw some life corks for Doris to catch on to," said Jessie, "otherwise I don't think she could have made it into the rocks. I then went over, and only just in time to save Doris & her Daddy for she was so numb from swimming that she could hardly hold on any longer. It was only touch and go there for us as the tide was coming in and the waves were now up to my neck."[19]

Faulk emerged from below decks and heard screams coming from the human chain stretching into the water. The surf rammed Doris against the rocks with their rasping barnacles. He gunned the cursed engine, raced over, hauled the thoroughly scourged and exhausted girl and her unconscious father aboard, then took the skiff in tow.

"I went back over the rocks and we dragged him up on the beach," Jessie Warren continued. "Faulk worked on him for awhile then went to Quatsino for help. After that we all took turns, the best we could (Doris numb and bleeding badly) but it was no use."

"It's funny how you react to things like that," Violet remembered, explaining how they took turns all day long straddling the corpse, kneading the chest, and lifting its arms to coax it back to life. Finally they dragged and rolled the dead weight up the ramp into the boathouse.

Faulk came back with three friends who spent a sleepless night trying to comfort the keening widow and seven children. Habit dies hard and sometime that night Jessie scrawled, "Syd got drowned," in her diary. "The boat is coming now to take the body to Quatsino and we are going too," Jessie wrote Wilby in that hollow dawn. She promised to leave two of the men in charge in case fog came up. Syd left no will so she asked to have his last cheque made out to her. "I am so upset that I cannot write any further," she closed. Later she added a postscript, promising to return the next day and run the light until they could be relieved. After the funeral she "made a risky trip back" to the station.

Jessie worked hard to ward off her grief. There was all that packing to do, including Syd's clothing with its familiar feel and lingering manly scent. She even found time for one last weeding of her garden. "Nearly all packed now," she wrote on 29 October with the house dead quiet around her. "Wish the boat would hurry up." Halkett came ashore in the *Estevan*'s workboat next morning. The silent sailors ferried all the crates out to the ship, then came back for Jessie and the girls. Halkett stood in the wheelhouse with them as the anchors came clattering up into the fo'c's'le. The ship shuddered, belched a black plume out of its funnel, and turned away from Kains. The superintendent was deeply moved by the courage of the girl who stood sullenly at his side, a mass of welts and scabs. "Great credit is due Doris Warren," he wrote Wilby that night, "a girl of sixteen years of age who immediately dove in and swam to her father and was cut by the barnacles and badly bruised by the surf on the rocks and was just conscious when she reached shore."[20]

Friends in town took in Doris and the oldest girls. Jessie spent two days and

nights on board the *Estevan* at the quay. She sat in her cabin with her diary in front of her after supper on Hallowe'en, overhearing the deckhands' banter as they took turns scraping stubble, splashing cologne, brushing their boots, borrowing each other's "best duds," and winking at the results in the mirror before clomping down the gangplank, bound for the costume ball. "Nearly all up now," she wrote. "Everybody getting ready for the dance. Good hunting tonight." Still a handsome woman at thirty-seven, she must have wondered if she would ever be anyone's quarry again.

Next morning Jessie swallowed her pride and borrowed some provisions from the ship's mess. Halkett opened his wallet and paid a teamster to haul the rest of her belongings away to a small rented house. She shook hands good-bye, then climbed up beside the driver and rolled off up Quatsino's main street to start life all over again, alone and away from the cruel sea.

Above: Veteran 1161-ton lighthouse tender *Estevan* served generations of keepers between 1912 and 1969.

Over: Julia Moe, who with her husband Ron started keeping Kains Island in the 1970's, has published two books of poetry about her life there.

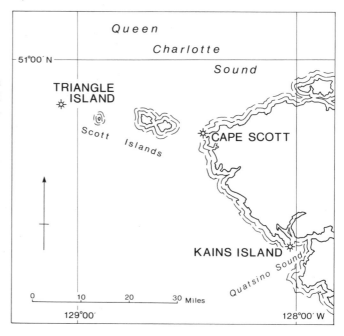

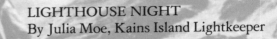

LIGHTHOUSE NIGHT
By Julia Moe, Kains Island Lightkeeper

All night the wind
comes and goes;
the storm can't quite decide
to come this way.
all night we watch the light turn
around and around:
a bad night for boats
skirting the cape.
here inside
the wind hardly rattles the windows,
the cats wheeze and twitch
in lost dreams;
night duty grows endless,
and oh how my body longs
to fall into the darkness of sleep.

(From *December Tide*,
Harbour Publishing, 1978.)

Estevan

No one will ever know if Colonel William Patrick Anderson, C.E., C.M.G., spared much thought for those isolated and impoverished families strung out five thousand miles away on the Pacific rim as he bent lovingly over his first-rate stamp collection in the evenings on Cooper Street, or sat in his club (the Rideau) savouring oysters with his peers in a fog of the finest Havanas. He had enough accomplishments of his own to count: decorated veteran of the Fenian raids, charter member of the Canadian Society of Engineers, executive member of the Geographic Board of Canada, chairman of the Canadian Lighthouse Board, chief engineer of the Department of Marine and Fisheries since 1891. He had stood at the elbows of ten successive ministers, including Laurier himself, and Sir Charles Tupper, too. Towering head and shoulders above the sour air of office politics, he was an artist with power. Marine agents on both coasts and the inland waterway were at his beck and call. He had only to bring his finger down on a map and reach for a T-square and slide rule to dispatch armies of labourers, shiploads of lumber, and tons of gravel and cement to transform an untouched wilderness forever.

The *Valencia* had been a bit of a blot, no doubt about that, but Gaudin had handled the enquiry well, and who in his lifetime would ever pick their way through the paper trail to stumble upon the real cause? Professionally he had taken on nature and had overcome every obstacle from St. John's to Prince Rupert. All that remained for him was to create a monument that would extend his reputation into the international sphere. And this he did at a place with the unlikely name of Hole-in-the-Wall, midway up Vancouver Island's West Coast on Estevan Point. The lighthouse taking shape at Estevan in the summer of 1909 would quite literally be Anderson's highest accomplishment, the boldest, most beautiful lighthouse in all British Columbia.

When the forms came away, the tower was one of the tallest free-standing concrete structures in the West. Erupting like a petrified geyser out of the stony beach, the eight-sided monolithic column soared 150 feet upward, embraced by flying buttresses holding it fast against the wind and rumbling earth tremors. The $35,000 first order classical lens on top was so huge that a man could spread a stepladder inside on the turntable, climb up, stretch out his arms, and not be able to touch any of its dazzling crystal prisms. In all, the beacon room, lens frame, clockworks, catwalks, and dome weighed twenty-five tons. An architectural triumph, the colossus at Estevan Point also stands as a graceful and fitting marker for one of Canada's most historic sites. Two momentous events that occurred two centuries apart give Estevan a unique and ominous significance.

Throughout the summer of 1980 British Columbians were bombarded with government advertising, complete with a bewigged "Captain Cook," to remind them it was two hundred years since native people discovered white men at Nootka Sound. The contrived hoopla was certainly wasted on the Nootkas at Friendly Cove, who had nothing to commemorate but their rendezvous with a bitter destiny. At any rate their oral history contends that their first European contact was neither with Cook nor at Nootka.

Their version, preserved by Father Brabant, a pioneer Catholic missionary, maintains that the first white men they encountered appeared off Estevan Point in June 1774. The Hesquiat band was astounded by the appearance of an immense bird out there on the water. As it drew near they assumed it was the long-awaited sacred canoe manned by their ancestors returning from the "land of the dead." When the oar-less "canoe" dropped anchor, they came face to face with bleached-out men clad in bizarre costumes, very much alive, who had iron to trade for furs.

The 1774 log of that Spanish vessel, the *Santiago*, commanded by Juan Perez, confirms the Indian account of

You could spread a stepladder inside the Estevan lens.

Estevan's famous flying buttresses (left) were duplicated at Father Point, Quebec (right).

the meeting place. Its description of the land mass seen from the anchorage—lowland rising gradually to rolling hills against a backdrop of snow-capped mountain peaks—is a clear description of the Hesquiat Peninsula.

Early in 1907 Anderson selected Hole-in-the-Wall, on the southern extremity of the peninsula, as his site, eighteen miles west of where *King David* had been wrecked a year before. There was no safe landing there, but supplies could be off-loaded near the Indian village of Hesquiat. A workgang hacked a trail five miles through dense underbrush, bridging ravines and rocks, and laid track for a horse-drawn tramway.

Without even the scant protection of a treaty, the Hesquiat people stood helplessly by as Indian Affairs surrendered their ancestral lands to Marine and Fisheries, and white men came crashing through the bush, scattering game. In May 1908, as soon as the Indian agent departed, their smouldering rage finally burst into flames. Five band members, led by Chief Amos, ransacked and demolished four buildings their agent had leased to the Marine Department for storing fodder and equipment. In a letter to the Indian agent Gaudin railed against "the man (Amos). . . responsible for this illegal action."[1]

But the Indians were the least of his worries. In late November 1908 a high tide, driven before a heavy southeast gale, carried away twenty-five yards of track and "pretty well chewed up" two hundred yards more. A.L. Gray, officer in charge, ordered his men to pack supplies on their backs and in wheelbarrows. "They become rather heavy after the first mile," he wrote, as they locked knuckles around the wheelbarrows' handles, plodded up slippery hills, and braced their heels for the down slopes with their loads of cement and gravel. Rain fell in a

Estevan supplies were unloaded at Hesquiat and hauled overland to the lighthouse, first by Jitney (top), then by truck.

continuous pelting curtain. Alfred Nelson, who took over the project from Gray on 26 January 1909, wrote Gaudin to inform him how that month's toil was all for nothing. The weather, he wrote, had been "simply awful. . . . Well, we went to work and screened about 20 yards of sand and then the horse got sick so we could not haul it away and now the high tide and wind the last month washed it all back to sea."[2]

Rotten food added misery to futility. One of the workers wrote Templeman in Ottawa one night, complaining bitterly about "the scandalous way" they were fed by "Mr. Humber of Victoria, the Foreman of the work." One of the gang had shot

Estevan Point Lighthouse.

a wild bull which provided ten days' fresh meat. "Then began a period of salt meat, day after day, morning, noon and evening." Leftovers were scraped off plates and dished up again as concoctions that were "on *many occasions sour*."[3]

In spite of all the trials, the tower with its winding staircase rose steadily higher with each bucket of concrete hauled up hand over hand, by rope and pulley. Finally they assembled the beacon room and its monstrous lens, with an imposing concentric configuration of crystal prisms, at the summit. In February 1910

Anderson proudly proclaimed the establishment of a "first class station . . . a very fine specimen of reinforced concrete work giving a monolithic column over 100 feet high, reinforced by flying buttresses." The new light and telegraph station would doubtless "prove of great assistance to transport steamers and local traffic alike," he boasted.

For its keepers, Estevan Point light held out some obvious advantages over its more isolated West Coast and island siblings. The station was a small, self-contained community, not unlike Pachena, since radio operators and their families were stationed there as well. Hesquiat lay within walking distance, though relations with the resentful band always demanded a good deal of diplomacy and tact. Supplies came "fairly regular," loaded onto canoes from the tender and landed at Hesquiat to be trucked down the slimey plank road to the station.

Still, the sodden climate and Estevan's location, perched on the precarious Pacific rim, took their toll of keepers. Otto Buckholtz, a veteran sealer who had helped clear the site and worked with the construction crew, was appointed Estevan's first keeper. In the autumn of 1909 he became embroiled in an argument with his assistant, Luckovitch. Luckovitch resolved it by shooting two of Buckholtz's cows. Jens Peter Jensen, Buckholtz's replacement, wrote Victoria:

Japanese submarine I-26, alleged to have fired the only hostile shells at Canadian soil since 1812. The gun was mounted aft because a small plane was launched on the foredeck. Imperial War Museum photo.

"Under present conditions with unusual weather and earthquakes find that I will have to be releaved either for a trip or for good. do not care which."

So life went on at Estevan much as at any other light. There were times of strife stemming from personality clashes between keepers and their assistants, or between the lighthouse and the radio operators. Boredom of the "bushed" advanced and receded. The department still appropriated "the whole time of the keeper," and a station with a tower that size, along with two dwellings and radio rooms, required it. But the quiet lighthouse life was shattered in June 1942, when Estevan Point became a household word in the most shocking manner imaginable.

According to the official version, Japanese submarine I-26 surfaced two miles off Estevan at nightfall 20 June and fired twenty-five 5.5 inch shells at the station. All the missiles landed short or overshot the tower and the village of Hesquiat behind. Estevan Point went down in history as the first place where enemy shells had struck Canadian soil since 1812. The events combined all the necessary ingredients of headlines: isolation, danger, a lighthouse. Like the Pattersons of Cape Beale some thirty years before, Robert and Eliza Lally, lightkeepers at Estevan Point, suddenly found their peaceful world thrust into the harsh spotlight of the nation's press.

Accounts published after the war left no doubt that the shellfire came from a submarine's deck gun. "The submarine pulled out on the surface and everyone could see her and hear the diesel engines quite clearly," the residents claimed. At the outbreak of war, lightkeepers were given crash courses in silhouette identification, and identification manuals lay within easy reach in their radio room, so their reports should be reliable. Commander Yokota of Japanese submarine I-26 freely admitted the attack.

Yet the incident at Estevan has always been treated with skepticism and derision by West Coast residents. "What a bunch of malarkey!" snorts veteran West Coast fisherman Robbie McKeand. "Just stop and think, why in the name of common sense would any kind of half-intelligent being ever surface and shell a lighthouse? All he would do would be give away his position. The Japanese navy was a pretty smart outfit, they didn't go around shooting lighthouses."[4]

Half a world away that summer of '42, a young destroyer captain in the Mediterranean opened a letter from home and was astonished by his mother's account of the incident. Looking back forty years later, Captain Gordon Stead, who, after the war, sat at the controls of the Department of Transport as deputy minister, clearly remembers reading that letter and thinking the whole story was a piece of lunacy. He had spent enough time chasing U-boats to know that no hostile skipper in his right mind would fritter away his position in a feckless attack on an aid to navigation that was as useful to him as it was to his enemies. And if, for some strange reason, he found himself doing so, how could his gunners get twenty-five straight misses around that huge 150-foot tower, sticking out like a clay pipe in a shooting gallery?[5]

Sinister theories were brought forward, often by those whose sons or husbands served in the navy and claimed to have information which would "curl your hair." The vessel in question, they affirm, was neither a submarine nor Japanese. One person from the lights, a contemporary of the Lallys, has even made veiled references to a visit paid by the RCMP afterward, who allegedly told them that the official version of the incident would be that a lone submarine was the culprit. Any statements to the contrary would bring dismissal and stiff prison terms—the War Measures Act was in force.

Obviously oral traditions and rumours, rampant in isolated places, must be handled with great care. But one fact flies in the face of the official version: by his own eyewitness account Robert Lally saw much more than a lone submarine that night. Whether it was a clandestine visit from the RCMP or not, something happened in the hectic hours after the event to make him change his story drastically.

The tale really began ninety miles to the north on the afternoon of 20 June. HMCS *Santa Maria*, a seventy-three foot patrol vessel of the "gum-boot navy," was rounding Cape Scott at the northern tip of Vancouver Island, her officers and crew vigilant for the wake of a periscope knifing through the water, and relieved that they had seen nothing. On an earlier patrol they had stumbled upon an abandoned, burned-out cannery which the Japanese had artfully converted to a watering station by diverting a stream into a galvanized outflow pipe. They were around, the "wily Nips," no doubt about that.[6]

Halfway around the Cape was an American halibut boat, the *Sea Breeze*. Her crew was frantically waving, whistling, and shouting to attract attention. When *Santa Maria* hove to within hailing distance, the excited fishermen told the sailors they had just had the scare of their lives. After setting their lines they had been attracted to an eerie turbulence in the water nearby. Suddenly a huge black shape rose through the bubbles and slithered out on the surface, water gushing out her compartments. When she spotted them, the submarine plunged under again. Twenty minutes later they saw her sinister profile some two miles to the west, steaming away south—surely an unlikely action for an enemy sub with an easy target in hand.

The fishermen had been too shaken to identify the submarine as Japanese or American, but they feared the worst. *Santa Maria* immediately radioed Maritime Command in Victoria and received orders to head south in hot pursuit. Captain Dave Ritchie ordered full speed and, with her engines roaring, *Santa Maria* swung around and set off after her quarry, armed with a few depth charges and .303 rifles. As darkness fell they plowed on, blacked out and chary at the prospect of ramming another vessel.

Down at Estevan Robert Lally strode out to the tower to light up. It was going on 9:15. Two days to go until the solstice, when darkness would begin to gain ground against the long summer days. He climbed up the 150 steps, wound up the weights, drew the curtains, and flicked the master switch to the thousand-watt bulb behind the prisms. Closing the tower door, Lally walked around to the beach under the huge windmill of light for a last look out to sea before heading home. A "moderate to strong" northwest wind came at him over a choppy sea. As the sun sank behind the rollers on the horizon toward Japan, visibility was unlimited. The time was 9:25.

Then he saw smoke on the horizon. And out of the smokescreen came a warship, zigzagging. Nothing unusual in that; Canadian warships had passed by that afternoon, and they had often patrolled offshore, blacked out, through the night. But this one began firing. When the first shells landed short of where he stood, Lally bolted for the tower, ran up the 150 steps two at a time, and cut power to the light. He had a commanding view from the catwalk in the beacon room. As he caught his breath, the lightkeeper took out a pencil and notebook and began to scribble a detailed account, unearthed by this author from the files of the Department of National Defense forty years later, with the help of a concerned MP:

Sighted warship on horizon SW light zig-zagging under heavy smoke screen. Time 9:25 p.m. Hostile warships shelled station. First shot "Marker" time 10 hrs. 14 min 30 Sec P.M. Put light out in tower 10:17 P.M. (on my own, no instructions). First salvo arrived crashed in front of light. 600 yards. Took up observation on landing outside lantern. Observed flashes from hostile batteries on horizon. (Second marker arrived 400 yards out. Second salvo arrived) Crashed 500 yards in front (Shots in line) (He is trying to stagger us) Shells falling faster and more in number. 3rd marker exploded 200 to 300 yards in front of light followed by a salvo from both barbettes on hostile warship on horizon exploded with terrific force tower shook. Three windows broke in lantern. (Stones flying and broken rock). Pieces of timber, etc. Six salvos fired in front light. Then he sent one salvo over. Made terrible racket like freight trains passing over bridge. Driving band must have tore off one of the shells for it started to "growl". Started down tower. Shells exploded about ¼ mile in bush. Saw flashes from explosion. Then run down stairs. Shell too close for comfort. Next salvo went over about ½ mile in bush then exploded. Four salvos sent over tower. One salvo burst near Hesquiat and another towards Antoine's beach (Inner Harbour).

During action observed white light approach from direction of warship (surface) towards submarine. No binoculars to observe same with. All women and children walked to Green Patch about ½ mile away (good cover) from shells or shrapnel. I did not mention white light to anyone as they might have thought it a landing party or demolition squad. No one excited or jittery, thought they were going to picnic. Roy, my son, was in Hesquiat fishing when shelling started. He came home. Said shells whistled and made awful row in bush. I asked him what he would do when shells landed close and believe it or not I nearly fell through the floor when he said Jump and run like H.... for the bush. He was laughing.[7]

There was pandemonium in Hesquiat where the Indians poured out of their shacks and ran for their canoes and motorboats. The rag-tag flotilla was underway even as the shells were still falling, heading for Boat Basin at the head of Hesquiat Harbour. They too watched a dim white light, "as if on a boat," head east of Estevan Point, reverse course, then head toward one of the sources of the shots. "These Indians," reported an officer from HMCS *Mooloch* who interviewed them a few hours later, "are certain that shells were coming from two different directions and came in volleys of three shots, one behind the other."[8]

O.E. Redford, senior radio operator at Estevan, sent off a message: "WE ARE BEING SHELLED," then scrambled for cover. Shortly after, naval headquarters in Victoria radioed the *Mooloch*, ordering her to proceed to Estevan Point to evacuate "women and children survivors." The effect of the plain language message in the *Santa Maria*'s darkened wheelhouse was electric. "My God! What's happened!" exclaimed her engineer, Dr. Joe Boucher. "Here we got news there's submarines in the area, and then the next thing we know there's a message to one of our sister ships to remove survivors from the point." Captain Ritchie "really got the wind up," and the crew strained to see any evidence of a raid or invasion through the butt end of the night and the encroaching dawn. "And to our utter amazement," Boucher remembered, "there wasn't a thing in sight anywhere... there were no aircraft, no ships, nothing—*nothing*!" They saw no sign whatever of search aircraft or other vessels anywhere near Estevan over the ensuing forty-eight hours.[9]

The *Mooloch* beat them to the Point, and sent a shore party over to Hesquiat. They interviewed the Indians, who told about the strange white light and the separate origin of the shells. Then the sailors set off over the greasy plank road to Estevan in a truck, to interview Lally and Redford, check for damage, and take out the women and children. "Most of the men here served in the last war and thus considerable faith may be put in their observations," the *Mooloch*'s officer in charge wrote shortly after he arrived. "Two people here definitely describe a light cruiser, other a submarine." Redford added that the shells came in rapid salvos, "25-30 shots fired in all, apparently from different sized guns."[10] A search party found a large shell fragment lying in a crater. Carrying the shell, the shore party left the station for Hesquiat, boarded the *Mooloch*, and set off south for Port Alberni. The "survivors" elected to stay behind and take their chances.

Within hours of *Mooloch*'s departure, *Santa Maria* rounded Estevan Point, dropped anchor at Hesquiat, and sent a party, including Dr. Boucher, ashore. The village was totally deserted. Walking from house to house was "the eeriest thing"; the shacks gave no hint whatever of the whereabouts of the people. The party tramped noisily along the plank road for a mile or more before realizing they might walk into an ambush. Fanning out into the underbrush, they crept up on the lighthouse, taking cover in the damp salal, rifles at the ready.

At first the station seemed as dead and deserted as the village. Then Robert Lally emerged from one of the buildings. The sailors hailed him, "scaring the poor guy out of a year's growth," and gathered round. The lightkeeper told them how a lone submarine had surfaced the night before and shelled the station, avoiding any mention of the cruiser, the white light, or the shells coming from different directions. He did, however, point out the tide pool where the shell had been found. The seamen were astonished to find that the water was bright yellow. "The shell that landed," Lally explained, "had a lot of Japanese writing on it in yellow paint and when the tide came in the paint had sort of come off... but it's rather strange," he went on, "the yellow paint characters were in Japanese yet there were English markings, numerals and whatever stamped in the base of the shell."

This was too much for the sailors. It just didn't add up. "The whole situation and *that* aspect of it as well created quite a bit of skepticism," according to Dr. Boucher. "You know, even amongst ourselves... this is... put on to remind people that there's a war on. That certainly was the predominant thinking at that time: that the way everything has happened this is not enemy action; this is more or less to stage a little bit of grandstand stuff to wake the people up." Shaking their heads in disbelief, the men hiked back to Hesquiat and resumed their patrol.[11] Life returned to "normal" at Estevan. But elsewhere across Canada the "enemy action," contrived or genuine, was greeted with anything but skepticism.

Colonel J.L. Ralston, minister of National Defense, met with a hushed clot of reporters in a corridor off the House that afternoon. "From the rate at which the shells were fired," he stated, "it would appear that there were possibly two enemy craft involved."[12] News of the incident arrived along with a much more ominous development: the fall of Tobruk, the Allied stronghold in North Africa. It was a gloomy day in Parliament and a notice marking the first anniversary of the Nazi invasion of Russia, full of purple prose about Soviet resistance, did little to dispel the pessimism. McKenzie King rose to inform the house about "the first time in this war that our country has been attacked on land," proclaiming, "It only goes to bear out what has been said so often that no one can take too seriously both the immediacy and the extent of the danger with which all parts of the world are confronted, and at this time our own part in particular."[13]

When pressed for further details of the attack, Ralston promised more, after a period of time to be determined "with the intelligence branches of the services involved." He did, however, state that flying conditions were "unsuitable" at the bases nearest to Estevan Point at the time of the attack (contrary to Lally's weather observation), but assured the press that aircraft "were out at dawn the next morning." None were spotted by *Santa Maria*'s crew. A bomber was reportedly dispatched but crashed on take-off, killing its crew.

The effect of the shelling in southern British Columbia was predictable. "You should have seen the panic when the Japanese submarine shelled Estevan," MP John Gibson recalled. "I was at a big party out at the air force base when the word came through. It was just like Pearl Harbour. Talk about a scattering of the brass—everybody drunk, of course. But it kind of brought home that the war wasn't just a big joke."[14] Truckloads of obsolete Ross rifles and Lewis guns arrived at Esquimalt and other bases, while Ralston laid plans to issue more arms to volunteer companies "in as great quantities and just as fast as possible."

Whoever peered into their range finders, pulled their lanyards, and sent those shells hurtling toward Estevan did the pro-conscription forces in King's government the greatest service they could have dared wish for. It was a quagmire, the conscription issue, right from the start. In Quebec, it seemed that no one—from the pampered sons of the rich, like Pierre Trudeau, to the lowliest farmers and blue-collar workers—relished playing the role of British cannon fodder in hopeless ventures from Hong Kong to Dieppe. The West was restless, always willing to believe the worst of the Quebecois, those "gutless frogs," who caroused in Montreal while *their* boys were bled white.

King tried to wiggle out of his long-standing promise to avoid conscription, by holding a referendum that would free his administration "from any past commitments restricting the method of raising men for military service." The outcome of the referendum was divisive. Overall, the country had given him a sixty-forty edge, but in Quebec, his power base, the referendum had failed by a four-to-one margin. His cabinet remained deeply split, with politically-disastrous resignations in the offing: his Quebec lieutenant, P.J.A. Cardin, promised to resign if conscription were legislated, while Ralston, minister of Defence, threatened to resign if it was not.

Heated debate on a controversial amendment to the 1940 National Resources Mobilization Act, which would permit conscription, had begun 19 June, *the day before the shelling*. No sooner did Ralston sit down on June 21, after reporting the attack, than Angus McDonald, the minister for Naval Services, rose to affirm his support for the proposed amendment "without any doubt or hesitation or reservation whatsoever." He took his seat to the thunderous pounding of desks and a ringing chorus of "hear-hear."[15]

With this one-two knockout punch the conscriptionists carried the day, and the bill passed final reading by July. Conscripts—"Zombies"—would have the option of volunteering for active duty overseas or could serve on the home front. Doing what? Naturally, after Estevan, the most crucial task they could perform would be "coastal defense."

The official report of the shelling arrived in Ottawa 1 July. Commodore J.R. Beech, commanding officer on the Pacific Coast, brushed aside the statements of eyewitnesses. "It would appear from the reports that the excitement during the bombardment may have caused those present to see and hear things which did not actually occur," he declared. The mysterious white light was undoubtedly the American halibut boat *Sea Breeze*, he explained, referring to the *Santa Maria*'s

Winter at Estevan Point.

patrol report. Yet that report, in the form submitted by Beech, differed radically from Dr. Boucher's recollection. It claimed that the fishermen had been brought aboard the *Santa Maria* and, when asked to locate the sub they had sighted, pointed on the chart to a position *"eight miles east of Estevan,"* a position which would put the submarine on dry land at the foot of the coastal mountains! At any rate, the *Sea Breeze* could never have appeared off Estevan Point ahead of the *Santa Maria*, which had left her behind at Cape Scott hours before.

"It is considered unlikely that a surface vessel was present during the bombardment since RCAF patrols failed to disclose any hostile craft," Beech affirmed. But according to Defense Minister Ralston, no planes were over the area at the time of the attack due to "unsuitable weather," and the *Santa Maria*'s crew, much to their astonishment, encountered no aircraft before, during, or afterward.

Beech concluded, "This bombardment was in all probability carried out by one submarine mounting 5.5" guns. . . . " The extract from Robert Lally's "Lighthouse War Diary" was never made public, and someone carefully filleted 20 June 1942 from the Lightkeeper's Logbook at Estevan.[16] Yet it is interesting to recall that, setting aside the question of the cruiser Lally and the others saw, their report of the firing described it as coming from a gun mounted "forward of the sub's conning tower." The I-26 had no deck gun forward of the conning tower. For Lally to gain that impression the sub would have had to surface in reverse—a physical impossibility.

Beech's version was confirmed by Commander Yokota's ready confession that his I-26 had carried out the attack. But Yokota was a questionable confessor at best. There's no more despicable trade in warfare than commanding a submarine. It takes a man with a shriveled soul to peer through a periscope, put the profile of an unarmed merchant ship on the open sea behind the cross hairs, and order torpedoes away. He can be sure there won't be many survivors. And it was just such an action, rather than carrier-based dive bombers, which opened hostilities between Japan and the United States that "day of infamy," 7 December 1941. The man behind the eye-piece was none other than Commander Minoru Yokota. He had slipped out of Yokuska on 19 November as part of Kempu Butai, the armada bound for Pearl Harbour, under orders to seek out and sink American shipping at the outbreak of hostilities. Early on the morning of 6 December Yokota sighted the 2,140-ton American freighter *Cynthia Olson*, bound for Honolulu with a cargo of lumber.

In his book *Infamy: Pearl Harbour and its Aftermath*, John Toland uses freshly declassified sources to document how Franklin Roosevelt and his chief of staff, General Marshal, knew of the impending attack on Pearl Harbour well in advance. They deliberately kept this intelligence, culled from cracked Japanese codes, from the navy and army commanders in Hawaii. Afterward, they saddled Admiral Kimmel and General Short with the blame, and the two joined Benedict Arnold in popular demonology of the day.[17]

In retrospect, FDR was wrong for the right reason. In order to enter the fray with the Axis the president had to lay low, once and for all, the powerful isolationist lobby which had grown out of the Nye Committee's revelations of shameless war profiteering in World War I. Though it must be cold comfort to the parents and widows of the hundreds of sailors entombed in the *Arizona*, and the 1200 more who perished in the infamous "sneak attack," Pearl Harbour held out the best opportunity to justify entering the war.

Commander Yokota very nearly gave the game away. On the morning of 7 December a radio operator aboard the liner *Lurline* heard the *Cynthia Olson* signalling "SSS"—the code for a submarine attack. The operator tried desperately to raise Pearl Harbour and San Francisco, but finally got through to the U.S. Coast Guard Radio Station at Point Bonita, California. Commodore Berndtson and chief radio operator Rudy Asplund logged the time: 7:00 a.m., fifty-five minutes before the first yellow planes with red suns on their fuselages appeared over Pearl Harbour.

This was surely an act of war, even more clearcut than the torpedoing of the *Lusitania* in the Irish Sea in 1917. Because of her buoyant cargo, *Cynthia Olson* took three or four hellish hours to go down with her twenty-five man crew. If word of the attack had reached Pearl Harbour it would certainly have alerted the forces clustered there like sitting ducks, and very possibly would have been intercepted by the enemy, causing them to call off the attack. But things went according to plan.

Toland carefully conducts his readers through a maze of lies and half-truths,

Unexploded 5.5-inch shells which landed near
Estevan Light June 20, 1942.

threading his way from General Marshall to intelligence officers who changed testimony and systematically destroyed evidence of their foreknowledge. When interviewed after the war, Yokota claimed he attacked the *Cynthia Olson after* 8:00 a.m., when dive bombers were pulverizing Pearl Harbour into a smoking ruin. It was a crucial hour on the clock of history, a discrepancy which rules out the element of surprise—the difference between an unprovoked attack and a cynical gambit to plunge a reluctant nation into global war. The implications are as clear as they are ominous: Commander Yokota either made an unthinkable error about the most pivotal hour in his nation's history, or he deliberately altered his recollections.[18]

For its part, the government of Canada still expects the world to take Yokota at his word about Canada's very own "Pearl Harbour" seven months later. "There is no doubt in the Department of National Defense regarding the shelling of Estevan Point Lighthouse," their Director of History wrote in 1982, "it was definitely done by the Japanese submarine I-26."

Maybe. But that official version leaves so much unexplained, and it depends on the evidence of Yokota to have credibility. Once Yokota's word is cast in doubt, that credibility vanishes.

Another scenario fairly suggests itself. There were American submarines, lots of them, slipping in and out of Dutch Harbour in Alaska, all with guns *forward* of their conning towers. There were cruisers too. The Canadian cruiser in the area was the lumbering ex-ferry renamed the *Prince Robert*. Official records show that she was in drydock that day, although contradictory reports have her on patrol. But there were American cruisers, and after the watershed of Midway, they would be the only other cruisers to be found so far into Allied waters. So the United States had the easy means and every opportunity to shell a target in British Columbia. And they may have had what Japan so obviously lacked: a motive. They would be giving allied military forces a leg-up out of a sticky political jam, assuring Canada the kind of total commitment to the war that would come with conscription. In principle, it wasn't so different from the Pearl Harbour gambit which had assured total U.S. involvement in the war. Military cooperation already existed at all levels, and Mackenzie King and President Roosevelt were known to consult informally on a first-name basis—although the ebullient president mistakenly took "Mackenzie" as the prime minister's first name, and shy Willie King was too chagrined to set matters right.

Top-level communication would result in the rendezvous between the submarine and one or more surface vessels off Estevan Point at nightfall. The men involved would be ordered to aim shells around the tower, and kick up a big fuss, but avoid civilian casualties, and above all, avoid damaging Colonel Anderson's masterwork. The need for strict radio silence would mean oral communication by dinghy, guided by flashlight as it zipped back and forth.

Opposite: Eyewitness Robert Lally on the night watch, Estevan Point Light.

Once word of the attack went out from the radio room at Estevan, the flotilla would scatter, confident that aerial reconnaissance would be delayed until they were well clear of the scene. Lally, in the meantime, would have doused the light and scribbled his factual on-the-scene report, ready for posting with the first of the gumboot-navy boats to visit the scene. It would be away before the RCMP or other government emissaries arrived to give Lally the "official version" of the incident, along with their warning that failure to cooperate could lead to imprisonment under the War Measures Act. Assuming Ottawa would know what to do with the dangerous true version once it arrived, Lally would later remove the lighthouse log's equally factual account, for his own protection.

Linda Weeden, wife of the lightkeeper at Estevan Point, went for a walk on 8 June 1973 and discovered another shell. Don Weeden radioed Victoria, and a Canadian Forces Explosive Ordnance Disposal team flew up from Comox. The shell was so badly corroded from three decades of salt water that they elected to blow it up rather than unscrew the fuse. It took three tries. When the projectile finally burst, it splattered surrounding rocks with lime-green picric acid. It was a marker, one of the first shells Robert Lally noted as he stood watching in disbelief and scribbling his record outside the lantern that night, thirty-one years before. "Dead men tell no tales," Robert Lally Jr. reflected forty years later. "But 'til the day he died my Dad swore it was a cruiser."

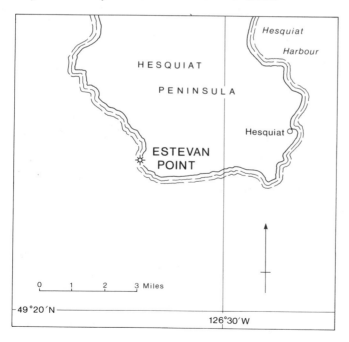

Nootka

It all began at Nootka. Captain Cook landed halfway up the West Coast in April 1778 on the southeast tip of Nootka Island. He sought the Northwest Passage but discovered sea otter pelts instead. Chief Maquinna of the Mowach-ahts gave Cook a lavish welcome (hence the cove's name) and in return, in an amusing twist of history, the explorer saddled them with the name Nootkas which, roughly translated, means "to go around." Standing aboard the *Discovery* when he met the people in their canoes, Cook had spread his arms to indicate he wanted the name of the place. Thinking he sought directions to a sheltered anchorage, they shouted, "Nootka-satl," and pointed to the cove.

The Spanish landed at Nootka in May 1789. They built a fort and occupied the area until March 1795 when Brigadier General Don Jose Manuel Alva, colonel of the regiment of Puebla, turned the bastion over to Lieutenant Thomas Pierce of the Royal Marines. While Spanish and British commissioners, and the curious Nootkas looked on, the Spanish flag was lowered, the Union Jack went up in its place, and all the white men left.

No sooner were the men-of-war out of sight than the Nootkas began dismantling the fort for its lumber and fittings. They even dug up the remains of Spanish soldiers killed off in a flu epidemic, and pried nails from their coffins to bend into fishhooks. Soon every physical trace of the Spanish in Canada was erased, except for a brick-lined well. But for over a century the Nootkas counted with Spanish numerals and observed Roman Catholic forms of worship. In 1859 band members rooting in a potato patch unearthed a Russian silver coin inscribed "Katherine II,

1775," which Captain McKay of the schooner *Morning Star* brought to Victoria.

To sail into Friendly Cove today is to witness first hand the decay and collapse of an advanced aboriginal civilization. Blackberries, themselves a foreign invader, have overgrown and choked the site where Maquinna feasted with Cook and his crew. Across a narrow channel from the lighthouse the government wharf, a dilapidated church, a boarded-up school, an abandoned fish-oil plant, and a scattering of Indian agency houses are all that remain of the once mighty Nootka nation outside the fenced graveyard. The Nootkas themselves have moved over to Gold River, lured by jobs in the pulp mill.

Like Victoria's Captain Nagle sixty years before, Herbert Smith, the storekeeper at Friendly Cove, set his own light up at its entrance in January 1906 to guide the mail steamers in at night. This was the light which the *King David* mistook for Cape Beale. Two years later, on 5 December 1909, a petition arrived in Victoria signed by "many of the settlers and others involved in the shipping interests of the West Coast of Vancouver Island." In a now-familiar refrain they "humbly prayed" for a light on Yuquot Point that would guide steamships on their run between Victoria and Quatsino Sound.

James Gaudin endorsed their proposal, claiming the light would enable coastal steamers headed for Tahsis Inlet to enter the Sound in rough weather, sheltered from the heavy seas hammering the West Coast. "The increasing commerce of the West Coast of Vancouver Island and the large number of passengers travelling on that run demand protection," he affirmed in a letter to Deputy Minister Johnston, making veiled reference to *Valencia*.[1]

Colonel Anderson answered the petitioners' prayers and authorized Gaudin to erect a light identical to the new one at Kains Island in February 1910. First, though, he must apply to Indian Affairs for the land. By September the agent had ironed out the details. San Rafael Island, the largest of the San Miguel Islands, would be ceded to the Department of Marine in exchange for $100 "for the benefit of the Indians," and a pledge to recruit "as much Indian labour as may be advantageously placed" during construction. Gaudin calculated that six men would be hired at $3.00 a day, including their board. "It must be understood," he cautioned the Indian agent, "that the Department will require efficient service and that indians or others engaged in their work will be subject to instant dismissal. . . if their labour or conduct are not satisfactory."[2]

The finished light exhibited a fixed white beacon from 108 feet up an "almost unscaleable" rock bluff. Landing was always perilous at Nootka, and supplies were winched up on a tramway. Herbert Smith, a close friend of H.S. Clements, the MP, was appointed lightkeeper in February 1911, in recognition of his voluntary services. His salary was $360 per annum—less than a third of the wages paid earlier to the Indian labourers.

Smith's first worry was the landing. He had no boat. By September he had smashed two canoes attempting to land supplies from Friendly Cove. He asked for a boat in August. In October the keeper disclosed, "In the recent gales I had my canoe smashed on the rocks & was thrown into the water." He reminded Captain Robertson, "I am *still* without a boat," and asked for caps and squibs to blast away the rock, and for some cement to pour steps down to the water.

Smith had emigrated with his eldest son. In June 1912 he obtained permission to sail to England and fetch his wife and remaining children. He left his boy, "22 years of age steady and reliable an abstainer & non smoker," in charge. He must have always regretted bringing his wife to Nootka; shortly after she arrived the arthritis invaded her. Smith received no fuel from the department. The nearest stand of timber lay two miles away by boat, and firewood had to be manhandled one log at a time up the "unscaleable" rocks.

In September 1913 his friend Clements came calling and was shocked to learn of Smith's difficulty in heating his clammy home. He promised to take the issue up with Captain Robertson and advised Smith to write the agent as well. The *Estevan* came up with two tons of coal in October and billed Smith $5 a ton. "Of course, it is a great Boon to have the coal delivered here," the keeper wrote thanking Clements, "but I understand it is the custom to supply Light Keepers Free where they cannot get wood around the Station." He asked the MP to let

Friendly Cove in the 1920's.

him know if this was correct, pledging, "If there is anything I can do for you in this district, I am yours to serve." A week later Robertson explained, "We have taken this matter up continuously with the Department and they do not feel justified in supplying coal to any lighthouse."[3]

In January 1914 Smith advised that "unprecedented Storms that have been raging on this coast during the past three weeks" carried away his landing, and "huge waves," using logs as battering rams, had beaten down the boathouse doors and stove in the boat's transom.

At least Smith was spared the routine of pumping a hand horn or keeping a fog watch. Only a single steamer called regularly at Nootka in 1915. Robertson replied to a request about the feasibility of installing a hand or power horn by stating that a steam plant was unwarranted. A hand horn, "to be operated by the Keeper in response to a steamboat whistle," would surely suffice.

In June 1915 J.W. Troup of C.P.R. Steamships called for installation of a flashing light as well as a horn after the *Princess Maquinna* mistook a fire on shore near Maquinna Point for the Nootka light. Fortunately, lead lines were cast. "Nootka light had not yet opened up," Troup related, "although from dead reckoning she should have opened up, but was behind time owing to adverse current." Realizing his error in time, the captain ran offshore, reshaped his course, "and in a short time opened out Nootka light properly."

If the Nootka light were flashing rather than steady, such a mistake would be unthinkable. As it was, Troup stood with the perplexed captain and his officers in the wheelhouse, and "watched the bonfire for fully half an hour. He remembered, "During the entire time we could not determine that the light we were looking at was not the Nootka light." That summer the department replaced the steady light with a fourth order lens fitted with a Duplex lamp and occulting apparatus, flashing every fifteen seconds.

In the summer of 1917 Smith joined his fellow keepers in the protest against their dismal wages. He began by writing Clements again, asking his old friend to arrange monthly rather than quarterly payment of his salary. "I can quite appreciate his position," the MP informed Alexander Johnston, deputy minister of Marine, "as he points out to me that the exorbitant price which now is being paid for almost everything in the way of his purchases for living, that the only chance he has is to pay cash for his supplies to make both ends meet." Smith, he added, was a close personal friend whom he visited once a year, and altogether a "very pains-taking and careful lightkeeper." Smith sent a copy of Clements' letter to Robertson, adding, "Prices of all food & clothing has nearly doubled."

Smith was not asking for a raise. He wanted monthly cheques because his suppliers balked at carrying credit for three months. But by July 1918 he had fallen too far behind. "I should esteem it a favour if you could find me a light with a better salary than this," he asked Robertson, or at least allow him to borrow against future wages by granting an advance. Freight rates from Vancouver and Victoria, coupled with "the increased cost of everything we eat and wear," were breaking them. Pointing out that he had "been in the Sound 12 years" and had only left to bring his wife out from England, he disclosed she was now "a confirmed Invalid with Rheumatism and cannot move unless carried and she is gradually becoming worse." Moreover, his youngest daughter was "only part educated." She *must* attend school. "I am laying this Matter before you for your consideration," Smith explained. "If you can do anything for Me, I shall be Glad, otherwise I Must look for Some More Lucrative Employment."[4]

In August Robertson offered Smith a transfer to Cape Mudge with its salary of $1020. Cape Mudge had a steam plant and Smith would have to use at least half his wages to hire an assistant, unless a member of his family was capable. He was glad to accept the agent's offer but he had a hard time persuading anyone to assume his position at Nootka. Finally he convinced a friend, William Taylor, to take charge on 15 October 1918.

Taylor telegraphed his resignation to Victoria three months later. "I regret having to take such a step," he explained. He had "given it a fair trial" for fifteen weeks but found his position "impossible," hunkered down against the battering wind and the hissing, tearing sound of the sea.

> My wife has contracted Rheumatism since being here owing to the dampness, we have had [so] many severe storms that it has been necessary to mop the bedroom floor during the night, and move the bed to the far corner of the room to escape the water. Since the Earthquake my Wife is nervous each time there is a storm as the building shakes, moreover When I go out in a skiff, my Wife is obliged to come and help to launch it, and then help me pull it up on the rocks, the only safe place to land owing to the surf, she refuses to stay and I have no desire to cripple my wife, as Smith did his, if Smith had been honest about the condition of things he would never have got me to relieve him.

"I am sorry, Dear Sir, to have to trouble you so much," Taylor apologized. Most of all he regretted Robertson could not "see things as they are during some of the Storms . . . as no one can realize what a place it is, unless they see for themselves."[5]

Taylor searched in vain for a replacement for six weeks, his own terrifying experience a poor advertisement at best. Finally, on 1 March 1919, Robertson enlisted P. Foley, a "returned soldier" serving as a deckhand aboard the *Newington*, who had once kept St. Mary's lighthouse in Newfoundland.

The department landed the long-awaited hand horn at Nootka in April. After a month on watch, Foley confessed he was no match for its rigours. On 8 May he asked to be relieved at the month's end. "I have been sick during the whole of April," he wrote, "and am not feeling any better, and am unable to do the work." His previous service on the East Coast may well have immunized him from the fear which had held the Taylors fast. He regretted "having to leave as I like the place, but I can't go against the Will of God." Sick as he was, Foley had done "all repair work and [painted] the tower."[6]

Once again the department faced the formidable task of finding a man willing to work in a god-forsaken place for next to nothing. Robertson had no luck in Victoria. Halkett hired another local, Arthur Marks, and dropped him off at the light 16 May. "I know nothing about the man as to his character and habits other than it was important to get a man for the vacancy," Robertson confessed to the deputy minister.[7]

As part of an arrangement with the department to survey conditions on the lights, a Red Cross nurse visited Nootka in 1922. Though Marks' wife had left him, he kept "his house in good condition," and was frequently entertained by friends at Nootka. "He was glad to get Carron Oil and Iodine from me as his supply was exhausted," the nurse reported. "He asked me to send him cabbage and flower seeds, also the Saturday Evening Post. Gets mail frequently from Nootka by launch or walks for it."

Marks resigned at age sixty in April 1927. Johnston, the deputy minister, complained, "The present salary seems high." He suggested Wilby either cut wages or fill the position on a part-time basis with a Nootka resident. The agent replied that the salary, $840, certainly hadn't seemed exorbitant to Marks: "I beg to state that the chief reason why the late lightkeeper resigned his position was on account of the insufficiency of salary paid," he explained. Marks had twice applied in vain for leave to go fishing to augment his wages. The agent pointed out that the local economy was on the upswing, with "the fishing and canning industry in a most flourishing condition, good wages. . . being made by everybody concerned." It was most unlikely that any local man would settle for government rates, and "if anyone did take the position at a smaller salary. . . it would not be long before they gave it up."[8]

In fact the salary at Nootka Light rose to $1860 with the establishment of a "first class fog alarm plant" in 1929. Tom Fish took charge that January, with instructions to provide and pay for an assistant. Fish's hand went through the derrick winch's main gear in June 1929, and came out with his fingers badly crushed. The coxswain of the Clayoquot lifeboat took him away to have two fingers amputated, an ominous beginning for the Fishes' stint at Nootka.

In March 1930 Gordon Halkett arrived for his annual tour of inspection. It must have been a harrowing yearly routine, never knowing what horrors he might encounter ashore. When he landed at Nootka the superintendent was relieved to find the Fishes all well and their station "maintained in a neat and clean condition." In spite of his injury, Fish "had carried out a lot of work around the premises," pouring a concrete stairway to the boat landing and laying out flower beds, "the soil for which [had] to a great measure been transported from the mainland." Clearly the Fishes were the right sort for the work—mentally and physically fit, and envigorated by solitude.

In August 1935 Annie Fish found her husband sprawled unconscious in his pampered garden at the foot of the concrete steps, with deep bruises on his head, shoulder, arm, and leg. Gilbert Fish helped his mother carry Tom up to the house

Nootka Lightstation from Friendly Cove, 1920.

where he lay comatose for several hours. He awoke "paralysed and his speech gone." Annie rang for the Tofino lifeboat. The crew landed a doctor "who pronounced it a Stroke and gave his opinion he could not live long." He advised it might be fatal to move Tom in his present condition.

For a month Annie and Gilbert kept a vigil at Fish's bedside while the delirious keeper weaved along his slender thread of consciousness. When the coiling carpets of fog rolled into the Sound, each blast of the fog horn sent him into convulsions. "HAVE TO MOVE MR. FISH TO QUIETER PLACE AS THE FOG HORN HITS THE HOUSE HARD," Annie wired Wilby in late August. "HAVING LONG RUNS OF FOG. HE IS VERY SICK, NECESSARY GET NEARER A DOCTOR'S CARE." The Fishes' eldest daughter, a trained nurse, was married to Ernie Dawe at Point Atkinson. Annie sought permission to move her husband there. At 10:20 a.m. on 31 August, Wilby telegraphed his approval, instructing her to make her own arrangements. "WOULD SUGGEST BY PRINCESS NORAH IF YOU CONSIDER THE MOVE SAFE AND DESIRABLE." Two hours later Gilbert rowed over to the operator at Nootka: "MR FISH DELERIOUS CONTINUALLY WHILE HORN IN OPERATION STOP IMPOSSIBLE TO GET HIM ABOARD PRINCESS NORAH IN PRESENT CONDITION." He asked Wilby to send up the *Estevan* with a shore party instead.

Annie Fish left with her husband aboard the *Estevan* a week later, leaving Gilbert in charge with an assistant. Down at Point Atkinson, Fish's condition improved somewhat, but he contracted pneumonia Christmas Day. Annie knew now there would be no return to Nootka. "It is with great sorrow that we leave Nootka Lighthouse," she wrote Wilby on 10 January 1936, "as we are greatly attached both to the Station and the many friends we have made during our stay there." Tom Fish officially retired in March. The department awarded him a gratuity of $1880. Annie thanked Colonel Wilby for his "kindly treatment" in their trouble." She still pined for Nootka and declared, "The time spent there will always be a pleasant memory." Fish died 29 May 1936. "I am rather tired after my long battle with death," Annie wrote Wilby. "Am taking his ashes to Nootka and committing them to the sea in front of the home he loved."

Howard Chamberlain, a cousin of Neville Chamberlain who had recently taken charge of the British Isles, moved over from Pine Island to relieve Gilbert Fish early in December 1937. His wife had been a victim of encephalitis as a young woman and her mental horizon had shrunk to that of a child. In July 1937 Howard admitted her to Vancouver General Hospital, confessing that his salary was insufficient to pay her mounting medical bills. Olive Cotsworth, director of the hospital's Social Service Department, wrote Wilby in September to advise him, "[Mrs. Chamberlain will] require institutional care, presumably for the rest of her life, and arrangements are being made to transfer her to the Provincial Home for Incurables at Marpole, B.C., when a vacancy occurs."

Cotsworth asked the department, on Chamberlain's behalf, to move him closer to Vancouver. He had three children who would soon reach school age. His brother, who worked as his assistant, also had three children, but his wife planned to quit Nootka for Nanaimo, leaving both men marooned with six children, including three girls aged six, five, and four. "Mr. Chamberlain has had quite a struggle to keep above water and does not wish to break up his home," she informed Wilby. As for her department, "we would be glad to assist Mr. Chamberlain any way we can."[9]

Wilby replied there were very few lighthouses near schools. Nor could he appreciate Chamberlain's difficulty. "There is no reason why the three children should not be well looked after, " he declared. "As a matter of fact, the father has really brought them up from infancy, and unlike men in other situations who have to leave their home practically all day in order to attend to their work, he is there continually and can properly take care of the children." Besides, there was now "a very excellent Provincial correspondence course."[10]

But money was still at issue. The hospital's administrator, W.R. Bone, could scarcely credit Chamberlain's claim that he made only $160.42 a month, out of which he had to pay $80 to an assistant and $20 for rent. Bone asked Wilby, "Kindly advise us whether or not this information is correct." Wilby pulled Chamberlain's file, which disclosed the keeper's net monthly salary stood at $162. His assistant's wage was "really no concern of the Department," but Wilby estimated that most keepers paid their assistants between $30 and $40 a month. "Board might be reckoned at $25 a month," he calculated. By Wilby's reckoning, Chamberlain's highest income would be $115 a month, to say nothing of his assistant's plight. Such was the perilous financial position of lightkeepers in 1937. In real financial terms they were worse off than George Davies had been when he worked for the colony at Race Rocks in 1860.

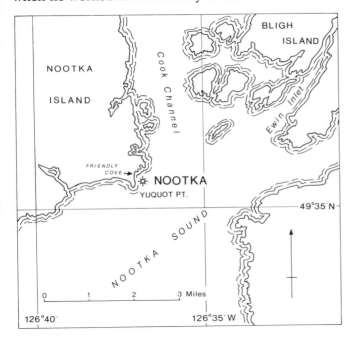

Triangle
Island

While they watch winter winds scale shingles off their roofs, lighthouse keepers from Race Rocks to Green Island on Alaska's doorstep can always console themselves with the maxim: "It could always be worse, we could be at Triangle Island." Triangle Island light was the worst ever. In the annals of West Coast navigation the very name conjures up savage weather, disaster, and death—complete and utter triumph of the elements over mankind. Established with a gush of enthusiasm under an ill omen in 1910, crowned with the worst calamity in the Department of Marine and Fisheries' history, Triangle would be abandoned as its costliest blunder ten years later.

Maritime events were always hot news in Victoria. When readers opened the *Colonist* or the *Times*, they first turned to the "Marine Notes" or "Shipping News" columns which heralded arrivals and departures and served up lurid accounts of wrecks. Reporters were permanent fixtures in the outer offices of the marine agency down on Wharf Street, constantly hectoring the agent and his underlings for scraps to carry back to their editors. They could also be found at any time of day down on the docks, rubbing shoulders with burly stevedores, notebooks at the ready as they waited for ships' officers and crew to disembark.

Late in the afternoon of 23 June 1909 their patience paid off when the lighthouse tender *Quadra* lumbered up to the government pier, home at last from laying plans for the "ultimate lighthouse." H.C. Killeen, the man of the moment, came down her gangplank and regaled them with an account of how he had staked out a site on Triangle Island—forty-two miles northwest of Cape Scott, 650 feet above the sea—for a powerful first order light which he was sure would "ultimately develop into one of the most important lighthouses on this coast." Rightfully predicting the "great development" of steamship traffic, the engineer declared that Triangle Island would serve as "a leading light which will be first picked up by the steamship captains and will give them their bearings whether they are bound for Puget Sound or Prince Rupert."

Triangle, as a special *Colonist* Sunday supplement exalted, stood out as "the furthermost western point of the Empire." It was the opposite bookend of British imperialism to Bombay's great gateway to India; a malevolent cone-shaped crag which had escaped the Ice Age, lurching out of the waves in flagrant, baiting challenge to the Marine Department's chief engineer, W.P. Anderson. After Anderson's heady architectural triumph at Estevan Point there was nowhere to go but up. And what kudos might come from humbling that awesome outpost, five times higher, destined one day to become "the key to wireless communication on the Pacific"! Crowning it with one of his distinctive concrete phalli would surely propel him into the ranks of his heroes—Great Britain's Stevenson, Douglas, and Halpin, the greatest lighthouse builders of all time, men who counted Eddystone and Skerryvore among their brainchildren. In a heated meeting on 5 March 1909 other members of the Lighthouse Board tried in vain to dissuade him, suggesting he build on Cape Scott, a more accessible site at the northern tip of Vancouver Island, instead. Their chairman was having none of that.[1]

It was one thing to draw the plans but quite another to translate them into steel and concrete on the cutting edge of a ceaseless hurricane. Gales howling down the Hecate Straits and Queen Charlotte Sound linked arms with storms swirling in like dervishes from the open Pacific to collide with Triangle Island. Jet-force winds crashing up its steep flanks enveloped the summit in updrafts from every point on the compass at once. Straining at her anchor chains in the heaving grey sea, SS *Leebro* disgorged supplies and gangs of navvies in workboats that summer.

Lightstation at the forbidding summit of Triangle Island.

They laid a ton and a half of steel rails that climbed 1820 feet up the rock face to a winch and donkey engine above.

During their off hours the workers explored the island. Crawling into a cave near the shore one evening, they held up their lanterns and recoiled in horror from a skeleton sprawled against the dripping rock wall, leering back at them, clad in a battered life belt and gumboots. No one ever uncovered the identity of the hapless "sentinel of Triangle Island," only that he was a white man who somehow made his way ashore years before. After an eerie lamp-lit ceremony, Captain Freeman of the halibut vessel *Flamingo* interred his bones in the cavern, but not before a radio operator with a grotesque sense of humour tucked the skull under his arm as a souvenir.

Up on top of Triangle the crouching workers dug, drilled, and blasted water cisterns, and framed a duplex dwelling and wireless shack. Fierce winds pried shingles and siding off almost as fast as they nailed them down. Carpenters harnessed in safety belts hammered up forms for the tower, then mixed, poured, and tamped the concrete. Once stripped, the tower stood forty-six feet tall. For three months they battled the shrieking gales to haul up and wrestle fifty-two half-inch-thick curved panes into place around the huge beacon room. Some days

Marine and Fisheries brass, 1913. Col. William Anderson at top with Captain Robertson (cane) on left and Gordon Halkett (goggles) on right.

the battering wind vibrated putty out of the frames faster than it could set. The iron lantern chamber was braced inside with stout beams, and anchored by cables and turnbuckles to the rock.

The first decade of this century seemed to promise that all Nature would be subjugated, bent to man's will through an enlightened partnership of labour, capital, and technology. Encyclopedias of the day portrayed a universe understood in all its complexity. This was the age of the *Titanic*, after all, the crowning era of steam and steel. In November 1910 the *Colonist* proclaimed in shouting capitals "TRIANGLE LIGHT IS SHOWN NOW," echoing Killeen's confidence in "the largest and most powerful of North Pacific Coast lights." And so it was. Its gargantuan lens, an identical twin to Estevan's, with outer prisms nine feet in circumference, rumbled around on a tub filled with nine-hundred pounds of shimmering mercury, and focused a million candlepower light from the kerosene wick through its bulls-eye in a slender cone that stretched fifty miles out towards Japan.

Back on Triangle, however, huddling out of the barbarous winds' reach, lightkeepers and radio operators looked down in disbelief upon the furrowed banks of cloud and fog, while mariners underneath searched in vain for the mighty flash in the night. The light was too high. As ugly rumours piled up Colonel Anderson came west to inspect Pachena, Estevan, and Triangle, all built since his last tour of inspection. If he had any reservations about Triangle, he kept them carefully to himself.

Life soon became unbearable for the tiny colony which inherited the dubious concrete achievement of Anderson's obsession. James Davies took over the station in July 1910 with his wife and three daughters. His assistant, A. Holmes, and the two wireless operators, Jack Bowerman and Alex Sutherland, doubled as school teachers.

Every hour after dark Holmes or one of the Davies family had to climb the tower and wind up the counterweights which spun the monster lens until they hit the floor. Sleep was often impossible thanks to the shrieking gales and the constant "evil lament of the huge sealions." Seven foot deposits of guano rendered Triangle's soil so caustic that it burned like lye and rotted leather boots. Occasional halibut, dropped off by sympathetic fishermen, were their only relief from the monotonous fare of canned food, but approaching and landing at Triangle was always a perilous venture. Davies once tried to enhance his family's diet by ordering a large consignment of apples, oranges, bananas, and vegetables. When the *Leebro* unloaded, the precious cargo oozed out from under thirty tons of coal. Two apples and half a banana survived. They tried keeping chickens and a cow, but the animals were driven over the cliff by the wind.

Since isolation magnifies trivia to gigantic proportions, it was hardly surprising that men confined under such abysmal conditions would turn upon each other, snarling like rats in an overcrowded laboratory. A dispute over a ton of coal soon escalated, on that wind-scoured outpost, to fisticuffs. When word of the rumpus reached Victoria an exasperated Captain Robertson, the new marine agent, issued standing orders to Davies: "You and your family. . . have no communication whatever with the wireless Station on Triangle Island, except when business necessitates it." The navy's Radio Telegram Branch reinforced the shaky truce with similar instructions to their men, so the people manning the very nerve centre of Pacific communications lived next door to one another, incommunicado.

In February James Davies called next door "on business," and sullenly handed the operators a message for Victoria: "MRS. DAVIES DANGEROUSLY ILL SOME TIME PAST, BAD HAEMORRHAGE CANNOT STOP, ESTEEM IT A FAVOUR IF VESSEL SENT DIRECT AS MATTER IS SERIOUS." Captain Robertson wired his superintendent of lights aboard the tender *Newington*. Gordon Halkett in turn ordered Captain Barnes "to proceed with all despatch to the station."

As she plied her way full speed toward Triangle, a freak wave overtook the *Newington*, poured over her fantail, filled her decks to the rails, twisted and wrenched out steam pipes, and swept away all the deck cargo. Cringing in terror, the crew clutched railing and bulkheads, and held its collective breath as water rose chest-high. The ship shuddered, then rose groaning from her grave under tons of the north Pacific.

Once at Triangle, Halkett leaped from the workboat, scaled the tramway, and found Violet Davies up at the house, "very weak from loss of blood." The deckhands lashed her to a mattress and lowered her down on the beach. They had a tough time hoisting her up the side and over the rails "owing to the *Newington* rolling badly." Halkett brought a doctor aboard at Alert Bay and he urged the superintendent to waste no time getting her to hospital. Fifty-six hours later an operator came across to Davies' house to tell him his wife had arrived safely in Victoria.

After signing on for two-month stints at Triangle, radio operators were often marooned, still living out of their suitcases a year later, bitterly complaining they had been "shanghaied." Even when, at long last, a ship came smoking over the horizon, weeks would slip by while the crew gambled their wages away, waiting for safe landing conditions. While their mother ship cut lazy circles offshore, workboats often stood little chance of abetting the islanders' escape, swamping in the surf and beating their way back to the tender.

The buildings atop Triangle looked like shriveled bugs, snared and sucked dry in a spider's web of cables and turnbuckles fastened into deadeyes grouted into the rocks. All the buildings were linked by cables—lifelines with burrs that sliced cruelly into fingers and palms. Even so, the dwellings teetered and swayed on their foundations so violently that their occupants became seasick. Windows bulged inward like lenses before they shattered. As a matter of routine, no one ever opened a door alone. Men groveled along on hands and knees between the buildings. To vacuum her house, Violet Davies needed only to open a window. The wind barged down chimneys and through walls to snuff out fires and spew billowing clouds of soot through the houses. Everything on the station stood poised to rush over the cliffs to the raging sea 608 feet below.

Supply ship *Newington*.

On 22 October 1912 the anemometer registered 120 miles per hour before the wind, furious at having its temper recorded, ripped it from its mounts, then assaulted the buildings, cleaving off six brick and iron chimneys at the roof line. A shed leapt off its foundation next to the tower and fled, somersaulting end-over-end, over the side into the sea. The wireless mast snapped like a straw, cutting off all communications. Down on the beach the raging surf reduced two storehouses to kindling. The two-ton donkey engine for the tramway crawled several feet away from its base.

Praying and shouting encouragement to one another, the two radio operators crouched in their dwelling like lunatics sharing a padded cell, becoming hysterical when the gale bashed in their windows and yanked the flapping doors off their hinges. The house shuddered and split in two. The attic water tank ruptured, flooding all the rooms. Preferring James Davies' company to the prospect of staying to be crushed, they inched along the walkway to the keeper's house, chins scraping the ground. And his dwelling "absolutely rocked in gale," he wrote, "not safe to be inside."[2]

While the gales caught their breath out at sea between storms, Triangle's stark terrain held out other dangers. Frank Dawson, another radio operator, went for a hike and tumbled two hundred feet over a cliff to a rock ledge. He had nearly screamed himself hoarse before a search party discovered his perch and hauled him up by rope.

By December 1913 Davies had clearly had enough. He begged Robertson for a transfer from this pest-hole of fear to "more congenial surroundings" as a reward for nineteen years' service. "Triangle is very hard on our nerves and a great strain on our constitutions," the former keeper of Egg Island confessed. Only two years old, his dwelling was already "unfit for habitation." Rain driven horizontally by the incessant gales "swamps us out," he complained, "as the building leaks, and it is an utter impossibility to keep a fire, as the place gets smoked out and we have sometimes to go a week at a stretch without a warm meal." Three winters at Triangle were too many; Davies wanted off before a fourth. "The way the wind circles around the buildings in whirlwinds makes keeping a fire out of the question," he told Robertson, "and you can imagine what a trial it is to myself and mine."[3]

Davies escaped with his family in March. In late January 1914 his successor, Thomas Watkins, sent a message off to Victoria, reporting that a gale had flattened the storage shed on the beach again, strewing 450 oil cans and five kegs of nails along the shore. "The roof is blown about 300 feet along the beach," he reported, "Sides & Floor about 150 feet from original position." Both dwellings "got a severe shaking"—the door of the spare house blew off its hinges and the chimneys

Left: Triangle tramway looked like the world's worst roller coaster. Right: Huge first order light shone in vain above Triangle's fog.

were scattered all over the ground again. By March there were only "two habitable rooms, a bedroom and a kitchen," in Watkins' house. That October the keeper was eager to transfer to a new station planned for Bonilla Island up north in the Hecate Straits—a "much more suitable place for a man with a wife and young children than Triangle is."

Watkins was succeeded in his turn by Michael O'Brien who had spent five years down in the hold of the Sand Heads lightship, where he had contracted rheumatism "owing to the confinement and dampness." He was "very desirous of being exchanged to Triangle Island" where he could live with his wife and family.

Triangle Island light may have been a nightmare for its keepers, but when the verdict came in on Anderson's accomplishment, his peers were unanimous. In 1913 F.A. Talbot published his definitive *Lighthouses and Lightships*, an ambitious study of the world's leading lighthouses, the latest and best survey of the state of the art. "Probably the most important light and certainly the loftiest on the Pacific seacoast north of the equator is that on the summit of Triangle Island, British Columbia," Talbot reckoned. He also lavished praise on the "Engineer-in-Chief of the Lighthouse Authority of the Canadian Government" for Estevan Point, placed in "a most romantic setting," and told how Anderson had laid a tramway through a "grand primeval forest" to haul concrete to the site.

The two lights confirmed Anderson's revolutionary reinforced concrete designs, with their ornate and functional buttresses, as "the last word in lighthouse building." Naturally neither could compare with Eddystone or Skerryvore as engineering feats, yet there was no denying that Anderson's "most powerful

Telegraph operator's dwelling with makeshift bracing against Triangle's hurricane-force winds.

beacons" were of "commanding character, representing as they do the latest and best in coast lighting."[4] Never one to rest on his laurels, Anderson altered Triangle's plan, stretching the tower out to twice its height and tapering the central column, for a masterplan to build new towers at Point Atkinson and Sheringham Point, each offering easy access for an appreciative public.

The nine years after Triangle Island first captured the public's imagination were nine years of war for its keepers and nine years of exquisite agony for its creator. For all his official preening, Anderson must have seen that Triangle's light was too high when he inspected his masterpiece the very first time, when he watched the shed on the beach slowly shrink to the size of one of his prized stamps as he rode up on the tramway. The chief engineer may even have ascended through the grey stratus which clung like cotton candy to the top two hundred feet of the eyrie most of the year. Surely he knew his mistake. The cardinal rule of lighthouse construction—never build higher than 150 feet—could be read on blackboards and in notebooks in every first-year engineering course in Canada. In his own annual report for 1906, only three years before he unrolled the plans for Triangle Island light, Anderson had reiterated, "*They should not be placed at an elevation exceeding 150 feet above the level of the sea on account of the prevalence of fog.*" So what must he have felt when all the praise pouring in was poisoned by grumblings and (even worse) derision in wheelhouses and shipping offices from Shanghai to San Francisco?

No one will ever know. Any complaints had to be put on paper and mailed off to the chairman of the Lighthouse Board of Canada. There was, of course, an endless barrage on every conceivable subject during Anderson's tenure. Petitions "praying" for new lights, complaints about existing ones, requests for foghorns, beacons, buoys, lifeboats, semaphore stations, and suggestions for changing characteristics of lights—handwritten pleas from lowly fishermen's cooperatives, or demands typed under the imposing letterheads of the world's most prestigious shipping lines—all piled into that in-tray in Ottawa, each one numbered and placed by harried secretaries on the Lighthouse Board's agenda. But there was not one letter about Triangle Island.

Whatever the explanation for the absence of any reference to the blind cyclops in the Board's minutes, Triangle Island was about to loom up and confront them all as the naval patrol vessel *Galiano* dropped anchor off the station shortly after noon on 29 October 1918 and sent off her workboat with supplies. It should have been a long-awaited day of deliverance for the radio operators. Sid Elliot was ecstatic—he was scheduled to "come off." Jack Neary would see his brother Michael, serving as a radio operator on the *Galiano*. For the lightkeepers there would be a sack of mail. But no one was permitted to go aboard or stay ashore since eight crew members had been left behind at Esquimalt, laid low by the dreaded Spanish flu running rampant in Victoria. Crestfallen, Sid learned that his stint would be continued; he plodded back up the thousand steps "home" while Jack caught up on news of friends and family.

By 1:30 that afternoon southwest winds began to muster their forces for another assault. The shore party hurriedly transferred cargo while clouds piled up in an ominous, dirty black anvil on the horizon. As the storm struck, Jack and Mike Neary quickly embraced and shook hands good-bye. Seamen dumped the remaining cargo onto the beach, snatched up Miss Brunton, a housekeeper who had been teaching the O'Brien children, thrust her into the workboat, and bucked the roller coaster swells back to their ship. *Galiano* wasted no time hoisting her anchors. As she steamed away the keepers piled freight on the tram, then climbed home to open their mail.

No one will ever know why the *Galiano* headed for the open sea rather than seek shelter in Shushartie Bay. She was a "cranky bitch" at best in foul weather, with decks and alleyways always awash when the wind was on her quarter. Her crew had long complained about their captain's inscrutable preference for riding out storms at sea, tempting fate.

Two hours later Art Green, the radio operator on watch, jerked upright in his chair, clamped his headset tightly to his ear, and grabbed for a pencil to scribble her last feeble message: HOLD FULL OF WATER. SEND HELP. He called Sid Elliot over and both took turns signalling till sunrise. There was no reply. Art looked over at Jack Neary snoring on his cot. "Shall I wake up Jack?" he asked. "No, let him sleep," Sid advised. Why wake him up to a nightmare? No one ever learned the *Galiano*'s fate. Fishermen on the halibut steamer *George Foster* gaffed Wilfred Ebb's body out of the water with a pike pole two days later; two other bodies were later found drifting two hundred miles away, east of Cape St. James.

Michael O'Brien left that winter to keep his own appointment with tragedy at Entrance Island light, and Alex Dingwell came down from Green Island to preside at the dismantling of Anderson's monumental mistake. In 1920 the Department of Marine grudgingly conceded defeat to Nature's fury and human error, a decade

Patrol vessel *Galiano*.

after the *Colonist*'s editor had gloated, "Triangle Island is at last to be put to the uses for which Nature apparently designed it from the beginning of things." Many of the same men who had bolted the beacon room together scaled it again to wrench off the rusted nuts. Piece by piece the curved glass panels, the nine-foot lens crystals, iron frame, copper sheeting, clockworks, and pails of mercury went down the tramway and out to a ship's hold. Some deckhand-photographer with a keen sense of history documented the surrender, capturing the last boat on its way out from Triangle Island.

The hulking lantern from the West Coast's "leading light" has been resurrected upon the tarmac at the new Canada Coast Guard base in Victoria, where it dwarfs tourists on Coast Guard Day. And way up in that punishing corner of nowhere, Colonel Anderson's squat monument still stands above the clouds, futile and permanent, a twentieth century Tower of Babel waiting to intrigue archeologists a thousand years hence. Who would have built it there, and why?

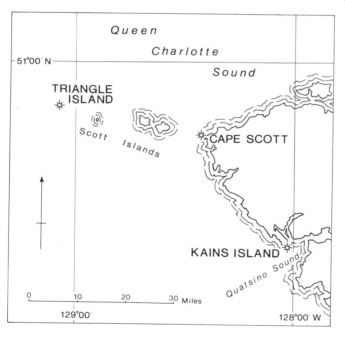

NOTES

THE IMPERIAL LIGHTS

1. Richards, report to Douglas, with letter, 23 October 1858. Great Britain, Kew Gardens, Public Record Office, CO 60/1.
2. Ibid., MT 9/9.
p. 41.
3. Ibid., CO 305/12.

FISGARD

1. *Rules and Instructions for the Guidance of Lighthouse-Keepers and of Engineers in Charge of Steam Fog Alarms in the Dominion of Canada; Together with Some Medical Directions, Etc., at Remote Stations* (Ottawa: Department of Marine and Fisheries, 1875).
2. Captain F. Revely, marine agent, to Amelia Bevis, 21 October 1879, Victoria, Transport Canada (hereafter cited as TC Victoria).

RACE ROCKS

1. T.W. Paterson, "Deadly Grip of Race Caught Poor Nanette," *Victoria Daily Colonist Magazine*, 23 March 1969.
2. *Victoria Daily Colonist*, 28 December 1866 (hereafter cited as *Colonist*).
3. Argyle to Pearse, 18 April 1870, Public Archives of British Columbia (hereafter cited as PABC), F 31/38.
4. George Inglis, "Race Rocks Treasure," *Colonist*, 20 February, 1977.
5. Albert Argyle to Senator MacDonald, 2 February 1889, TC Victoria.
6. Fred Arrow and J. Sydney Wells, "Committee to Canada and the United States. 1872, 4 November 1872" (London: Trinity House Corporation), pp. 39:40.
7. George Inglis, "Race Rocks Treasure," *Colonist Magazine*, 20 February 1977.
8. Argyle to Senator MacDonald, 2 February 1889, TC Victoria.
9. Argyle to Hon. Simon Tolmie, 2 February 1889, TC Victoria.
10. Transcript of Enquiry, Victoria, 18 September 1900, Ottawa, Public Archives of Canada (hereafter cited as PAC) RG 42, vol. 524.

CAPE BEALE

1. Thomas E. Appleton, *Usque ad Mare: A History of the Canadian Coast Guard and Marine Services* (Ottawa: Department of Transport, 1968), p. 232.
2. Ibid., p. 233.
3. Mrs. Francis Morrison, "Some Recollections of Victoria and Cape Beale Lighthouse ca. 1880," PABC, Aural History Division, 1299-1.
4. Mrs. P. Alexander Haslam, Ibid., 309-1.
5. Minnie Patterson, from notes of an interview with unidentified *Seattle Times* correspondent, ca. December 1906. University of British Columbia Library, Special Collections Division.

6. *Victoria Times*, 11 August 1962 (hereafter cited as *Times*).
7. Minnie Patterson, op. cit.

POINT ATKINSON

1. Nora M. Duncan, *The Heroine of Moodyville: An Epic of Burrard Inlet*, 1936.
2. *Rules and Instructions for the Guidance of Lightkeepers*....
3. Ibid.
4. Walter Erwin to William Smith, deputy minister of Marine and Fisheries, 1 March 1890, PAC, RG 42, vol. 526.
5. Walter Erwin to Captain James Gaudin, marine agent, 26 December 1906, Ibid.
6. Hon. William Templeman to R.G. McPherson, MP, 9 April 1907, Ibid.
7. Robert Hood to H.H. Stevens, MP, 13 December 1926; and to A. Johnson, deputy minister of Marine and Fisheries, 5 May 1927, Ibid.
8. Point Atkinson Lightkeeper's Log, 11 January 1933.
9. Ibid., 6 October 1933.
10. Petition submitted by Messrs. Wood et al. to Colonel A.W.R. Wilby, marine agent, 6 October 1934, TC Victoria.
11. Lightkeeper's Log, 6 June 1935.
12. Peter N. Moogk, *Vancouver Defended: A History of the Men and Guns of the Lower Mainland Defenses* (Surrey: Antonson Publishing Ltd., 1978), pp. 96-100.

PROSPECT POINT

1. Gaudin to Francois Frederick Gourdeau, deputy minister of Marine and Fisheries, 21 March 1889, TC Victoria.
2. John Grove to Gaudin, 9 February 1910, TC Victoria.
3. Ibid., 11 April 1913.
4. Grove to Captain Robertson, marine agent, 13 August 1916, TC Victoria.

BROCKTON POINT

1. Gaudin to Colonel W.P. Anderson, chief engineer, Department of Marine and Fisheries, 20 March 1901, TC Victoria.
2. "The New Lighthouse at Brockton Point," *Vancouver Province*, 19 April 1902 (hereafter cited as *Province*).
3. Gaudin to Gourdeau, 29 June 1905, TC Victoria.
4. *Province*, 19 April 1902.
5. Fred Rogers, *Shipwrecks of British Columbia* (Vancouver: Douglas & McIntyre, 1980), pp. 227-231.
6. Gaudin to Hon. W. Templeman, acting minister of Marine and Fisheries, 27 August 1907, TC Victoria.
7. W.D. Jones to Gaudin, 9 January, 12

February 1910; 7 August 1911, TC Victoria.

8. Secretary-Treasurer, Returned Soldiers Club, to E.H. Scammel, Military Hospitals Commission, Ottawa, 7 December 1916, TC Victoria.

9. Urquhart and Buckley, *Historical Statistics of Canada*, p. 204.

10. Civil Servants' Superannuation Act, 24 Geo. 5, c.69. Only one civil servant had reason to rejoice; MP's inserted a clause granting the Clerk of the House of Commons $2500 each year for life upon retirement.

11. Jones to Wilby, 29 January 1925, TC Victoria.

CAPILANO

1. E. Harris to Wilby, 17 March 1925, TC Victoria.

2. Capilano Lightkeeper's Log, 17 August 1930, copied and loaned to the author by Gordon Odlum.

3. Ibid., 16 November 1944.

4. Ibid., 6 January 1942.

5. Ibid.

6. Sheringham Point Lightkeeper's Log, 15 June 1946, copied and loaned to the author by Gordon Odlum.

ENTRANCE ISLAND

1. *Nanaimo Daily Free Press*, 10 June 1876.

2. Captain G.E. Robertson to E.D. Perdue, 19 December 1914, TC Victoria.

3. Perdue to Robertson, 18 December 1914, TC Victoria.

FIDDLE REEF

1. Gaudin to M.A. McInnes, MP, 14 October 1898, TC Victoria.

2. Gaudin to Gourdeau, 27 February 1905, TC Victoria.

3. D.H. McNeill to Wilby, 22 May 1924, TC Victoria.

4. C.D. Stuart to Hon. C.D. Howe, minister of Marine and Fisheries, 27 December 1936, TC Victoria.

THE PACIFIC GRAVEYARD

1. Captain Archie Phelps, "Hazardous Pacific Coast," *Colonist Magazine*, 3 October 1971.

2. R. Bruce Scott, *Breakers Ahead! On the Graveyard of the Pacific* (Fleming-Review Printing Ltd., 1970), pp. 65-71.

3. Report of a Committee of the Executive Council, 10 May 1887, PAC, RG 12, vol. 1500.

4. Anderson to Gourdeau, 2 May 1891, TC Victoria.

5. "Life-Saving Stations on Vancouver Island," memorandum to Sir Louis Davies, 17 April 1894, TC Victoria.

6. Appleton, "Marine and Fisheries Lifesaving Stations in 1914," *Usque ad Mare*, pp. 309-311.

CARMANAH

1. Carmanah Point Lightkeeper's Logs, PABC GR 307, Marine and Fisheries.

2. Ibid., 5 August 1908.

3. Gaudin to Daykin, 15 November 1894, TC Victoria.

4. Scott, *Breakers Ahead!* pp. 71-6.

5. Gaudin to Daykin, 31 December 1903, TC Victoria.

6. Daykin to Robertson, 26 August 1911, TC Victoria.

LENNARD ISLAND

1. Francis C. Garrard, "Reminicenses," PABC Add. MSS 46.

2. Gordon Halkett to F.C. Garrard, 24 April 1907, TC Victoria.

VALENCIA

1. Rogers, *Shipwrecks of British Columbia*, pp. 132-3.

2. Seattle Federal Archives and Records Centre, Transcript of Hearing Held before Local Inspectors Bion B. Whitney and Robert A. Turner, Seattle, 27 January 1906, RG 41, vol.1 (Washington: US Government Printing Office, 1906), p. 48.

3. Gordon R. Newell, *SOS North Pacific: Tales of Shipwrecks off the Washington, British Columbia and Alaska Coasts* (Portland: Binfords & Mort, 1955), p. 128.

4. Ibid., pp. 129-30.

5. Rogers, p. 138.

6. Transcript, p. 693.

7. *Province*, 27 February 1906.

8. Clarence H. Baily, "The Wreck of the Valencia: The First Complete Account Published of the Recent Disaster off the West Coast of Vancouver Island," *Pacific Monthly*, March 1906.

9. Gaudin to Anderson, 30 July 1906, TC Victoria.

10. Gaudin to Daykin, 27 August 1906, TC Victoria.

11. *Colonist*, 3 October 1906.

PACHENA POINT

1. Gaudin to Anderson, 6 November 1908, TC Victoria.

2. T.W. Paterson, *British Columbia Shipwrecks* (Langley: Stagecoach Publishing Co. Ltd., 1976), pp. 147-50.

3. Ibid., p. 150.

4. Wilby to Hawken, 31 October 1921, TC Victoria.

5. Dr. C.T. Hilton to Wilby, 6 July 1923; W.H. Trowsdale to Wilby, 9 July 1923, TC Victoria.

6. R.E. Wells, *The Stranding of S.S. Uzbekistan, USSR, on the West Coast of Vancouver Island* (E.W. Bickle, 1974).

AMPHITRITE

1. R. Bruce Scott, *Breakers Ahead!* p. 94.
2. William L. Thompson to Wilby, 14 December 1914, TC Victoria.
3. Secretary, Ucluelet Relief Committee, to Wilby, 14 December 1914, TC Victoria.
4. H.S. Clements, MP, to Robertson, 6 February 1915, TC Victoria.
5. Robertson to Wilby, 8 February 1915, TC Victoria.
6. James Frazer to Robertson, 10 March 1919, TC Victoria.
7. Wilby to Alexander Johnston, deputy minister of Marine and Fisheries, 8 August 1927, TC Victoria.

KAINS ISLAND

1. *Colonist*, 1 January 1907.
2. J.H. Sadler to Robertson, 2 December 1915, TC Victoria.
3. Letter to H.S. Clements, MP (signature illegible), 1917, TC Victoria.
4. "Locked from World on Northern Island," *Colonist*, 5 January 1919.
5. Dr. O.M. Lyon to Robertson, 9 September 1918, TC Victoria.
6. Halkett to Robertson, 20 September 1918, TC Victoria.
7. Ibid.
8. Lyon to Robertson, 7 October 1918, TC Victoria.
9. Robertson to Lyon, 11 October 1918, TC Victoria.
10. Robertson to Stanton, 16 December 1918, TC Victoria.
11. Wilby to Hawken, 30 April 1920, TC Victoria.
12. Halkett to Wilby, 24 October 1921, TC Victoria.
13. Quinn to Wilby, 11 November 1921, TC Victoria.
14. Dickenson to Wilby, 1 June 1925, TC Victoria.
15. Wilby to Sydney Warren, 16 June 1925, TC Victoria.
16. Violet (Warren) Cummings, interview, 4 October 1983. Mrs. Cummings allowed the author free access to her mother's diary and ledgers.
17. Halkett to Wilby, 7 September 1929, TC Victoria.
18. Violet (Warren) Cummings, interview, 4 October 1983.
19. Jessie Warren to Wilby, 24 October 1929, TC Victoria.
20. Halkett to Wilby, 5 November 1929.

ESTEVAN

1. Gaudin to A.W. Neill, 20 May 1908, TC Victoria.

2. Alfred Nelson to Gaudin, 26 February 1909, TC Victoria.
3. H.C. Brown to Hon. W. Templeman, 15 December 1909, TC Victoria.
4. Robbie McKeand, Sound Heritage Series Number 33, PABC.
5. Gordon Stead, interview, 1983.
6. Dr. Joe Boucher, interview, 28 May 1982.
7. Lighthouse Control Emergency, War Diary, 20 June 1942, obtained from the minister of National Defense by Terry Sargeant, MP. Lally's son attests that the account is one filleted from the Estevan Point Lightkeeper's Log for 20 June 1942.
8. Patrol Report, HMCS *Mooloch*, 21 June 1942, obtained from minister of National Defense.
9. Dr. Joe Boucher, interview, 28 May 1982.
10. Patrol Report, HMCS *Mooloch*.
11. Dr. Joe Boucher, interview, 28 May 1982.
12. *Hansard*, 22 June 1942, 3507.
13. Ibid.
14. John L. Gibson, interview, PABC Aural History Division, 3878: 25 & 26.
15. *Hansard*, 22 June 1942, 3508.
16. Roy Lally, interview, 8 July 1983.
17. John Toland, *Infamy: Pearl Harbour and its Aftermath* (New York: Doubleday & Co. Inc., 1982).
18. Ibid., pp. 306-7.

NOOTKA

1. Gaudin to Johnston, 7 December 1910, TC Victoria.
2. Gaudin to Niell, 14 September 1910, TC Victoria.
3. Robertson to H.T.W. Smith, 24 October 1913, TC Victoria.
4. Smith to Robertson, 4 July 1918, TC Victoria.
5. William E. Taylor to Robertson, 18 January 1919, TC Victoria.
6. P. Foley to Robertson, 8 May 1919, TC Victoria.
7. Robertson to Johnston, 12 June 1919, TC Victoria.
8. Wilby to Johnston, 27 April 1927, TC Victoria.
9. Olive V. Cotsworth to Wilby, 3 September 1937, TC Victoria.
10. Wilby to Cotsworth, 7 September 1937, TC Victoria.

TRIANGLE ISLAND

1. Ottawa, Transport Canada Library, *Dominion Lighthouse Board Minutes*, 5 March 1909.
2. Robertson to Anderson, 25 October 1912, TC Victoria.
3. James Davies to Robertson, 1 December 1912, TC Victoria.
4. F.A. Talbot, *Lighthouses and Lightships* (London: William Heineman, 1913), p. 174.

INDEX

Page numbers in bold face refer to illustrations.

Photograph credits: B.C. Provincial Archives pages 15, 51, 53, 61, 103, 111, 104, 157, 165, 181(a), 183, 185. Cadieux Collection 10, 22, 23, 28, 37, 40, 63, 65, 75, 76, 78, 90, 93, 94, 100, 129, 131, 140, 150, 204, 224, 227, 257. Canada Coast Guard 28, 39, 41, 42, 49, 85, 86, 99, 108, 120, 124, 126, 141, 143, 155, 181(b), 185, 187, 194, 195, 200, 201, 228, 229(b), 230, 253, 254, 258, 259. Elsie Coombs 65. Violet Warren Cummings 211, 214, 217, 218, 219, 222. Imperial War Museum, London 231. Roy Lally 227, 237, 239, 240. Gordon Odlum 25, 58. Public Archives of Canada pages 10. Jim Ryan 5, 13, 14, 17, 24, 29, 33, 47, 106, 115, 149, 162, 181, 192. Vancouver Maritime Museum 171, 197. Vancouver Public Library Historical Photograph Collection 13, 57, 81, 89, 245, 249. R. E. Wells 139. Our grateful thanks to all of the above, as well as Donna Williams, for assistance received.